Official
Know-It-All
Guide™

Easy Entertaining

Edith Gilbert

Frederick Fell Publishers, Inc.

Fell's Official Know-It-All Guide / Easy Entertaining
FREDERICK FELL PUBLISHERS, INC.
2131 Hollywood Boulevard - Suite # 305
Hollywood, Florida 33020
954-925-5242
e-mail: fellpub@aol.com
Visit our web site at www.fellpub.com

This publication is designed to provide accurate and authoritative information in regard to the subject matter covered. It is sold with the understanding that the publisher is not engaged in rendering legal, accounting, or other professional service. If legal advice or other assistance is required, the services of a competent professional person should be sought. From A Declaration of Principles jointly adopted by a Committee of the American Bar Association and a Committee of Publishers.

Library of Congress Cataloging-in-Publication Data

Gilbert, Edith
    [All about parties]
    Fell's official know-it-all guide : Easy Entertaining / Edith Gilbert.
        p. cm.
Originally published: All about parties / Edith Gilbert. New York:
Hearthside Press, 1968.
    ISBN 0-88391-068-3
1. Entertaining. 2. Parties. 3. Cookery. I. Title.
    TX731 .G5 2001
    642'.4–dc21
            2001006260

Interior Design by Linda M. Parker
Cover Design by Elena Solis

Acknowledgments

The most pleasant part of authoring a book comes at this moment when one is privileged to say "thank you" to all the wonderful people who helped make this Easy Entertaining book possible, especially those who have taken the time to help test favorite recipes using modern equipment. That includes my good neighbors, Doris Lundteigen and Kay Heise, my daughter-in-law, Vicky Gilbert, and friend, Sally Blackwell. To Nancy Porter, hostess par excellence, I am indebted for always acting as my sounding board when I'm trying to make decisions on what to include and what to omit. I especially thank Wes Westhoven, wine authority and owner/chef of the Rowe Inn, for his expert advice in suggesting the right wines to accompany the meal. I am grateful to Linda Parker, copyeditor, proofreader, and typesetter, for her valuable expertise in fine-tuning the text. Illustrator Jon Beuchel's delightful drawings add just the right finishing touch.

It's impossible to list all the friends who have wined and dined me and are still my inspiration when planning a party. You know who you are! Still, my high school chum, Noyon Berg, was an early influence, as were my frequent co-hostesses, Connie Wineman and Gertrude Kasle, and for final authority and role model for creative entertaining, I am indebted to Joan MacGillivray. I thank them all for showing me, with their special brand of warmth and kindness, the real definition of gracious hospitality. Finally, there are important contributors to this book, bless their hearts, who live only in my memory.

Contents

Introduction

"A host is like a general: adversity reveals his genius, prosperity hides it."
—Horace, Roman poet, 65 B.C.

Many of the glamorous parties that I've been privileged to attend are described here with nostalgic delight. One posh, private party at the Waldorf, that still ranks high on the list, is the time Bob Hope jumped out of a birthday cake and sang "Happy Birthday" to our surprised host!

Then, too, there are memorable photographs of low-fuss, low-stress glimpses of family gatherings, when there was a sainted cook in the kitchen. There are pictures of intimate get-togethers with good friends—cookouts on the beach, and after-ski, laid back gatherings around the fire.

People who like to entertain will do so just because their garden is in bloom or because their team is going to the Rose Bowl. Nothing stops them from inviting people again and again, and they don't fall apart, no matter how many disasters they may have encountered. Speaking for myself, I recall with a mild shudder the time we planned a formal dinner party for 100 guests in a downtown hotel, and on that very afternoon—there was a waiters' strike! Or what about the time my cat had kittens under my bed, just as the doorbell was ringing and guests were crossing the threshold? Then there was the day all the electricity went off at dinner time, and we ate in the dark by candlelight. (Thank heaven we had a gas grill to prepare the food.) How about the time I forgot-—whoops!—to confirm the date with the caterer? These are things we laugh about today, because somehow it was all handled then, and long forgotten now.

It's the good times we like to recall and I have done so, step by step, in this book. People who like to cook will find kitchen-tested recipes. Power-house party givers, who are used to calling in professionals, will still be able to gather ideas from tried and true menus for both stand-up receptions and sit-down dinners. For creative people, there are many mix-and-match recipes and menus to play with. For people who like to entertain, there are loads of new ideas, and for those who are hesitant, there is encouragement here.

Although wines and cocktails are suggested, those who prefer to abstain from alcohol are free to omit them.

You will notice that I have included a new category before each recipe: "Equipment." This will prevent you from looking for something on the top shelf, while the telephone is ringing and the timer is buzzing. It's entirely up to you if you care to stir the dough with a wooden spoon or use a shiny stand mixer.

I won't apologize for not having any fat-free recipes here. Instead I tend to agree with Julia Childs that, in order for food to taste good, one needs to use butter! You may feel free to substitute margarine for butter, but I prefer using sensible portion control to counting calories. Also, you won't find much about fruits and vegetables because I am depending on you to buy fresh fruits and vegetables in season in the zone where you live. You probably already know that vegetables are best steamed, don't you?

When pressed for time, I am not—and I hope you are not, either—above supplementing a meal with a specialty from a gourmet shop, ordering from a chic catalog, or picking up a carry-out from a nearby restaurant or bakery. I recall an elegant Fourth of July party with a red, white, and blue table as spectacular as an exploding firecracker, only to be told that the delicious fried chicken came from the Colonel! It all depends on my schedule whether I do the fresh flower thing, spend hours creating a glamorous centerpiece, or order a seasonal arrangement to be delivered by a florist at the last minute. Sometimes I invite guests out to dinner because, as my old high school chum remarked, "Don't knock yourself out—I know you can cook!"

When I entertain, I do think of presenting food in an appetizing and appealing way, of course, considering color, soft and crunchy texture, and sweet or sour taste—but this does not mean I try to compete with fancy restaurants, who build complicated Eiffel towers on their dinner plates.

On the other hand, there are special times, when it gives me enormous pleasure to set our table with my mother-in-law's Wedgewood china, ring my grandfather's silver dinner bell, or toast an honored guest with a crystal goblet that we received as a wedding gift from my favorite aunt.

Finally, please allow me to share an amusing incident that took place after a lecture I gave at the fashionable Greenbrier resort in White Sulphur, W. Va. During my slide talk, I casually mentioned that I lived in Northern Michigan. Later, while autographing books, a lovely lady asked me very politely, "Isn't there a little bit of New England in you?," to which I laughingly replied, "Not a drop!" I did spend two of my baby years in nearby New York City, and the rest of my life was divided between a dash of Hamburg, Shanghai, San Francisco, Beverly Hills, and Detroit. It was quite evident that this lovely lady could not imagine that someone from Northern Michigan would have a clue how to set the table!

The Charlevoix area, where I now live, ought to be more renowned than it is for its fine dining cuisine. Irma Rombauer spent her summers "Up North" before she wrote her popular book, *Joy of Cooking*. For a number of years, a steady stream of retirees from all over the United States has chosen this historic summer resort for their second home. A favorite indoor sport is to rate the outstanding restaurants in the area. One is praised for its fine wines, another for its service, a third for its decor, a fourth for its menu, and each has its devoted following.

These are the names of few successful restauranteurs in the area, given according to the date of their establishment. Wes Westhoven, chef/owner of the Rowe Inn, has received the "Fine Dining Award" by Distinguished Restaurants of North America (DIRONA). Pete Peterson, chef/owner of Tapawingo, has received the James Beard "Best Chef Award of the Midwest" four times. Owner/chef Dave Beier of the Walloon Lake Inn was recently mentioned in *Condè Nast Traveler* magazine as the "best kept secret in Michigan." Another chef/owner, Bob Stark of Andante, has received the Wine Spectator Award of Excellence. Chandler Symons of Chandler's, and chef Rick Travis of Latitude in Bay Harbor, are both fairly new and bear watching. Chef Garrett Scanlan of the Charlevoix Country Club has been honored with the Silver Medal, European Culinary Olympics.

Yes, with our fine restaurants on the one hand, and with our woodsy ski and shore environment on the other hand, we have the best of both worlds! Deer wander through our back yards, and flocks of wild turkeys circle the golf courses, while we dine par excellence!

It is a good place to write as well, and it is my fond hope that you will be stimulated by the easy entertaining tips described here, and that you will enjoy entertaining your family and friends in this exciting new century, as much as I have in the past.

Chapter One

Keys to Successful Entertaining

The more, the merrier; the fewer, the better fare.

—Old Proverb

My favorite parties are those filled with delightful memories of people, of lights and glitter, delicate fragrances, of warmth and love and kindnesses. Some of my favorite parties have been huge affairs with the correct number of guests per square foot, with cold drinks and hot music, where it's fun striking up a conversation unexpectedly with someone whose passion for a particular play, or Imperial jade, or a fast game of tennis, is as great as one's own.

Then again, sometimes my favorite parties run small because here I can chat with all those interesting people one never has the chance to enjoy visiting with at large receptions. At intimate coteries I can sit down and listen to people exchange ideas instead of merely information: where a wise woman asks an intelligent man, "What do you think?" instead of telling him what she thinks; where contacts are made, not exploited; where small talk, spiced with wit, is appreciated and not considered a waste of time.

Small Touches Count

These memorable, magical parties, both large and small, don't just happen, and we'll tell you why chapter by chapter. One of the keys to successful party-giving is not so much what is served but *how* it's served!

Let me recount an incident that took place on a yacht where I overheard the steward ask a guest if he'd like something hot or cold to drink.

"Something cold."

"Hard or soft?"

"Just a plain glass of water, please," came the reply.

"Vichy, Polin or Mountain Valley Water, sir?" pressed the steward.

"Plain water," sighed the visitor.

In a jiffy the steward returned. "Anything else?" he inquired as he offered a clear glass of cold water beside a folded monogrammed napkin on a silver tray. And floating on top of the water was a paper-thin slice of lemon, proving that it's quite possible to serve a plain, cold glass of water with as much flair as a chilled bowl of caviar!

Now, when the postman rings your doorbell on a hot summer day and you offer him a glass of water with a thin slice of lemon, he may think you're some kind of kook, but the group from your neighborhood block meeting will vote you hostess with the mostes'.

Some Hosts Are Fussy—And Some Are Flexible!

Chances are your block sports two types of people, just like my block does. Remember the "Odd Couple" in that well-known play? There are the fussy types, the kind who keep all their possessions wrapped in cellophane (this type even have slip covers for their slip covers!) and never remove the cellophane from any lamp shades. If you are allowed into this home, they will sit like watch-birds and watch every move you make! They are always checking to see that no one drips or spills, scratches or burns, creases or musses anything. They regiment their guests, and people don't have much fun here.

Then there's the second type—the flexible person—who also takes pride in his or her surroundings, but never loses sight of the fact that one's home and its furnishings are meant for the enjoyment and comfort of people, and these folks don't allow themselves to become the slaves of inanimate objects. They entertain even at the last minute. They entertain whether their walls have been freshly painted or not, whether the house is full of children or not, whether this year's income is up or down. They are flexible and manage to shift the scene, expand the menu, cut corners and still come up with a memorable evening. Because they are confident, relaxed, and poised, they enjoy themselves whenever or wherever they entertain.

Speaking of being relaxed and poised always reminds me of this classic story that happened at a small dinner party in Shanghai, China, many years ago. During dinner the waiter approached the dining table carrying a beautifully garnished goose on a silver platter. He tripped and the goose slipped to the floor. Calmly the hostess turned to him and said, "Please bring in the other one!" Naturally most of the guests were pretty certain there was no "other" goose in the kitchen. Yet, after the bird was brought around a second time, everyone tactfully raved how delicious the other goose tasted. Well, who knows? Perhaps there was another goose in the oven!

Fabulous Females—Marvelous Males

According to one of the top management consulting firms in the country, playing it cool is the key to success in our digital age just as it was in the pioneer age; and entertaining know-how has always been money in the bank.

What we mean is that if someone is at home in a variety of social situations, life is more pleasant and enjoyable. The gorgeous creature dripping in sequins and jewels who dances through the pages of *W* today is often the same woman who knows how to whip up a fondue tomorrow at that little ski hideaway, or who can prepare a platter of tantalizing hors d'oeuvres in the poolhouse kitchen, or plan a benefit dinner for a thousand people. Today, a man should know how to prepare for company, or the exact time to put the casserole in the oven. For special occasions, he needs to know what to expect from a caterer.

But how can entertaining know-how lead to a successful social life? Do we need to suffer through a stretch of stuffy, formal functions? Heavens no! All we mean by a successful social life is to have friends with whom one shares one's home, one's time, and one's interest in a congenial, pleasant atmosphere. Ever since Eleanor Roosevelt served hot dogs to the king and queen of England, Old World formality flew right out the White House window, and the free-wheeling American host and hostess with their natural charm and lighthearted manner have come into their captivating own.

Budget Time and Energy

With our food processors, nonstick pans, and bread-making machines, the modern hosts accomplish miracles in their spacious living-dining-kitchen area. They know how to save time and energy. But all too many people forget that savings are meant to be spent! A slice of time saved by automation is profitably spent in leisure social activities—a casual cook-out, a relaxing cocktail, a stimulating dinner party, or a glittering dance.

Naturally, it takes a sense of balance to budget one's time and energy, to find energy for things that are important and things we enjoy. Budget time for marketing, cooking, exercising and chauffeuring—yes, but budget time for rest? Too many people forget that this important consideration should come first. When one is over-tired, it's easy to be crotchety and impatient with those around us. Let washing windows go another week if it means giving up your rest period. Your devoted friends are coming over to enjoy your sparkling face, not your sparkling windows!

Of course, the best stimulant to energy is happiness. Thomas Wolfe said, "There's no spectacle on earth more appealing than a beautiful woman in the act of cooking dinner for someone she loves!" The corollary of this statement is: Don't be pushed into giving a party for people you don't like! We all know things (and people) that make us unhappy, angry, or fearful. When energy is directed towards battling hostile elements, there's little left for the job at hand. On the other hand, if you look forward to entertaining, if you think that you are going to give a fun party, you'll find plenty of time to get everything taken care of cheerfully.

I have found the trick to relieving the monotony of any job is to think up ways of improving it. How to give a prettier, livelier, more amusing party might be the answer for those who find entertaining a monotonous chore.

Party Price Tags Need Not Show

And while we're on the subject of budgeting our time and energy, let's take a minute to talk about budgeting the cost of our entertaining too (Chapter Six). All of us, I'm sure, entertain simply at times and splurge at other times, but simple entertaining to one person may mean splurging to someone else. When in doubt, remember this rule: It's better to serve a tasty stew than a tough steak! The magic ingredient of a swinging party has never been an unlimited $ budget. We've all been to dull, *duller,* the **dullest** parties that have cost, *cost,* **cost!**

When we talk of budgets, let us remember we're talking in comparative terms. Inviting friends for brunch is ordinarily less costly than having friends for dinner. Entertaining at home, if you prepare the meal yourself, is a lot less expensive than dining and wining your friends in an elegant restaurant or club. Making your own invitations is not only less expensive but often more fun than ordering printed invitations. Renting equipment may be better budget-wise than buying something you'll never use again or have no room to store. Today more people are hiring a caterer to take the place of Grandmother's full-time help.

To Market, To Market, To Buy a Fat Pig!

People always ask about quantities. Here are a few basic principles that I follow when marketing for a party, but age, sex, and weather are variables. For example, people eat more outdoors than in; heavy drinkers eat less than light drinkers. When planning a cookout for young men and women, double the quantity. For college athletes, triple the quantity. For a ladies' luncheon, reduce the quantity.

Hors d'oeuvres: Before dinner: Allow 3 pieces per person or 1/8 pound seafood such as shelled shrimp, crabmeat, lobster, etc. For cocktail parties allow 8 pieces per person.

Main course: Allow a full 1/4 pound boneless meat such as hamburger, cubed beef, etc., per person. Meat with bone, allow 1/2 to 1 pound, depending on amount of bone.

Cooked potatoes, rice, vegetables, etc.: Allow a minimum of 1/3 cup per person, or 1 medium whole vegetable as cooked potato, baked tomato, etc.

Coffee: One pound coffee and 2 gallons water equals 40 to 48 servings.

Tea: One pound loose tea equals 150 servings.

Mix-and-Match Menus and Recipes

We've tried in the following chapters to give you enough variations so that you can mix and match your party menus and decorations to suit any strings attached to your budget, whatever they may be!

You'll notice as you read along that oodles of our recipes are also mix-and-matchable. Many appetizers do as well on the tea table as on the cocktail table; green spinach salad with anchovies blends as smoothly with grilled fish as with cheese fondue; and our Bundt

Kuchen recipe and pecan rolls could truly be called the classics in a trousseau of recipes.

We hope you won't feel bound by any hard and fast rules as you experiment with a few of our suggestions. Instead, you'll perhaps find it easier in the future to coordinate a menu with a party theme whereby you'll create a mood, a style, and a personality so completely your own, people will say, "That party is you!"—but not a monotonous you!

Which Wine with Which Food?

This is a question that intrigues many and intimidates some. The simplest solution to the problem of matching wine with food is to serve champagne or a chilled rosé throughout the entire meal. Champagne will certainly add gaiety to any dinner party. Rosé is excellent with light or cold foods. Still, it might be more fun to be a little more adventuresome in selecting the right wine, considering the effort we go through to prepare a fine meal.

For gala dinners, a few wine lovers may taste their way through the menu before the big event. Others claim that any wine goes with any food—if it suits you. But it might be better to try traditional pairings of food and wine because we have learned from experience that they go well together.

Don't be intimidated by the glamour and mystery heaped on the subject of wines. One of my favorite cartoons is by James Thurber, who spoofs the self-styled critic, seated at the dinner table and raising his glass, saying, "It's a native, domestic burgundy without any breeding, but I think you'll be amused by its presumption."

Here is a brief, reliable guide of traditional combinations of food and wine.

Hors d'oeuvres: Salads and antipasto do not lend themselves to wine because they are acidy, but quiche may go well with the wine you have selected for your main course, and a paté may go well with a Riesling.

Soup: No wine is needed with a cream soup, but with a consommé one might offer a sherry or Madeira.

Fish: Usually a light white wine like a Pinot Chardonnay, Alsation Riesling, Petit Chablis, or Pouilly-Fuisse. For shellfish a traditional Chablis is a good choice, especially with oysters.

Pork and Veal: White wines, such as a Riesling or a Graves, go well with lighter flavored meats. If you prefer a light red, a Beaujolais or Zinfandel will do nicely. A rich pork dish, as served in Germany, calls for a Rheingau.

Chicken and Other Fowl: Both red or white, light or full wines are all served with poultry. Much depends on how the dish is prepared. A red Bordeaux goes well with roast chicken or duck. Chicken in a rich sauce calls for a white Burgundy. Moselle or chilled rosé are good with cold chicken.

Pasta: A native Italian Chianti Classico enhances all pasta dishes.

Beef and Lamb: A fine red Bordeaux with roast beef, or burgundy with lamb. Stews are best with Beaujolais, or a Cabernet Sauvignon.

Ham: A light red wine like a Pinot Noir goes well with baked ham, or a chilled rosé is also good with ham, when it is accompanied with something sweet like pineapple.

Game: Pheasant or quail is nicely complemented by a light red wine, such as a Pinot Noir or Merlot. Strong game, such as venison or wild duck, calls for a heavier wine, such as a Cabernet or Chateuneuf-du-Pape.

Curry Dishes: Highly seasoned dishes do not require any wine, but one might suggest a Gewurztraminer.

Cheeses: Delicate cheeses such as Havarti go well with almost any wine. Heavier cheeses like Roquefort or Liederkranz may overwhelm the delicate flavor of a fine Medoc or aged Burgundy or Port.

Dessert: A sweet wine, like a Sauterne, a cream sherry, or a German Spatlese or Auslese Rhine wine, goes well with a cake, soufflé, or fresh fruit. A port is a perfect accompaniment to walnuts or other nibbles after dinner.

Fruits in Liqueurs

The following liqueurs seem to go well with the accompanying fresh fruits as listed, but please don't feel these suggestions are binding. With a bit of experimenting you may discover your own special favorite combination. Of course fresh fruit and liqueur may be served at any time, either before or during a meal. When served as a dessert, add a scoop of sherbet.

Bourbon—peaches and pears
Brandy—strawberries, raspberries, peaches, pineapple
Champagne—peaches, berries, melons
Curaçao—oranges, pineapple, mandarin oranges
Grand Marniér—grapefruit, oranges, tangerines
Kirsch—bananas, cherries, melons, peaches, pineapple
Kummel—figs, peaches, pears
Port—raspberries, nectarines, melons, plums

Red Wine—peaches and strawberries
Rum—bananas
White Wine—apples, pears, purple plums

After-Dinner Liqueurs and Cordials

*"I thank you for your welcome which was cordial,
and your cordial, which was welcome!"*

While we settle world affairs after dinner while seated in our dining room chairs, each with comfortable arm rests, lively dinner conversation keeps flowing. It's the perfect time to offer guests the pleasant taste of an after-dinner cordial or liqueur—served in tiny cordial glasses—such as: Crème de Menthe, Kahlua, Cointreau, Courvoisier, or Bailey's Irish Cream.

Borrowing—A Mixed Blessing

Once in a while most people need to rent or borrow an extra card table, a few chairs, or a coffee maker when entertaining a large group. We've faced this reality throughout the book, frequently referring to borrowing equipment of various kinds in spite of Shakespeare's solid good advice, "Neither a borrower nor lender be; for loan oft loses both itself and friends."

Certainly there are some things we never want to risk loaning and surely it's our privilege to say so. One might easily say something like this: "No, I am sorry but I just can't let you borrow this crystal punch bowl. It belonged to my grandmother and I'd feel terrible if something happened to it."

If we do decide to make a loan to a friend or neighbor, then let's protect ourselves by making it a habit to put our name on the article we're loaning. Return postage labels printed with your name and address work like charms to bring home stray records, trays, etc. If the label does not stick to the surface, write your name on freezer tape or adhesive tape. I can't tell you how many items have been returned to me because they were labeled.

Of course, people who borrow should return the article as soon as possible, preferably the following day, and in perfect condition. Copper and silver should be brightly polished; anything broken or damaged should be repaired or replaced after reporting the accident to the owner.

18

Casting a Party

My friends were giving me the rundown on a recent dinner party catered in a fashionable home. There were twenty guests, soft lights, good music, imported caviar, fine wines, yet it was as dull as yesterday's headlines.

We wondered why and finally agreed that there are times when a host may turn himself inside out for nothing. The fault lies with the guests.

There are guests who feel that their mere physical presence is all that's required. They arrive promptly. Remove their wraps carefully. Eat quietly. Drink moderately and thank their hosts politely before putting on their things to leave. They feel if they don't spill or break something they're conducting themselves admirably.

But these dullards contribute nothing! They don't listen attentively; they don't smile appreciatively; they don't sigh sympathetically; they don't join eagerly; they don't communicate enthusiastically . . . . they just *don't!*

The trouble with this kind of person is that, like a bad apple, he can spoil the whole barrel of fun.

Elizabeth Carpenter, White House press secretary to Mrs. Johnson, told me, "For a really good party, have on your guest list a few people who make almost a career of going to parties. They're the ones who will turn themselves inside out to make yours go!"

There are people who don't invite people to parties—they cast them! For zest and balance, one needs a variety of personalities, including a sprinkling of "doctors, lawyers, Indian chiefs." An architect friend of mine makes it a rule to have people of different ages to his "Thank-God-It's-Friday" cocktail parties. Balance and variety, yes, but the perfect guest list will surely include a beautiful woman along with a man of accomplishment.

A popular guest usually is an experienced party-giver, who knows it's a treat to be invited into one's home. He'll never "make an appearance," rushing in late from one function and leaving early for the next! (If one must leave early, it's best to thank the hostess in advance and explain why one must leave, then slip out quietly and unobtrusively. In France they call this "taking English leave," and in England it's called "taking French leave," but no matter what it's called, this is a thoughtful way to depart without disrupting a group.)

Party Pill Is My Name

> *I never answer invitations*
> *I cancel at the last minute*
> *I telephone a half hour before the party*

I always arrive early—or late
I like to bring my children and pets
I don't mingle with the guests
I monopolize the conversation
I tell off-color stories
I make amorous advances
I enjoy heated, controversial discussions
I like to drink too much
I don't want to go home
I don't write or phone my "thank you's"

Thank the Lord for those precious, lovable guests who may do the most outlandish things but, because of their particular charm, become even more endearing. They're cheerful, not boisterous; courteous, not fresh; and if they are a little fresh, not obnoxious. They are serious, not somber; they tease, but don't hurt; they're sweet, not gooey; they are sharp, not cutting.

A guest who everlastingly endeared himself to his host way back in 29 B.C. was described by Horace in *A Rich Man Dines.* When a canopy fell from the ceiling on the dining room table and the elegant Roman meal was covered with black dust, Balatro complimented his host with the ultimate *bon mot* by saying:

"A host is like a general: adversity reveals his genius, prosperity hides it."

To this the host replied, "Heaven grant you all that you pray for! You are so kind and considerate a guest!"

Hostess—With Apologies

Of course, guests are not the only pet peeve in this great, big, wide, and wonderful world. There are some hostesses I'd gladly nominate for a one-way passage to the moon. Edgar Guest said it first and cleverly:

The Sorry Hostess

She said she was sorry the weather was bad
The night that she asked us to dine;
And she really appeared inexpressibly sad

Because she had hoped 'twould be fine.
She was sorry to hear that my wife had a cold,
And she almost shed tears over that,
And how sorry she was, she most feelingly told,
That the steam wasn't on in the flat.

When the dinner began she apologized twice
For the olives, because they were small;
She was certain the celery, too, wasn't nice,
And the soup didn't suit her at all.
She was sorry she couldn't get whitefish instead
Of the trout that the fishmonger sent,
But she hoped that we'd manage somehow to be fed
Though her dinner was not what she meant.

She spoke her regrets for the salad, and then
Explained she was really much hurt,
And begged both our pardons again and again
For serving a skimpy dessert.
She was sorry for this and sorry for that,
Though there really was nothing to blame.
And I thought to myself as I put on my hat
Perhaps she is sorry we came.

—From Edgar Guest's "Just Folks"

Invitations—Verbal, Written, Last-Minute—But Specific!

Old-fashioned formality reached such extremes during the early 19th century that, in some Parisian societies, if one neglected coming to dinner after having accepted an invitation, one had to forfeit 500 francs or about $60.

In today's society, we may be billed on our credit card after making a reservation at a hotel banquet whether we're there to eat the creamed chicken or not, but generally our social life is much more informal and invitations, too, are more casual than ever. Herein lies a danger that's reaching significant proportions.

This happened to a friend of mine who invited a casual acquaintance a little too casually for dinner. When her doorbell rang on the appointed day, at the correct time, the hostess almost fainted when she saw her guest dressed in a formal dress when all she'd planned was a cozy meal with the kids!

Inviting someone for a game of bridge can become awkward unless one spells out exactly whether one plays for fun or money—and how much. A quarter could easily mean twenty-five cents or a quarter of a cent a point—a big difference!

Surprises do give a party special appeal—except when it's a fundraising appeal! It's never in good taste to invite someone to a party and then surprise him by asking for a donation. If the party is given in behalf of charity, this should be clearly stated in the invitation and solicitations should be done by letter or phone the day after.

It's amazing how often people who should know better invite friends while they're at another party or meeting. Sometimes they even rely on a husband to relay the invitation to the wife—a lamentable idea. To avoid misunderstandings, be considerate and follow any casual mention of an invitation with a follow-up telephone call. This gives people a chance to circle the date on their home calendar, because it's a darn shame holding dinner only to learn that your guests thought they were invited after dinner—if they remembered the invitation at all!

Sometimes people are under the false impression that it doesn't make any difference whether they go to a reception or not—it's going to be a large affair with lots of people coming and going and their absence won't be noticed. Wrong! Most hostesses screen their guest list carefully, they do count heads and are disturbed when an expected someone turns into a "no-show"! Often questions are raised: "Did so-and-so say they were coming?" "Shall we call the house?" "Do you think something is wrong?"

Every invitation should be answered "yes" or "no" within a few days either by note, telephone, or e-mail. If this is impossible, then an explanation is in order.

When invitations are mailed and one does not receive a reply within a reasonable time, it's best to check why. Perhaps the invited guest is out of town or the invitation has been mis-addressed or gone astray.

Of course everyone dreads last-minute cancellations, yet there are times when this too is unavoidable. We bump into Mary hastily filling a prescription in the drug store for her feverish husband and she cries, "We're so disappointed we won't be able to be with you for dinner tomorrow!"

"Horrors," you think. "We need another poker player, but how can I invite someone at the last minute?" Well, why not? Now's the time to call your best friend and be honest, "We're giving a small dinner party tomorrow night and the Plunkets can't come. Will you be a sport and fill in for us?"

Or Bob calls at six o'clock. "Jane's plane is grounded! I'm so sorry she can't be with us tonight." Too late to get a substitute, OK. But rather than leave an empty place at the table, it's so much more congenial to remove the place setting which only takes a minute. No one likes being seated next to a vacant chair, yet I've seen this happen more than once.

All invitations, verbal or written, should give the exact date, time and place and sometimes dress (black tie or blue jeans). There should be an R.S.V.P. or Please Reply in one corner with a return address or telephone number. One of my pet peeves is to receive an invitation from Mary and Bill or Jane and Tom without a last name. It's thoughtless to make people play "Guess Who?," unless of course you're deliberately planning a Mystery Party!

In addition, one may write when the party is supposed to be over. Open House from three to five o'clock. Cocktails from five to seven. Tea from two to four o'clock, or whatever one decides. On the phone one might say, "We're having a few friends over for Frank and Dorothy on Wednesday evening—it won't be a late evening because they're leaving on an early flight for the South the first thing Thursday morning."

There was a day when it was considered gauche even to have a clock in the living room, but those were the days when people knew how long to stay and when to go home. Glenville Kleiser has written these appropriate words on the subject.

The Ideal Hostess—	*She gleans how long you wish to stay* *She lets you go without delay.*
The Ideal Guest—	*She is not difficult to please;* *She can be silent as the trees.* *She shuns all ostentatious show;* *She knows exactly when to go.*

Keep an Open Heart—and Table

It's true remaining loyal to old friends is an admirable trait, but psychiatrists caution us that in order to keep a healthy mental outlook, we must not become isolated in later life. Therefore we must continually make new friends.

While interviewing a moody patient, a psychiatrist brought up the subject of friends and asked, "Do you meet new people easily? Are you broadening your circle of friends?"

"Why should I make new friends," replied the cynic, "when I don't like the ones I already have?"

Evidently the Greeks had a healthier mental outlook than the cynic because their word for "guest" is *xenos*, which also means "stranger," making it impossible to translate the friendly American cowboy expression into Greek: Be my guest, stranger!

Hospitality is never a matter of inviting the Joneses because we owe them or including a neighbor in order to show off our new carpet. It's more than feeding a crowd or housing a stranger. While listing the intangible gifts of the spirit, the brothers Overstreet (educators, authors, professors) head their list with the Spirit of Hospitality.

"We can welcome our fellow humans when they enter the door of our homes by our manner which says, 'I'm glad you've come. If you feel tired, beset by chores, battered by the demands of life, on the defensive, you can rest here. And you can safely be yourself. If you don't agree, I'll respect your ideas as yours, I won't call them silly or shout you down. Come in . . . . be at home. There is room for you here!'"

In a home that does more than serve as a hostel, it's possible to schedule as little as one day a month—perhaps on the weekend—when one's table is set with extra loving care, when good china and crystal are given an airing, when dinner is served leisurely, graciously, with thought given to both taste appeal and eye appeal. The French have developed the fine art of eating to its highest degree. Dinner is not only a time to satisfy our hunger, but a form of recreation, a ritual to be enjoyed. The Germans call it "Gemutlichkeit," wherever good food, good living, and good companions meet. We can't define, it but we can experience it!

Creating a pleasant atmosphere at mealtime is not only a matter of aesthetics, but also vital to health. Doctors agree that digestion is definitely improved and appetites stimulated when meals are relaxing. The Bible reminds us, "Better a dry morsel and quietness therewith, than a house full of feasting with strife" (Proverbs 17:1).

It's just a skip and a jump from planning a family dinner to entertaining friends. Then why do we meet with resistance among some people? What's the problem?

In many cases the problem is basically that too many people are unsure, afraid. They worry that their homes are not fine enough or the refreshments won't please or the guests will be bored. Some say it's impossible to entertain until the couch has been recovered or the children are older or the bank account is larger. Excuses, excuses, excuses!

Nor is that all. There are other drawbacks. In some marriages one of the partners is more sociable and outgoing than the other. "She" loves to go out for a fun evening or adores having company at home, while "he" couldn't care less! It could be the other way around. "She" is the quiet one who'd rather stay home and read a book than entertain the boss for dinner. What to do? The solution, as in all successful partnerships, is to establish a give-and-take. In this case a good compromise is for "he and she" to sit down together and budget the family entertaining on a fair and compatible basis in one of the following ways. One couple may decide to have a few friends over regularly once a week or once a month.

Another couple may occasionally prefer dividing "his" and "her" friends into separate stag affairs and hen parties. Another couple may choose to go all out and invite everyone they know to a huge bash once a year or so. Some may decide to entertain jointly with another couple or a small group. (See Chapter Five.)

Whatever the decision, this one social rule always holds fast. No matter how charming, bright, attractive, or witty one is, it's not possible to have a successful social life unless hospitality is reciprocated. Now it doesn't necessarily matter if one reciprocates on the same level, tit for tat, but reciprocate one must to the best of one's ability. It is much better to invite someone to lunch or plan a picnic—even after being invited to an elegant catered dinner party—than not to reciprocate at all.

Poet-publisher Joseph Addison put it neatly when he wrote in 1702, "For my part I can no more accept a snuffbox without returning my acknowledgements than I can take snuff without sneezing after it."

Efficiency—Efficiency!

The efficient hostess is not always the hardest worker. When asked, "How do you manage to get so much done?," she's apt to reply, "I'm basically really very lazy. I always try to think of the simplest shortcuts!"

A useful shortcut for lazy people like me is to keep a party log or diary similar to the call board used in the theater. (A call board is a meticulously contrived chart showing exactly what should be happening during rehearsals and where.) Referring to your notes speeds things up a lot when organizing your next party.

The queen in *Alice in Wonderland,* by Lewis Carroll, sums it up rather accurately.

"The horror of that moment," the king went on, "I shall never, never forget!"

"You will, though," the queen said, "if you don't make a memorandum of it."

Not only is a party log a time-saver in the long run, but it's as much fun to browse through as a photograph album or a first baby book. Sometimes I include photographs of my table, and even thank-you notes. It's a snap to make your own by using a looseleaf binder where a page might look like this:

Party for	Where	Date	Time
Dress			
Guest list	Accept	Regret	

Menu:
Recipes:
Special shopping list or
  food specialties to send for

Caterer or extra help	Tel. number

Beverages:
Liquor:
Equipment to borrow or rent,
  folding chairs, tables, bars:

Flower arrangement	Florist

Table setting theme
Music
Comments:

House Check List

Is the house number visible—or hidden behind an overgrown bush?

Is the driveway clear—or will Johnny be heartbroken if someone drives over his new tricycle?

Is the car in the garage—or is it taking up good parking space in front of the house?

Are the garage doors closed—or wide open, leaving a hole about as decorative as a missing tooth?

During warm weather, are the sprinklers turned off along the sidewalk? Presumably everyone has already had a shower.

Is the garden hose draped across the walk—or neatly rolled out of the way?

In the winter, is the walk free from snow and the steps clear of ice—or do you carry lots of insurance?

Check List for a Large Party

Parking space
Coat racks and hangers
Table skirt and cloths
Flower decorations, candelabras
Candles, matches
Cloth napkins
China
Table glassware
Flat silver
Service silver
Serving trays and platters
Warming stoves, ovens, grills
Coffee maker

Bar Equipment:

Cocktail napkins
Bar table, linen, glassware
Bottle openers, stirrer, etc.
Wines, spirits, mixes, punches
Garnishes for drinks, lemons, limes, olives
Ice cubes, crushed ice, ice molds

Chapter Two

Come for Brunch or Lunch

"Spend more imagination than money."

—Lyndon B. Johnson

Brunches, Lunches, and What to Wear

The charm of a combination breakfast–lunch is that it's such a genial way to entertain at home! Sometimes we need to be reminded that hosts and hostesses don't invite guests because they think they're hungry, but because they want to entertain friends! Instead of only food, think about a congenial guest list, diverse seating arrangements—who will enjoy meeting whom—and the table setting with a nice, low centerpiece. By its nature, a brunch ought to be a casual affair, and I just can't bring myself to enjoy the formality of dressing up for a brunch for a large crowd at a swank hotel with crystal chandeliers!

It follows then that the setting of a memorable brunch is far more important than the menu. In warm climates, dining on a shady terrace, a Spanish patio, beside a sparkling pool, under a latticed gazebo—or anywhere in a well-appointed garden—is my first choice. Dress, of course, should be casual sport clothes. During football season, in the winter, or just for relaxation, a brightly lit fireplace helps melt any possible friction into spirited congeniality.

It's up to the host or hostess to prepare us for an *al fresco* setting when we are invited by suggesting what to wear. On the phone, we might be told, "Please come for brunch Sunday to meet our houseguests. We'll be dressed from church, but if it's a nice day, you'll enjoy a dip in the pool, so won't you bring along your suits and towels?"

Human beings are, by and large, conformists and dislike appearing singular. Customs vary so from group to group and locale to locale that it's difficult for even the most experienced traveler to always be right when it comes to dress. In southwest resorts you'll find some tuxedos, but they are mostly worn by the waiters. In San Antonio western shirts and Levi's predominate, while in Palm Beach one's best linen dress can be spotted at 10:00 A.M. on Worth Avenue.

Today's dress requirements are often odd, ambiguous, and confusing.

Casual or **Dressy Casual** can mean different things in the city, suburb, or country. Generally speaking, this means either leather jackets, sweaters, turtlenecks, and jeans.

Informal or **Elegant Casual** sounds dressier than casual. A man might wear a tie or turtleneck with his sportcoat and a woman might wear either a skirt or slacks.

Business Attire or **Coat and Tie** usually mean that one is coming directly from the office, where men and women wear suits.

Black Tie Optional means if you own a tuxedo please wear it, but don't rent one.

Black Tie is less formal than White Tie and means a tuxedo for the man and a dressy cocktail dress, long dress, or silk suit for the woman. Again, in different countries the dress means different things. For instance, in the United States, Black Tie is considered formal, but in England it is considered informal.

White Tie is considered truly formal everywhere, and women wear long dresses or ball gowns, gloves, and best jewelry.

Travel agencies make it their business to inform us exactly how little one needs when traveling to faraway places, and so do steamship companies. If you're uncertain what to wear to a party, do a little advance sleuthing. Most people will be flattered by the question, "What are you wearing to the Smiths' on Sunday?" Haven't we all had an unhappy experience in our lives when we wished we'd remembered to ask this simple question? I know I have! One summer I was invited to a cocktail party at five o'clock. I raced home early from the beach on a beautiful, hot summer day, showered, dressed myself in heels and my best linen, drove to the party, and noticed through the garden bushes that everyone there was still dressed in casual beach attire. Without stopping the car, I returned home, changed into a fresh pair of shorts and T-shirt and arrived at the party, breathless, late, but properly "undressed"!

A noted dress designer believes that the color of a woman's dress must be becoming to her mind, and isn't this particularly true for the hostess as well? Always wear something you like, that's comfortable, that isn't too loose or too tight or too warm, if you wish to remain cool, calm, and collected. Take time out during the party to freshen up a bit. A few secret moments by yourself to run a comb through your hair will do wonderful things for your nerves. Your serenity will help give the impression all's well—even if there's chaos in the kitchen!

Poolside Brunch

Whenever we're invited to an outdoor affair I'm reminded of this story about a woman who planned a garden party and didn't invite her neighbor because she was annoyed with her. At the last minute she relented and telephoned her neighbor, who without hesitation replied, "It's too late—I've already prayed for rain!"

Well, we prayed for sunshine and fortunately on the day of the brunch everything appeared in readiness around the pool. We were offered the choice of a Bloody Mary or a Bullshot or a non-alcoholic Red Orange Juice, each already mixed ahead in a pitcher to be poured over ice. (Both Bloody Marys and Bullshots are made with vodka, a drink that has rapidly overtaken gin in popularity in the United States.)

It's wise not to serve drinks in breakable glasses around a pool—too many bare feet. There are clear, plastic containers that are disposable or can be washed and used over and over again, and won't break if dropped.

Sunday Chef Poolside Brunch

Bloody Mary (see Chapter Four)
Bullshot
Red Orange Juice (mix an equal part of cranberry and orange juice and serve chilled)
Garlic toast
Crispy cheese sticks
Omelet with herbs, chives, cheese, bacon, onions, red caviar or jam
Muffins
No-yeast Bundt Kuchen
Tea or Coffee

Omelets with a Flair—Any Time

Sunday chefs who delight in demonstrating their culinary skills might do well to take a tip from a prominent caterer and professional omelet-maker extraordinaire. He combined a bit of legerdemain with his culinary ability—why else was he flown from one end of the country to the other, preparing from twenty to thirty thousand omelets a year for leading figures of the stage and screen?

An omelet chef turns out omelets not only for wedding breakfasts and hunt breakfasts, but for Christmas Eve gatherings, New Year's Eve parties, after-theater parties, and just about any happy occasion. I have watched such a chef perform magic against a backdrop of blue delphinium at an outdoor wedding breakfast. Bringing his own equipment, including two portable, propane-fueled burners and two 10" omelet pans, he deftly set up his equipment on two long tables covered with white cloths. On the tables he placed numerous small bowls filled with a choice of chopped herbs, chives, parsley, onions, grated cheddar cheese, bits of bacon, red caviar, sour cream, apricot jam, and powdered sugar.

It doesn't take long before the orders come hot and fast! "Make mine cheese!" or "I'll try the caviar and sour cream!" or "One apricot jam and powdered sugar!" And to our astonishment, the chef delivers in seconds—thirty seconds to an omelet, to be exact!

Here's a tried and true omelet recipe for 25.

Basic Omelet

Equipment: Portable propane-fueled burner, 10" omelet pan, 10 small bowls

1 cup cold water
1 tablespoon salt
1 teaspoon Tabasco sauce
5 dozen fresh eggs, room temperature
3/4 lb. butter

1. In a small bowl mix water, salt and Tabasco.
2. Break eggs into very large bowl (5- or 6-quart capacity) and beat until well blended with an egg beater. Add salt water and Tabasco mixture to beaten eggs and stir well. Set aside until ready to use.

3. Heat individual omelet pan to medium and melt one tablespoon butter until it bubbles.
4. Select any one or combination of several ingredients now i.e., chopped herbs, parsley, chives, crumbled bacon, finely chopped onion, or mild grated cheddar cheese, and put in pan.
5. Add a dipper of 3/4 cup egg liquid and stir with a fork flat on the pan making one fast circular motion. This movement will distribute the herbs or bacon etc. evenly throughout the omelet. While making the circular motion, shake the pan to and fro until the eggs congeal and the bottom of the pan is covered with egg. Roll onto heated plate and garnish with parsley.

Serves 25.

Addenda: Always use salted butter. Keep pan on a medium flame with the heat readily adjustable. Have ingredients and things to be added within reach. Banish everything but the care of the omelet from your mind and concentrate on the eggs. Serve immediately. Make only one omelet at a time.

Red Caviar Omelet for One

Before risking inviting two dozen neighbors, you might like to try an omelet with red caviar and sour cream for yourself first.

1 tablespoon water
1/4 teaspoon salt (scant)
Dash of Tabasco sauce
3 eggs
1 tablespoon salted butter
1 tablespoon red caviar
2 tablespoons sour cream
1 tablespoon chopped parsley

1. Mix water, salt, and parsley in a cup.
2. Break eggs into small bowl; beat slightly.
3. Add salt-water mixture to beaten eggs and stir well. Set aside until ready to use.
4. Heat omelet pan to medium and melt one tablespoon butter until it bubbles.
5. Pour egg mixture into pan and stir with a fork, holding it flat on the pan and making one fast circular motion. Shake the pan to and fro until eggs congeal and

the bottom of the pan is covered with egg. Roll onto heated plate.

6. Make an incision lengthwise (about 3 inches long) and spread it apart and neatly spoon the mixture of red caviar and sour cream into the opening. Sprinkle with parsley and eat hot.

No-Yeast Bundt Kuchen
(*Bundt* is the German word for "circle")

What would we ever do in our house without this Bundt Kuchen, because we use it constantly for almost every occasion year 'round—morning, noon, and night. It's especially dazzling served during the winter season because when the cake is lightly dusted with powdered sugar, the effect always reminds me of freshly fallen snow on a hilly countryside. Naturally, it requires a bundt form. Mine is a heavy, old, copper antique with a crown pattern which I found years ago. Bundt forms are advertised in numerous catalogs and are available in any well-stocked cooking section of a kitchen supply store. There are also bundt pans on the market that look like muffin pans. These are shaped in individual, miniature bundt forms instead of muffins. (See Sources of Supply.)

Most bundt recipes call for yeast, but we've had such good luck with our modified no-yeast version and so many people have asked for the recipe, here it is! It's one of those cakes that freezes well and is better on the second and third day, if there's any left.

We set the eggs and butter out of the refrigerator the night before and take the milk out of the refrigerator the first thing in the morning or at least one hour before starting to make sure everything is at room temperature. This recipe is made in an 8-1/2-inch bundt form.

Bundt Kuchen is good made the day before. When freezing, let cake cool down first or it may become soggy. After defrosting it for a couple of hours, sprinkle lightly with powdered sugar.

Equipment: 8-1/2" bundt form, large mixing bowl, electric beater, sifter

1 cup butter
2 cups sugar

5 egg yolks, slightly beaten
3 cups sifted flour
3 teaspoons baking powder
1 cup milk
5 egg whites, stiffly beaten
1 teaspoon vanilla
1/2 cup raisins
Rind of 1 lemon, grated medium fine
3 tablespoons powdered sugar

1. Cream butter and sugar together in a large mixing bowl until the mixture is light and fluffy. You can use an electric beater or the back of a wooden spoon.
2. Add slightly beaten egg yolks to butter and sugar.
3. Sift flour three times (even pre-sifted flour, because you use less flour after sifting). Measure out 3 cups and add 3 teaspoons baking powder and sift again.
4. Add to butter mixture in bowl and alternate with 1 cup milk.
5. Fold in stiffly beaten egg whites, vanilla, raisins, and lemon rind.
6. Bake in 350° F. oven for 45 minutes (with heavy-duty copper form, allow an extra 20 minutes).
7. Cool. Just before serving, sprinkle lightly with powdered sugar.
Makes 16 servings.

Clove Cake

A spicy variation of the Bundt Kuchen, also baked in a high tube pan or bundt form. It stays fresh for several days and freezes nicely. Set eggs, butter, and milk out of the refrigerator for at least one hour before mixing or until room temperature

Equipment: Sifter, large mixing bowl, high tube pan, or bundt form

3 cups flour
1 tablespoon powdered cloves
1 tablespoon cinnamon
1/4 teaspoon salt
1/2 lb. butter
2-1/4 cups sugar

5 eggs
1 cup sour or buttermilk
1 teaspoon baking soda

1. Preheat oven to 350° F.
2. Sift flour twice. The third time sift together with cloves, cinnamon, and salt.
3. In a large mixing bowl, cream butter and sugar; add eggs one at a time. Beat well until light and fluffy.
4. Alternate flour mixture with 1/2 cup milk (no soda) adding to creamed butter mixture.
5. Last, add 1/2 cup milk mixed with baking soda.
6. Grease and flour tube or bundt form well. Place in oven and bake for 1 hour or until done.
 Makes 16 servings.

Champagne Brunch

For those dear people who do not choose to be "center stage" flipping omelets or crêpes and who much prefer preparing things as far ahead as possible, this menu should suit just fine! Practically all that needs doing on the day is to pop the cork for the champagne—that is, if you set the table the night before.

Champagne Brunch Menu

Champagne Séc
Sherried sweetbreads and mushrooms rolled in crêpes
Mini-marmalade sandwiches
Bibb lettuce salad
Fresh berries and fruits
Coffee

Sherried Sweetbreads

Sherried sweetbreads and mushrooms rolled in crêpes may be done in three simple stages. The crêpes can be made weeks ahead and frozen. (See crêpe recipe, Chapter Six.)

The day before the brunch, cook the sweetbreads, sauté the mushrooms, and combine with sauce. On the morning of the brunch, spread sweetbread mixture over defrosted crêpes, roll, and warm in oven until ready to serve.

Equipment: Medium-sized skillet, oblong baking dish

2 lbs. sweetbreads
1 teaspoon salt
1 tablespoon vinegar
1 lb. fresh mushrooms
4 tablespoons butter

1. Soak sweetbreads in cold water for 20 minutes. Drain.
2. Cook 20 minutes in a quart of boiling salt water with vinegar. Drain water and plunge sweetbreads into cold water.
3. Chill in refrigerator. Remove pipes and membranes; cut or break sweetbreads into small pieces.
4. Slice off the end of mushroom stems and rinse under a light stream of cold water and drain. Slice mushrooms.
5. In a heavy, medium-sized skillet, heat butter then add mushrooms. Turn with a pancake turner as edges begin to brown slightly and mushrooms turn golden, about 5 minutes.
6. Combine sweetbreads and mushrooms.

Sauce

3 tablespoons butter
3 tablespoons flour
1 chicken bouillon cube
1 cup hot water
1/2 cup cream
Dash of salt
Dash of paprika
3 tablespoons sherry wine

1. Melt butter in saucepan and add flour. Stir. Place chicken bouillon cube in cup of hot water until dissolved and add to heated mixture while stirring.
2. Add cream. Bring to boil while still stirring. Add seasoning and sherry.
3. Combine sweetbreads, mushrooms, and sauce and refrigerate until ready to serve. Save a little sauce to pour over the finished crêpes.
4. Defrost the crêpes. Preheat oven to 275° F. and spread sweetbread and mushroom mixture over crêpes.
5. Roll and place in an oblong baking dish ready for serving and cover with remaining sauce. Warm in oven for 20 to 25 minutes.

Makes enough for 12 crêpes or 6 servings.

Mini-Marmalade Sandwiches

Remove the crust from thin slices of white bread. Spread with soft butter and orange marmalade. Put two slices together. Melt a tablespoon of butter or margarine in frying pan and fry slowly on both sides until golden. Cut diagonally twice into quarters before serving.

Addenda: You can prepare this one hour ahead and keep it toasty in a warm oven. The butter keeps bread from drying out.

Egg Roulades—with Creamed Mushroom Filling
An alternative suggestion to crêpes

Roulades may be made a day ahead and reheated. Light as a feather and delicious!

Equipment: Two 10" x 15" x 1" deep jellyroll pans, wire whisk, rubber spatula, wax paper, large sauce pan, or cast iron skillet

8 tablespoons butter
1 cup flour
4 cups milk, heated
2 teaspoons salt
1/4 teaspoons cayenne pepper
2 tablespoons cognac
2 tablespoons sour cream
8 eggs, separated

1. In a large saucepan melt butter over low heat and blend in flour. Cook, stirring until golden and bubbly. Remove from heat and gradually stir in milk with wire whisk, removing all lumps. Return to heat and stir until thick. Add salt, pepper, cognac, and sour cream. Beat egg yolks lightly and add to mixture.
2. Preheat oven to 325° F. Butter two jellyroll pans, then line with wax paper, leaving a couple of inches overlap, and then butter paper again really well.
3. Beat egg whites to stand in soft peaks. Thoroughly fold in 1/3 egg whites into sauce mixture, then lightly fold in the remaining 2/3 of egg whites. Divide mixture between two jellyroll pans and spread evenly with rubber spatula.
4. Bake 40 minutes or until golden on top. When done, remove from oven. Invert pan onto a large sheet of wax paper. Loosen paper from the pan, then peel it from the roll. If some sticks, gently loosen with knife. Trim edges of egg roll with sharp knife. Using rubber spatula, spread with filling, then gently lift wax paper to form into a fat roll, like a jellyroll. Transfer to a warm serving platter and add rest of filling on top.

Creamed Mushroom Filling

12 tablespoons butter
1 lb. mushrooms, sliced
1 tablespoon lemon juice
Salt, freshly ground pepper
6 tablespoons flour
1-1/2 cups milk, heated
1 cup whipping cream
1/2 cup chopped parsley

1. In a large sauce pan or cast iron skillet, melt 6 tablespoons butter, add mushrooms, and sauté quickly, sprinkle with lemon juice, salt, and pepper. Set aside.
2. Melt the remaining butter in a saucepan, blend in flour, and cook over medium heat, stirring until bubbly and golden. Whisk in hot milk carefully so sauce doesn't lump and keep stirring until thick. (Tip: If sauce is still lumpy, put it through a food processsor.)
3. Add salt and pepper to taste. Mix in whipping cream and parsley. Add sautéed mushrooms and heat.

Servings: Two egg roulades with mushroom filling will serve 12.

Farçies a la Princesse
Another luncheon suggestion

Years ago, Princess Grace of Monaco shared one of her favorite recipes with me for Farçies. Farçies are stuffed vegetables which can be served hot or cold along with a large tossed green salad. Here is the Princess' own recipe for this delicacy.

You may fill either tomatoes, eggplant, or zucchini or a combination of all three with the following ingredients, but this quantity is sufficient for 8 large tomatoes. There are no hard and fast rules to the recipe, and every woman has her own way of making them. Some prefer, for instance, to use rice in place of the potato; others also add a bit of raw spinach. The overall characteristic of Farçies is that they are usually peppery and well flavored with garlic.

Equipment: Electric blender, 14" baking pan

8 large tomatoes, unpeeled
1 medium-sized boiled onion
3/4 lb. boiled ham
1 crushed clove garlic
2 tablespoons mashed potatoes or rice
1/4 cup finely chopped parsley
3/4 cup finely grated Italian Parmesan cheese
1 large beaten egg
Large dash of freshly ground pepper
Salt to taste
3/4 cup bread crumbs

1. Preheat oven to 400° F.
2. Cut deep narrow hole in firm, large tomatoes. Scoop out inside and save. In your blender mix boiled onion, ham, garlic, cheese, potato, parsley, seasoning, and to-mato pulp at medium speed for 15 seconds.
3. Remove from blender and bind together with beaten egg. Fill tomatoes with mixture.
4. Top with dry bread crumbs and bake in oven for 15 minutes.
Makes 8 Farçies.

Addenda: To substitute tomato cases with eggplant or zucchini, cook the vegetable whole in boiling salted water with a slice of onion added for flavor. When tender but still firm, drain and cut in half. Blend the ingredients for the filling as given above, stuff and bake as directed.

An Invitation to Lunch

Giving a luncheon is a pleasure—to be as free and creative as one likes—and there's usually a delightful reason for celebrating! A bridal shower, baby shower, a farewell or welcome-home, a birthday, an award ceremony, or graduation are all popular occasions for a luncheon.

When there's a ready-made theme, easy entertaining is a breeze for the hostess with a flair who steals a few tricks from the theater, where entertainment is king. Her invitations announce coming events like the theater lights on a marquee.

An invitation may be as informal as a personal postcard or printed on white vellum. It may be a jingle of your own or a champagne glass mailed in a box of popcorn that's marked, "To be filled at—." It can be as sentimental as a locket or as corny as a bandana!

As far back as 1847, Lady Goon was plagued with the desire to mail an original and unusual invitation. She went to a great deal of trouble and arranged for the printing of a special issue stamp showing the profile of a lovely lady somewhat resembling Victoria. One of these unused Mauritius stamps sold many years later for over $20,000 in London.

One can't help but speculate why all the stamps were not used for mailing her invitations. Did Lady Goon black-pencil a name on her list in anger—or with regret? Or had she, with foresight, ordered extra stamps? We can only guess.

But the urge to be original still persists, for I've noticed invitations that have come through the mail with special commemorative stamps that jibe with the party theme. For instance, a yacht club sent invitations to their closing Commodore's Ball by using the commemorative stamp of a sailboat race!

Sometimes it's not easy to find just the kind of printed invitation one is looking for on the market. Then it's fun to improvise. This is what I had to do when I looked for a "Bon Voyage" invitation for my friend, Caroline. I found some informals with a pale green marine scene across which I scrawled "Bon Voyage!" in green ink. On one page inside I put the date, time, and place; on the other page I wrote "Please bring an intangible gift—a travel tip, a timely hint, a suggestion or a word picture of a memory, a scent, a sound or image; a toast."

Bon Voyage Luncheon

All the guests arrived with amusing anecdotes of experiences and memories of their travels, some in poem, song or rhyme, with loads of advice for our peripatetic friend as to where and where *not* to eat, shop and stay.

After a glass of sherry and throughout the meal these poems were read, memories kindled, toasts given, and information shared with the prospective traveler.

There's no question when guests are involved it's bound to help make things go! To this day Caroline cherishes her Bon Voyage scrapbook and the memory of a very personal, hearty send-off.

Bon Voyage Luncheon Menu

Sherry
Hot cheese cookies*
Shrimp and artichoke casserole
Rice with chopped parsley
Spinach salad**
Clover leaf rolls
Chocolate mousse
Coffee

*Hot cheese cookies recipe under Hors d'Oeuvres in Chapter Four.
**Spinach salad recipe in Chapter Five.

Shrimp and Artichoke Casserole

This shrimp and artichoke casserole recipe with an international flavor came from the family kitchen records of Adlai Stevenson's mother. When Stevenson was U.S. Minister, Chief of U.S. Delegation for the United Nations, he served this dish to President Kennedy and U.N. Acting Secretary General U Thant. Even though Stevenson had eaten the same dish the day before, he enjoyed it so much that he asked the chef to prepare it again on the following day when lunching with the president. I have served it many times for lunch or dinner and it always brings rave reviews.

Equipment: Medium-sized saucepan, small skillet, double boiler, 2-quart oven-proof casserole baking dish

1 lb. shrimp, fresh or frozen
2 tablespoons salt
1/4 lb. fresh or canned mushrooms, sliced medium
2 tablespoons butter
1-1/2 cups cream sauce
3 tablespoons butter
3 tablespoons flour
1-1/2 cups milk
Salt and pepper to taste
1 can (20 oz.) artichoke hearts
1/4 cup dry sherry wine
1 tablespoon Worcestershire sauce
1/4 cup grated Parmesan cheese
1 teaspoon paprika

1. Plunge washed, deveined frozen shrimp in 1-1/2 quarts of boiling salted water and cook 10 to 14 minutes or until tender. (Fresh shrimp take less than 3 to 5 minutes.) Let shrimp cool in liquid.
2. Slice mushrooms and sauté in butter in a small skillet at medium temperature until golden.
3. Make cream sauce: In a double boiler heat 3 tablespoons butter, 3 tablespoons flour, 1-1/2 cups milk, salt, and pepper. Beat with egg beater to prevent lumps from forming. Cook for about 5 minutes.
4. Drain water from artichoke hearts and arrange hearts in a buttered 2-quart baking dish. Spread shrimp and sauteed mushrooms over artichokes.
5. Add sherry to cream sauce, stir and add Worcestershire sauce and stir again. Pour cream sauce over shrimp and artichokes. Sprinkle top generously with Parmesan cheese and paprika. Bake for 30 to 40 minutes in 375° F. oven and serve hot.
Makes 6 servings.

International Smorgasbord

Give travelers a rousing send-off by serving a native product from each country on their itinerary. On a large platter arrange a mixture of cold cuts and place a matching flag of the land on the Swiss cheese, Danish ham, Portuguese sardines, Italian salami, Greek olives, Russian rye bread, served with German beer or French wine.

One can enjoy an international smorgasbord at any time—for luncheon, dinner, or an evening snack. (See Sources of Supply for party props.)

A Symphony Luncheon Menu

Once in a while there's an occasion when a "little" luncheon at home for both men and women is a pleasant diversion. I attended such a gathering in honor of a visiting conductor and his wife, where the theme for the decor was musical, of course. Our imaginative hostess used sheet music for table-mats, and a violin and a bow set among potted violets as the centerpiece on a base of records—a nice low arrangement to help span lively discussion.

Naturally the stereo was turned on softly playing some symphony recordings while we were lunching.

Symphony Luncheon Menu

Chicken bouillon
Crabmeat on Holland Rusk
Celery, olives, green pickles
Vanilla ice cream with crème de menthe sauce
Tea

Crabmeat (or Tuna) on Rusk

Crabmeat on rusk is very popular with men, so be prepared to serve seconds!

Equipment: Cookie sheet, 2 medium-sized bowls

6 oz. cream cheese
1/8 lb. butter
1 tablespoon lemon juice
1 teaspoon Worcestershire sauce
1 tablespoon minced onion
1 (7 oz.) can lump-style crabmeat or tuna
1 package Holland Rusk
2 large tomatoes in 6 slices
6 slices Old English cheese
3 strips partially cooked bacon

1. Preheat oven to 450° F.
2. Cream the cream cheese with butter, lemon juice, Worcestershire sauce, and minced onion in a medium-sized bowl.
3. In a separate bowl flake crabmeat and remove bones. (If tuna fish is used instead, drain tuna.) Add to cream cheese and mix together.
4. Divide mix and shape into six patties. Put each on a piece of Holland Rusk. On top place a slice of tomato, a slice of Old English cheese, and half a strip of partially cooked bacon.
5. Bake on cookie sheet for 10 minutes in 450° F. oven and 5 more minutes (check carefully) under broiler or until cheese melts and bacon is crisp.
6. Serve on individual plates and garnish with olives, pickles, celery.

Makes 6 patties/servings.

Sub-Teen Birthday Luncheon

Wouldn't every "Little Miss" adore dressing up for a luncheon preceding a Saturday matinee or swimming party?

Our doorbell begins ringing promptly on the appointed hour. As soon as the youngsters finish "ohh-ing" and "ahh-ing" over the presents, the group moves on to the dining room, where a pink and white table is set.

My all-time favorite centerpiece for this celebration is composed of an ordinary small leafless branch with numerous twigs that's been sprayed a shocking pink and placed securely in a deep flower pot filled with sand. An ice cream cone is tied on to each twig with a pink ribbon. Nestled in the ice cream cone is a bright pink carnation corsage—a souvenir for every young lady present.

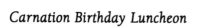

Carnation Birthday Luncheon

Chicken salad
Tomato wedges, olives, hard-cooked eggs
    garnished with bouquet of watercress
Hot biscuits or scones (see recipe in Chapter Three)
Iced chocolate float
Vanilla cookies

Serve on individual plates garnished with parsley, olives, wedges of tomatoes, and hard-cooked eggs.

Iced Chocolate Float

Chocolate syrup
Ice cubes
Whipped cream
Root beer
Chocolate ice cream

Put two tablespoons of chocolate syrup and an ice cube into a tall glass. Fill with root beer and a ball of chocolate ice cream. Top with a teaspoon of whipped cream. Garnish with carnation petals.

Trick or Treat Trifle

Once in a while it's nice to have a trick up your sleeve that can be prepared on the spur of the moment: a quick, easy dessert for unexpected company; something that doesn't need to be baked because we already may have a casserole or roast in the oven; something that doesn't need to sit in the refrigerator overnight; something that tastes so divine, your guests will swear you've spent the day in the kitchen! And unless your cupboard is bare, chances are you might not even need to go marketing—if you're one who likes to improvise.

This recipe is not new, it was old in Martha Washington's day, and I'm sure she cherished it as much as I do today.

What's it called? It's called "trifle," a puzzling name, but one of the dictionary definitions for the word is "trickery," which explains a lot, because it's merely a combination of leftover cake, custard, jelly, fruit, liquor, and topped with whipped cream if you like, and sprinkled with nuts if you have some. It's most appealing when served in a large glass bowl because then one can clearly see the variety of different layers.

This is the way we like it best, but I'll give you the substitutions just for fun too.

Trifle

Equipment: Double boiler

To serve, a glass bowl shows up the variegated layers of trifle best.

Custard
Made from scratch

(Or if you prefer use 1 package vanilla pudding mix instead. Use 2 packages if you omit whipped cream.)

2 cups milk or cream
3 tablespoons granulated sugar
4 egg yolks
2 teaspoons vanilla

1. In the top of a medium-sized double boiler, heat cream and sugar.
2. In a medium-sized mixing bowl beat egg yolks, then add them to the liquid on top of double boiler, stirring until it forms a thick sauce in about 3 or 4 minutes. Let cool.
3. Add vanilla and stir.

Cake
• 3 dozen ladyfingers or cookies, macaroons, leftover yellow or gold cake or any combination you have

Jelly
• 1/2 cup red currant jelly or apple jelly or whatever you fancy

Fruit
• 1 cup applesauce or bananas or fresh berries

Liquor
• 1 jigger Cointreau or brandy, sherry or white wine

Topping
• 1-1/2 cups whipped cream or whipped topping or extra portion of vanilla pudding

Nuts
• 2/3 cup toasted, slivered almonds or chopped pecans, Macadamia nuts or walnuts

1. Spread ladyfingers on bottom and sides of a glass bowl (it's pretty to see the various layers of cake, custard and fruit through the glass) or china serving bowl and sprinkle with Cointreau, brandy, or wine until the liquor is absorbed by the cake.
2. Top the ladyfingers with jelly and applesauce, cover with some custard, add another layer of ladyfingers and repeat, alternating with liquor or wine, jelly, applesauce, custard. Put in refrigerator to chill until ready to serve.
3. If you like, top with whipped cream and nuts.

Surprise Box Lunch

A variation of our usual dessert luncheon is to have each person bring a box lunch for one. After everyone has arrived, the boxes are exchanged with the person to the left. (No favoritism, please!) The hostess serves coffee and cake.

Many of the guests enjoy decorating the boxes as artistically on the outside as they do the goodies on the inside and one of the perkiest box lunches I ever saw was wrapped simply in red and white striped sailcloth (a paper design) and tied with matching red rick-rack.

Surprise Box Lunch Menu

Imported beer
Cold meatloaf on whole wheat bread
Chinese hard-cooked egg (Chapter Four)
Ring of green pepper, carrot and celery sticks
Midget pickled corn on the cob (sold whole in glass jars)
Black olives
Chocolate peppermint wafer

Creamy Meatloaf—Hot or Cold

I must confess that this meatloaf recipe has followed me all over the United States. Everyone agrees it is just as delicious served cold as hot.

Equipment: One large bowl, 8" x 12" Pyrex pan

2 lbs. ground round steak
2 eggs
2 slices whole wheat bread
1 lb. cottage cheese
1/2 cup yogurt
1 package Lipton dehydrated onion soup
Dash of beau monde seasoning (Spice Islands)
1/2 cup catsup

1. Preheat oven to 250° F. In a large bowl mix everything together except the catsup (I do it by hand) and let stand in refrigerator for half an hour.
2. Shape into loaf and put in an 8" x 12" pan and bake uncovered for two hours.
3. The last half hour, cover with catsup. Serve cold or hot.
Makes 10 servings.

Very Special Box Lunches or Suppers

Box lunches or suppers are popular for five or five hundred, and are ideal for business meetings, club meetings, garden parties, picnics, outings on chartered bus trips for theater parties, football games, etc. It's fun to decorate the containers for men with a festive bowtie or boutonniere and the ladies' box lunches or baskets with a fluffy bow or corsage. When serving chicken, it's also a good way to distinguish dark meat from white meat.

For elegant "cotillion" suppers—where the menu might include such fancies as rock lobster tail which has been removed from the shell then replaced and garnished, served with ravigote sauce—you can line a basket with a linen napkin or roll the silverware in a linen napkin topped with a corsage, and enclose a split bottle of wine.

Menu for Box Lunch or Supper

Choice of baked ham, corned beef, roast beef, cold steak or sliced chicken sandwich
Hard-cooked egg, or olives
Mandarin orange, banana, or apple
Choice of container with potato salad, cole slaw, cottage cheese & chives, potato chips
Choice of brownies, doughnuts, French pastry, peppermints

Beverages

Depending on the climate, with lunch or supper serve hot or iced coffee or tea, or soft drinks, beer or wine. Sometimes a mug of hot soup first (recipe below) hits the right spot.

Beautiful soup, so rich and green
waiting in the hot tureen!
Who for such dainties would not stoop?
Soup of the evening, beautiful soup!
           —sung by the Mock Turtle in *Alice in Wonderland*

Soup Stock

Some people love to gnaw the rib bones of roast beef or steak privately, or pick at a leftover turkey, but I prefer to use them as soup stock.

I would be remiss if I didn't mention this basic stock made from scratch. Later you can add choice scraps of meat, fowl or sausage to the basic stock and have a complete hot meal with a crispy loaf of bread to serve after skiing, or during the holiday season.

In a large soup kettle or stock pot, barely cover leftover roast beef bones (or turkey or chicken bones and scraps) with cold water. Add an onion, cut up piece of celery with leaves, a carrot, a few sprigs of parsley, herb seasoning such as thyme, one tomato (raw or stewed). Bring to a boil, then reduce heat to simmer and cook for several hours (the longer, the better!). Remove from stove and strain stock through colander into mixing bowl and let cool. Discard remains in collander. Place stock in refrigerator several hours or until fat forms solid crust. Be sure to skim fat from top and discard.

This clear stock is delicious when you simply add bits of meat or fowl, cooked vegetables such as peas, carrots, spinach, broccoli, lima beans, cauliflower, etc. You may also add noodles, pasta, or rice. For creamed soups use 1 cup chicken stock to 1 cup milk.

Discovering Mint and Other Herbs

For years I was intrigued by pictures of herb gardens and recipes using herbs. I was fascinated by magazine articles describing in detail how to freeze them, dry them, and store them. I admired shiny bright photographs showing fresh herbs growing in neat little squares bordered by red brick walks or planted inside the spokes of an old wagon wheel.

But the closest I ever got to an herb were the dried jars on my grocer's shelves.

Though I longed to have a formal herb garden of my own, I was intimidated by these ancient aristocratic plants. Decorative herb charts threw me into a panic. Suppose I put the wrong herb in the stew? What would happen if I used too much marjoram or not enough basil?

It wasn't until a friend came along who knew all there was to know about herb gardening that I overcame my timidity. With her encouragement and advice, I plunged into this new culinary adventure with a vengeance. She readily convinced me that herb gardening was really quite simple. Growing mint and other herbs is no more complicated than growing any ordinary house plant, and it's so much more rewarding!

First, she helped me select the right spot in my garden. She chose a small triangular plot, not much bigger than a throw rug, next to the kitchen door. The area is sunny and the soil happens to be slightly acid as required.

With some old brick that was lying around in the back of the garage, we divided the plot into twelve sections. Next, we bought a basic selection of herbs from the local florist, a nearby supermarket, and a friendly farmer. We planted thyme, chives, marjoram, basil, dill, chervil, and two kinds of mint—peppermint and curly leaf as a start. We placed the tall herbs, such as dill and basil, at the rear and the short ones, such as thyme and chervil, in the front. We still had a few squares left, so we decided to use one for parsley and another for cherry tomato plants, which our children love to pick.

Before too long, I began plucking tender young sprigs from the garden which I rinsed in the kitchen sink. Then carefully I removed the leaves from the stems because my friend cautioned me that stems have a bitter taste. While chopping herbs with one hand, I conscientiously balanced an herb chart in the other.

That first summer everything we ate was complimented with herbs! We had mint in our juleps, chives on our eggs, thyme in our stew, basil on our tomatoes, chervil on our fish, dill in our potato salad, and marjoram in our soup.

The only thing served pure was milk!

Then one glorious day, I discovered a recipe using a variety of herbs mixed with butter and placed between thick slices of French bread. The whole thing is then wrapped in foil and heated in the oven. Delicious!

French or Vienna Herb Bread

1/2 lb. melted butter
1 teaspoon basil, chopped
1 teaspoon thyme, chopped
1/2 teaspoon marjoram, chopped

Cut Vienna or French bread into thick slices and spread with herb butter and wrap in aluminum foil. Place in an oven preheated to 350° F. for 10 minutes. Serve in wicker basket.

By that time, even I had to admit I'd gone overboard on the herb bit. I pledged to myself that from then on I would only season one dish at a meal with herbs. And, happily, I've been able to stick to this sensible resolution. At this point, I also stopped referring to the chart incessantly and began using herbs indiscriminately in our cooking.

What's so great about herb cookery, one might ask? Well, it gives your tired old recipes a lift. It makes them taste new and special. The flavor of herbs themselves is hardly discernible. They're far more subtle than seasonings, such as salt, pepper, onions, mustard and catsup. People will rarely notice the flavor of thyme or marjoram, but they will notice your stews, gravies, salads and soups tasting extra good! And herbs make such a lovely garnish on platters, too.

Fresh Mint Sauce

And speaking of mint, when Sir Walter Scott and his wife were taking a stroll in the meadows of Abbotsford, his country home, they stopped to admire a field where a herd of sheep were grazing. "It's no wonder," exclaimed Sir Walter, "that poets and philosophers have always made the lamb the emblem of peace and innocence."

"They are indeed delightful little creatures," agreed his wife, "especially with mint sauce."

1 cup water
1 cup vinegar
2 cups sugar
1 cup firmly packed mint leaves

In a medium-sized saucepan, cook water, vinegar, and sugar for 3 minutes, then add finely chopped firmly packed mint leaves.

Remove from heat and let stand overnight. Strain and seal in hot sterilized jars.

Ten-Day Mint Julep

The ancient Greeks and Romans called herbs the "wit" of cooking and, I might add, of drinking as well.

1/2 cup sugar
2 jiggers brandy
Rye or bourbon
Fresh mint sprigs, crushed

Pour sugar into 1-quart mason jar. Tightly pack with tiny sprigs of fresh crushed mint until full. Add two jiggers of brandy, then fill to top with rye or bourbon. Do not stir, but keep jar refrigerated and invert the jar each day for 10 days. To serve, pour 2 ounces of mint concentrate over crushed ice. Garnish with fresh sprig of mint.

Makes 1 quart.

Chapter Three

Tea for 2 or 102, and Introductions

*"There are few hours in life more agreeable than the hour dedicated to
the ceremony known as afternoon tea."*

—Henry James, author

What magic turns the simple act of serving a cup of tea into a bewitching ceremony? Answer: The more paraphernalia, the better! The secret may well lie in the "conspicuous consumption of goods," a theory as described in Thorstein Veblen's *Theory of the Leisure Class*. For instance, drop in to the Vier Yahreszeiten, in Hamburg, Germany—one of the ten most renowned hotels in the world. Here a trim waiter will bring, along with your tea, an assortment of fifteen utensils (I've counted them): a cup, saucer, plate, teapot, pot of hot water, pitcher of cream or milk, sugar—both cubed and granulated—wedges of lemon with a lemon squeezer on a plate, silver tea strainer, plus silverware. All this is presented on a fresh white tablecloth with white linen napkins and a nosegay of fresh flowers.

The tea ceremony in Japan is even more precise. Hot tea is served in delicate porcelain bowls to guests seated on cushions on the floor of a specially designed teahouse. In the Near East one is served hot tea in a glass. In England tea is brewed and served in an antique china cup in front of a small glowing fire. Wherever tea is served one delights in this lovely ceremony when it is staged correctly.

Deliver us from stiff affairs where a large assortment of gooey pink and green cream cheese sandwiches are consumed in a hushed atmosphere. And why, oh why should this

55

be, when the real reason for a tea is always an auspicious, happy occasion, such as moving into a new home, graduating, announcing an engagement, honoring a bride, welcoming a new college president or any V.I.P., thanking volunteers for a job well done, entertaining sorority sisters, dedicating a building, or hosting visiting friends and family.

Let's run through a fresh bouquet of ideas, starting with an elegant small tea, then a Devonshire tea, an Easter Sunday tea, a Strudel Tea, and winding up with a very cheery Champagne Tea! These are affairs to remember!

Decorate the Front Door

How can we create a jovial mood that the stylish tea-time custom deserves? One way is to pamper our guests with tender loving care from the very moment they approach the house. I like to decorate the front door or entrance not only during the Christmas season but for any kind of a party at home or at a club with just a small accent that carries out the party theme and sings out a warm welcome. In the summer it may be no more than an arrangement of potted geraniums on the stoop, whereas for a bridal party we once used white paper doves nestled on the door knocker, and on Easter Sunday we made a wreath using wire coat hangers trimmed with real carrots, and in the middle of this bounty sat what appeared to be a very contented stuffed rabbit.

Greeting Guests

Have someone stationed inside the door to greet guests with a pleasant "hello" and help them with their hats and coats; or, I like the whimsical idea of hanging a fancy bonnet over the bedroom door to help guide the way to this improvised coat room.

Be sure to designate a bathroom for your guests and alert the family to be especially careful to leave it as polished and bright as they find it. Convenient fingertip guest towels are available in either disposable paper, linen, or terrycloth in attractive colors and designs or monograms. Keep a bottle of air freshener handy, check on the supply of toilet tissue, and place a few additional conveniences within easy reach, such as safety pins, aspirin, etc. A tiny fresh flower arrangement or just a single perfect bloom next to the mirror is a cheerful touch.

After removing jackets or coats, our guests first greet the hostess and chat with people they know, are introduced to newcomers, or in a large group they will take the initiative and introduce themselves, "for the roof," as they say, "serves as an introduction." If the tea is given in honor of someone, the hostess should see to it that all the guests are introduced to the honored guest, and at a large party it's a good idea for her to ask close friends to help make these introductions.

This Business of Introductions

How many times have we heard someone say, "Oh, she's stuck up! I've been introduced to her twice and she doesn't remember me!"

Listen with relief to what the New York Society of Self-Culture had to say in 1904:

An introduction may be cordially recognized ten years after it has taken place or it may be worth nothing after two hours. It's not necessary to bow and strive to recall the names of all those persons to whom one has been hurriedly and informally introduced at a large reception, unless the meeting proves to be agreeable and conversation ensues.

And what to do with that forever coy, foolishly irritating soul who saunters up to us and says, "I'll bet you don't remember me, do you?" Three cheers to the courageous fellow who replied, "Lady, you win that bet!"

How grateful we are to that special someone who kindly says, "My name is George Smith. We met at the Wilsons' last month. It's nice to see you again!"

Emily Post condoned only one category of information to be conveyed during an introduction (that of family relationship), but I've often wished I could assign name tags with a few pertinent remarks describing the idiosyncrasies of each guest. One might print, "Don't ask her about her health—she'll tell you!" or "Talk about anything except taxes!" or "This one likes to flirt!"

Unfortunately the day will never come when we can use these name tags, but we can brief our guests when we're entertaining a prominent personality.

At a posh party recently, a friend of mine struck up a very pleasant conversation with another guest—he didn't catch the name:

"It's been so enjoyable talking to you, where are you from?"

"I'm from Norway," the guest replied.

"How interesting. And what do you do there?"

"I'm the king," was the simple reply.

An Informal Tea

One of the most charming continental hostesses I know does much of her informal entertaining with "little teas"; so much so, in fact, that she even had a large, low, revolving coffee table made to order—a king-sized Lazy Susan—and on this she places assorted finger sandwiches, cookies, and cakes that taste as good as they look. In the summer she moves this table onto a screened porch off the garden and serves iced tea in tall glasses with a sprig of fresh mint. It's a treat to visit with this jolly lady and to meet the medley of interesting people she always seems to attract.

I've always yearned for just such a lovely revolving table, but unfortunately most of us have to make do with what we have: either a stationary coffee table, TV snack tables, a tea cart, or a bridge table covered with a pretty cloth for a small group, or the dining room table for a larger group. On this we set a tray with our tea things and while pouring from our china or silver teapot, we inquire, "Lemon, cream, or milk? Saccharin or sugar? How many lumps, please?" We hand the cup and saucer (or cup and dessert plate) along with a dainty napkin and spoon to the person seated closest to us, while other guests come over to us for their cup. (Of course, fancy paper napkins are acceptable, especially for a large group, but don't you love the feel of linen?) Everyone helps themselves to an assortment of tiny sandwiches, dainty muffins, or slices of fresh cinnamon toast on pretty little platters. Sweets such as cookies, coffee cakes, or brownies, mints or glazed nuts look especially tempting and take up so much less space when they're arranged on two- or three-tiered serving dishes.

A Chic and Elegant Small Tea

Giving a tea party for fifteen or twenty should be a joyful experience, and one should not be trapped in the kitchen refilling the teapot, coffee pot, creamer, and replenishing platters! Ask a close friend (or train your cleaning woman or babysitter) if necessary, to help do these simple chores for you, and remind her please to keep an eye on the tea-table during the rush instead of waiting in the kitchen watching the clock! I know it's not easy, but do be firm about this.

When there are more people than the hostess can informally handle herself, it's best to set the tea things on a tray on a large table, such as a dining table, from which everyone helps themselves to sandwiches and sweets. One or two ladies may be asked to be alternately seated at the table and are given the honor of pouring, never for more than half an hour each, usually fifteen or twenty minutes is enough. With a very large group, tea and coffee may be served from both ends of the table to speed the service.

I learned from Mrs. Edsel B. Ford how to overcome the bane of large, picked-over platters. At her large benefit teas catered at her lakeshore estate in Grosse Pointe, Michigan, she had waitstaff pass numerous 10-inch plates filled with hors d'oeuvres. These are easy to pass in the crowd and are quickly refilled—a trick worth remembering.

Tea Talk

Whether you serve hot tea or iced tea is up to you, but I prefer loose tea to tea bags. A good brand of loose tea is available in upscale grocery stores and may be flavored with orange and spice if you like and brewed in a preheated teapot. Then let the conversation flow—hot and spicy as the tea!

Brewing a Good Cup of Tea

There are four golden rules tea-lovers from Ceylon to San Francisco agree should be followed:

1. For full flavor, bring fresh cold water to a full rolling boil. (Water that has been preheated on the stove gives tea a flat taste.)
2. Preheat the teapot with hot water.
3. Empty hot water from teapot and refill with boiling hot water. Measure one teaspoon of tea for each cup of water.
4. Allow to brew in the pot from three to five minutes before pouring.

Elegant Small Tea

(Optional: A glass of sauterne or sherry)
Assorted mini-sandwiches
Open-faced sandwiches
Toasted mushroom triangles

London tea squares
Pecan rolls
Spiced tea
Coffee
Mints
Nuts
(Mini-sandwich recipes are at the end of this chapter.)

London Tea Squares

If you or a friend can manage to do a little quick and easy baking on the morning of your tea, London tea squares are as delicate a sweet as you'll find anywhere. The pastry is covered with a thin layer of jam and topped with meringue and sprinkled with nuts. (I wish I could tell you they keep, but they're best eaten within hours!)

Equipment: Sifter, bowl or stand mixer, 9" x 13" x 1/4" pan, medium bowl, egg beater

2 cups all-purpose flour
1/4 teaspoon soda
1 teaspoon vanilla
1/4 cup skim milk
1/4 pound butter, room temperature
1/4 cup sugar
3 egg yolks
1 cup of your favorite jam

For meringue:
3 egg whites
1/2 cup sugar
1/8 cup of your favorite nuts, chopped

1. Preheat oven to 350° F.
2. Sift flour (even pre-sifted flour) once in a small bowl and then add soda. Combine vanilla and milk in a cup.
3. In a medium-sized bowl, cream butter and 1/4 cup sugar. Add egg yolks and beat until light. Add flour alternately with milk and blend thoroughly.

4. Pat dough into a 9" x 13" pan to 1/4-inch thickness and spread with jam.
5. Beat egg whites until frothy and add sugar gradually and beat until egg whites come to a point. Spread meringue over jam and sprinkle with chopped nuts.
6. Bake in 350° F. oven for 25 minutes. Cool and cut in small 2-inch squares or rectangles.

Makes about 25 little pieces.

Pecan Rolls or Schnecken

This recipe, without a doubt, has become the most popular recipe in this book! Several professional chefs that I know have gone into business offering this mouth-watering treat for sale to their customers, and orders pour in from all over the country. I used to send schnecken as Christmas gifts to my children, but thank heaven, they now have learned how to make them—some even use their bread-making machines to process the dough. Admittedly it's a time-consuming process, but well worth the effort. They can be made weeks ahead and freeze beautifully.

Individual pecan rolls or schnecken are made with yeast. If you've never tried baking with yeast, this rich dough is well worth a try. They're best served warm. They can be prepared in two steps on successive days or all in one day if you start early in the morning.

Pecan rolls are good for breakfast, lunch, tea, or served with coffee as dessert after a cocktail supper. (The dough can also be used for rolls, stollen, or fruit ring.)

Equipment: 3 muffin pans, measuring spoon, wooden spoon, sharp knife, measuring cups, 2" brush, large bowl, medium-sized bowl, rolling pin, small cooking pot, cooling racks, stand mixer (optional)

Three muffin pans make the job go much faster. There are various sizes of muffin pans for small, medium, or large pecan rolls.

Dough

This may be made in a bread-making machine, following directions, with the same ingredients as with the traditional method. (Dough does not need to be rolled and beaten by hand.)

2 packages yeast
1 cup warm milk, not just lukewarm
1 cup butter, unsalted
2 eggs, beaten
4 tablespoons sugar
1 teaspoon salt
4 cups all-purpose flour (no sifting necessary)

Bread Machine

1. Pour 1/2 cup of really warm milk into machine and add yeast. Let sit for 15 minutes.
2. Add rest of milk with melted butter.
3. Add eggs, sugar, salt, and flour. Press button. Observe timer and check container.
4. After mixture has risen twice, remove from bread machine and place in a large bowl and cover with a cloth.

Traditional Method

1. In 1/2 cup of really warm milk, soak yeast for 15 minutes.
2. Melt butter in other 1/2 cup of milk.
3. In a large separate bowl, beat eggs with sugar, salt, and combine with both yeast and butter mixture.
4. Add four cups unsifted flour, beat well.
5. Cover dough with a clean dish towel and let rise in a warm place (with no drafts) for 5 or 6 hours or until double. Or you may put the dough in the refrigerator overnight covered, but if you do, be sure to let the dough and bowl reach room temperature again, so that it may rise again for 5 or 6 hours after removing it from the refrigerator.

Filling

1 cup melted butter, unsalted
1 cup sugar mixed with 1 tablespoon
    cinnamon

1 or 1-1/2 cups raisins
1-1/4 cups chopped pecans
2 cups pecan halves

1. Punch risen dough down with your fist. Take 1/3 of the dough and roll on a floured board with a floured rolling pin to 1/4 thickness. Brush with melted butter.
2. In a separate, medium-sized bowl, mix sugar, cinnamon. Sprinkle 1/3 mixture of chopped pecans and raisins and 1/3 mixture of sugar and cinnamon on rolled-out dough.
3. Fold the dough over once and brush with melted butter. Repeat until you have a nice long roll like a jellyroll.
4. With a sharp knife, cut into 1-inch pieces. Repeat until you have used all the dough.

Syrup

1/4 lb. butter, unsalted
1 cup dark brown sugar
2 tablespoons water

In a small saucepan, over medium heat, melt butter, add sugar and water and stir with a wooden spoon until slightly thick, about 3 minutes.

Assembly

1. Preheat oven to 350° F. Brush muffin pan with melted butter, fill each section with about 1 tablespoon syrup, and 2 or 3 pecans.
2. Place rolls in each section, brush with melted butter, cover with cloth, and let rise again in a warm place for about half an hour or until puffy. Repeat until all dough is used.
3. Bake in 350° F. oven for 20 minutes or until brown. Remove from oven and let pan cool for about 30 minutes. Invert pan on cookie sheet. If any pecans fall off, merely put them back on top of the pecan rolls.
4. Cool on wire racks. Serve caramel side up. Best eaten warm.
Makes 2 dozen.
To reheat, baptize schnecken with a few drops of water and put them briefly (frozen, 15 sec.) in microwave.

A Bonnie (Non-Alcoholic) Devonshire Tea

"Much may be made of a Scotchman if he be caught young."
—Dr. Samuel Johnson

Catching a young fellow today isn't any easier than it was 200 years ago, especially if he's under 21, for parents who are anxious to give a homecoming party where liquor can't be served to those under that magical age.

Our club, like many private clubs and organizations, wished to entertain for the young college set during vacation, but the entertainment committee's hands were tied with an age group that's too mature for bubble gum and too young for beer!

We solved this dilemma by sponsoring a "Devonshire Tea," featuring those heavenly Scottish scones, a kind of super biscuit. Both lads and lassies were invited at 4:30 in the afternoon to the golf club, an ideal masculine setting, for you'll recall that the game of golf originated in Scotland. The "Devonshire Tea" is the counterpart of our American cocktail party—but no alcohol is served. Oh, 'tis a bonnie affair, ne'ertheless! Instead of the more traditional string orchestra, the committee engaged a talented young folk singer with an electric guitar, and before long the rafters were ringing with song, while some people took "the high road" and others "the low road" and half the group got to Scotland 'afore anyone else!

The committee set up a long buffet table in the center of the room, accessible to everyone from all sides, covered with a bright red, green, and white plaid cloth. For a centerpiece we used a large copper teakettle filled with flowering thistle (allowing the florist plenty of time to order the flowers). Because tea-table centerpieces should always be high, the arrangement was elevated on a 12-inch base also draped with Scotch plaid material and trimmed with branches of Scotch pine, the tips lightly sprayed gold. A dozen tall green candles set in teacups trimmed with sprigs of Scotch pine circled the centerpiece.

Getting back to the menu: Originally scones were served with clotted cream, a specialty of Devonshire County, England, but cream cheese is usually substituted nowadays. Members of the clan split their own scones, first spreading them with soft cream cheese, mixed with a little sour cream if one likes, and strawberry preserves. It's also fun dipping fresh strawberries, with stems attached, in sour cream sweetened with sugar, or in just plain powdered sugar.

Addenda: You may expand the Scotch menu by including additional native items such as trout and herring, along with superb Angus or Aberdeen beef, venison, and grouse.

64

Devonshire Tea Menu

Assorted mini-sandwiches
Open-faced sandwiches
Scotch scones
Scottish smoked salmon on party rye
Strawberry, blackberry, orange preserves
Fresh strawberries with powdered sugar
Assorted nuts
Licorice mints
Black, green or a variety of teas

Fresh Scottish smoked salmon is available frozen through specialty catalogs or many upscale grocery stores. The fish goes a long way and should be sliced almost flat and as paper-thin as possible and eaten at room temperature.

However, if you live near the Great Lakes, new plantings of co-ho salmon are now revolutionizing the commercial fishing industry. Smoked co-ho is a real treat.

Invitation to a Devonshire Tea

Lads and Lassies—
Let's go to a Devonshire Tea
(Don't be a fool, Mac, it's free!)
There'll be music on bones
With lots of hot hot scones
4:30 is the time for our spree.

Scotch Scones

Scotch scones are served hot like biscuits and there are some ready-mixes on the market, but in case you'd like to make your own, here's a tasty recipe. (We love them with chicken or turkey salad too!)

65

Equipment: Sifter, large bowl, egg beater, stand mixer (optional)

2 cups all-purpose flour
4 teaspoons baking powder
2 teaspoons sugar
1/2 teaspoon salt
4 tablespoons butter
2 eggs
1/3 cup cream
Sugar-cinnamon mixture: 1/4 teaspoon cinnamon and 2 tablespoons sugar

1. Preheat oven to 400° F.
2. Mix and sift flour, baking powder, sugar, salt in large bowl. Cut in butter and mix to consistency of coarse cornmeal. Add well-beaten eggs and cream.
3. Turn on lightly floured board, pat and roll to 1/2" thickness and cut into diamonds about 2 inches wide or into small triangles. Brush with a little egg white and sprinkle with sugar-cinnamon mixture and place on floured baking sheet. Bake for 15 minutes.

Makes 12 scones.

Easter Sunday Tea for Children and Grown-Ups

One lovely year our anniversary fell on Easter Sunday, so my husband and I decided to invite some close relatives and friends with their children to an Easter Sunday tea party.

At about 3:30, five or six families arrived on a cool but sunny day, and to everyone's surprise and delight there was a real-live welcoming rabbit in our living room! (He was quite safe in a sturdy playpen covered with chicken wire.) The gimmick for this afternoon's entertainment was to have each child draw an egg from a nest of hard-cooked, colored Easter eggs, on which we'd inscribed every child's name—twelve children, twelve eggs, twelve names. The child who drew his own name first would win the rabbit as his very own to keep, and we didn't need much else in the way of entertainment. Every child present hoped he'd be the lucky one to take the live bunny home, and every parent present hoped somebody else's child would be the "lucky" one!

In the family room we set up two large bridge tables with portable round tops for six children each, and we covered the tables with brightly flowered print cloths. In the   center of the table we filled a basket with small favors from the dime store, and tied animal-shaped balloons filled with helium to the handles. We gave each child a small tray, cafeteria-style, on which he could put his mug of hot chocolate, sandwiches, cookies, and cake.

Grown-ups served themselves from a buffet spread on the dining room table, which was covered with a matching flowered print and in the center stood a spring arrangement of hyacinth in a pastel wicker basket. But before the grand drawing, we fortified the adults with a welcome cup of hot tea spiked with a spoonful of flaming orange curaçao.

Easter Sunday Menu

Watercress sandwiches
Cucumber sandwiches
Pimento cheese carrots on crackers
Peanut butter and jelly sandwiches
Minced chicken sandwiches
Petite pecan rolls
Fudge cake
Snow balls
Easter egg candies
Orange curaçao tea for adults
Hot chocolate with marshmallow topping for children

Fudge Cake

I coaxed forth this treasured family recipe from a great cook of my acquaintance. It is quick, easy, and very rich, just the kind most children as well as grown-ups will enjoy.
Equipment: 8"x 12" pan, sifter, large bowl, egg beater, stand mixer (optional)

1 cup butter, room temperature
2 cups sugar
4 whole eggs beaten together
I cup cake flour
1 cup walnuts, chopped fine
I teaspoon vanilla

Icing

1 tablespoon butter, melted
3 tablespoons cocoa
2 cups powdered sugar
1 teaspoon vanilla
1/4 cup hot water

1. Preheat oven to 400° F. In a large mixing bowl, mix butter with sugar until fluffy. Add well-beaten eggs alternating with flour.
2. Add walnuts and vanilla.
3. Bake cake in shallow pan, 8" x 12", for 20 to 25 minutes. Get icing ready while cake is baking and spread over cake the minute you take the cake from the oven. If icing is too stiff, just add a little more water.
Makes 24 small pieces.

Flaming Orange Curaçao Tea

Try a little *abracadabra* magic by serving a flaming tea. Use a black tea and it's best if tea is not too strong. Curaçao comes in a bottle, and this alcoholic beverage is available in any party store. Pour Curaçao into a teaspoon and hold over tea to heat for about a minute. Then light and gently lower spoon into tea and stir.

Snowballs

Equipment: Shallow cake pan and egg beater

Follow directions on 1 package white cake mix. For 3 dozen snowballs cut entire cake into 1-1/2" squares. (For 1 dozen snowballs, use only 1/3 of cake.) Each square, after it's covered with icing and shredded coconut, makes a 3-inch snowball.

Classic Icing
for 1 dozen snowballs

2 cups sugar
2/3 cup water
2 tablespoons light corn syrup
2 egg whites
1/8 teaspoon salt
1-1/2 teaspoons vanilla

1. Cook sugar, water, and corn syrup over low heat until sugar is dissolved.
2. Boil without stirring to 238° F. or until icing forms a soft ball when dropped into a small bowl of cold water.
3. When sugar syrup is almost ready, beat egg whites with salt until stiff but not dry. Pour hot syrup over egg whites in a fine stream, beating constantly. Add vanilla and continue beating until frosting is of spreading consistency.

Coconut

For 1 dozen snowballs, use one 14-oz. package of coconut flakes or 1 fresh coconut (2 lbs. yields 14 oz. shredded coconut). Using canned coconut flakes is a convenience but grinding a fresh coconut tastes better and is infinitely cheaper.
To break open fresh coconut, see Chapter Six.
Grate by hand and spread in a shallow pan.

Assembling Snowballs

Drop individual squares one at a time into icing, coating cake on all sides. With a large spoon, scoop out iced cake, and roll lightly in coconut flakes. With your hands pat additional coconut and form into a perfect snowball.
Makes 1 dozen snowballs.

Viennese Strudel Tea

Sometimes a tea becomes memorable simply from hearing about it. This is the case with a Strudel Tea a friend of mine gave in behalf of one of her favorite charities. Nothing else was served but an assortment of Viennese Strudel: apple, apricot, cherry, plum—all garnished with generous dabs of real whipped cream.

They tell me there were merry violins playing those marvelous Strauss waltzes among potted palms (rented, of course). Guests sat at those dear little café tables and chairs (also rented) lost in a world of lace handkerchiefs, duels of honor, and romance.

Some strudels can be bought ready-made at a fine bakery. In our house it was more fun to tease Mother into making one. For an extra large strudel she always cleared the dining room table, covered it with a fresh white table cloth, and rolled the dough out as far as possible to the edge. Then began the delicate pulling of the dough with light fingertips until it was almost transparently thin right up to the very edge of the table. (Please don't panic if a few holes appear because the dough is all rolled together with apples, nuts and raisins anyway into a long loaf.)

Mother's Viennese Apple Strudel

Equipment: Sifter, 2 medium bowls, rolling pin, clean, old tablecloth, 11" x 16" pan

Dough

2 cups flour
2 eggs
1/2 teaspoon salt
2 tablespoons cold water
1/4 cup shortening (or olive oil)
1/4 cup lukewarm water

Filling

5 lbs. apples
1 cup chopped walnuts
1 cup white raisins
1/2 cup sugar
2 teaspoons cinnamon
1/4 pound butter, melted
1/4 cup powdered sugar

1. Sift flour into a medium-sized bowl and make a well in center. In a separate bowl, stir 2 eggs mixed with salt, water, and melted shortening. Add to flour and keep stirring until smooth. Remove from bowl and knead dough into a ball. Bounce dough on table several times until there are no more air bubbles. Form into ball and place on a floured plate. Pat lukewarm water on top of dough so the top does not dry. Cover with bowl and let stand for 1/2 hour or more.
2. Peel and slice apples into thin wedges. Chop nuts, medium fine, add raisins, sugar, and cinnamon and combine with apples in a separate bowl.
3. Spread a tablecloth over large kitchen or dinette table. Sprinkle with flour and roll the dough with a floured rolling pin until very thin. Dust hands with flour, then start pulling dough by sliding hands under dough and lifting from center. With fingertips very gently tease and stretch dough until paper thin all the way to the edges. With a scissor cut away thick edge that may be left.
4. Preheat oven to 350° F. Brush melted butter over dough; sprinkle half the apple mixture all over dough. Lift tablecloth at one end and gently roll strudel, allowing air bubbles to form in roll. Now keep adding apple mixture until it is all used.
5. Place strudel—which now looks like a large jellyroll—on a well-buttered shallow pan about 11" x 16" or on a large, well-buttered cookie sheet in a 350° F. oven for 1 hour or until golden. When strudel has cooled, sprinkle lightly with powdered sugar and serve at room temperature.

Makes 8 to 10 servings.

Champagne Tea

Staging a tea in honor of a bride or to announce an engagement is about as nice an assignment as one can look forward to.

Let's think pastels because most young ladies prefer soft pastel blues and yellows above any other color. Let's think music because most girls love to be serenaded. Let's think lace and velvet bows and flowers, because most girls love doo-dads.

Let's think champagne because this is a once-in-a-lifetime affair! Let's think about reading tea leaves because most girls love to dream of the future! Pastels, music, lace, bows, velvet, flowers, champagne, gypsy fortune tellers—mix them all together and you have a gala champagne tea that will be remembered for a lifetime.

The prime focus of this party is a lavishly decorated table about 8 feet long, or a large round table is pretty too, covered first with a pastel-colored petticoat and then a cloth of nylon net. With a rectangular table it's fun to gather the net in each corner into a pouf by pinning it with a straight florist's pin. The pouf is bound with dark green or blue velvet ribbon tied in a lush bow with long streamers. In addition the net can be trimmed with artificial small cloth flowers that are either lightly pinned or stitched to the net. (See Chapter Eight for more table decorating ideas.)

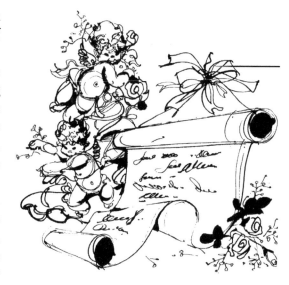

When the challenge of giving a bridal tea was put to me, the image of rococo cherubs, yellow roses, green leaves, and dreamy maidens languishing under a tree came to mind. (Luckily, my mother-in-law let me borrow her tall Dresden ornament for this special occasion.) Two tall epergnes filled with yellow roses and Bristol fairy flowers—similar to baby's breath—flanked the centerpiece.

While party shopping for paper napkins in a gift shop, I found a hanging scroll designed for guest signatures, and the bride thought it was a lovely sentimental souvenir of the day.

(It's simple to make a scroll by using two strips of wooden dowels 15" each, obtainable at any hardware store. Glue a roll of heavy shelf paper, as long or as short as one wants, around the dowel at each end. Reenforce the edge of the shelf paper with mastic tape to prevent tearing. To hang scroll, add a braid or silk ribbon attached to the back of the dowel with two screw eyes. If one is artistically inclined, the scroll could be further decorated with ink sketches or decals. Start the ball rolling by signing your name first.)

To honor the bride, I ordered flowered party mints with the young couple's name from my favorite candy store.

Champagne Tea Menu

Champagne
Hot mushroom triangles
Hot cheese rolls

Hot lobster canapés
Merry-go-round pie sandwich
Stuffed cherry tomatoes
Open-faced sandwiches: cold turkey, ham, or assorted mini-sandwiches
Silver champagne punch (see Chapter Three)
Petit fours
Cream puffs
Crispy lace cookies
Tea
Coffee
Flower mints

Crispy Lace Cookies

What could be more suitable for a champagne tea than crisp lace cookies so delicate one can peek through them? They can be made days ahead and keep very well. Lace cookies may be served flat or shaped into cones while still warm. Men like them just as much!

Equipment: Medium-sized skillet, wooden spoon, rubber spatula, 2 cookie sheets

2/3 cup packaged almonds
1/4 lb. butter
Dash of salt
1/2 cup sugar
1 tablespoon all-purpose flour
2 tablespoons milk

1. Preheat oven to 350° F. Grind almonds medium-fine.
2. Melt butter in medium-sized skillet. Add salt, sugar, and flour and stir over flame with wooden spoon until sugar melts. Add milk and almonds, continue to blend until mixture is thick and no longer runny.
3. Use rubber spatula and drop 1 teaspoon dough on buttered and floured cookie sheet 3 inches apart as cookies spread out flat. (Remove skillet from stove and cover. It's best to use 2 cookie sheets of medium size, and make cookies quickly as the dough has a tendency to dry out.) Re-flour and butter cookie sheet each time.

4. Watch timing carefully when baking in oven for about 10 minutes. Remove from oven; let cool for 2 minutes before removing from cookie sheet with spatula or they may crumble. Place cookies on cooling rack and they will become nice and crisp. Or they can be shaped into cones while still warm.

Assorted Mini-Sandwiches

There are a few simple rules to follow in making not only attractive but tasty fresh mini-sandwiches.

1. In my opinion, If you avoid combining all cream cheese recipes with bread, your battle's already won. Cream cheese on soft white or whole wheat bread is about as tasty as Elmer's glue! Tinting the cheese pink or green and mixing it with chopped olives or nuts doesn't help the texture either. (Cream cheese is good only as a spread on crisp crackers, chips, bagels, brown bread, or biscuits.)

2. Use thinly sliced white, whole wheat, and rye bread. Spread bread lightly with softened butter to prevent the filling from soaking into bread.

3. Use an "assembly line" technique with plenty of countertop space for cutting and spreading sandwiches.

4. Certain types of sandwiches can be prepared in advance and frozen, but fillings containing hard-cooked egg whites, raw vegetables, and mayonnaise do not freeze successfully.

5. Use a sharp knife for trimming off crust and cutting bread or it will tear.

6. One cup of filling will spread on about five dozen mini-sandwiches.

7. To estimate the number of sandwiches and other tidbits for teas or receptions, it's a safe rule to provide five pieces for each guest, regardless of the number of varieties served. (For cocktails, allow a minimum of seven pieces because drinking promotes appetite for hors d'oeuvres.)

If three cups of filling make 15 dozen mini-sandwiches, allow about three hours to make 180 sandwiches from scratch. Of course, the job goes faster with someone to work along with you and keep you company. Making sandwiches can be broken down into stages.

The day before: Make the fillings. Spread the ribbon sandwiches and wrap whole after cutting. They will stay fresh and moist in plastic wrap.

The day of the party: Open-faced sandwiches are best made fresh in the morning on the day of the party. Put them on a serving tray or platter and cover with a damp-dry towel and then cover with plastic wrap.

Sandwich Spreads

The following three basic sandwich spreads taste delicious separately or blend well together between alternate layers of white, whole wheat, and rye bread: 1) yellow cheese; 2) Braunschweiger liver sausage; and 3) chopped egg mixture.

There's an infinite variety of sandwiches to be had when combining three kinds of spread with three types of bread and cutting the bread into various shapes (circles, squares, triangles), plus making open-faced sandwiches that in turn can be cut with a variety of cookie cutters into heart shapes, tree shapes, spades, clubs, or diamonds, and finally decorated with a sliver of olive, a strip of pimento, or a sprig of parsley.

Two-layer sandwiches can be cut criss-cross into either small squares and triangles while three-layer or ribbon sandwiches are made by alternating rye bread, liver-sausage spread, whole wheat bread, chopped egg spread, white bread, cheese spread, and rye bread or in any combination you would wish. With a very sharp knife, trim the edges of the sandwich, then cut the bread in four parallel strips.

Yellow Cheese Mixture

Equipment: Hand food chopper, sharp knife

1/2 lb. medium sharp store cheese
3 strips red pimento for color
1/4 cup mayonnaise
1 teaspoon minced onion

With food chopper, cut cheese, mix with pimento, mayonnaise, and onion until smooth.
Makes 1-1/2 cups.

Braunschweiger Liver Sausage Mixture

1 package 8 oz. Braunschweiger liver sausage
1/4 cup mayonnaise
1/4 cup sweet pickle relish

With a hand food chopper cut liver-sausage and add mayonnaise and pickle relish
and mix until smooth.
Makes 1-1/2 cups.

Chopped Egg Mixture

3 hard-cooked eggs
1/4 cup mayonnaise
1 teaspoon dried parsley flakes
1 tablespoon finely chopped fresh onion (less, if you don't care for onion flavor)
2 tablespoons chopped celery, very fine
Salt and pepper to taste

With hand food chopper, chop eggs. Add mayonnaise, parsley, onion, celery, salt, and
pepper and mix until smooth.
Makes 2 cups.

Pimento Cheese Carrots

1 jar (5 oz.) pimento cheese spread
1 package 4 oz. grated cheddar cheese
White oval crackers

Mix cheddar with pimento at room temperature. Make carrots using 1 teaspoon of
mix to each carrot and roll into shape. Garnish top with sprig of parsley and place one tiny
carrot on a oval, white cracker.
Makes 50 carrots.

Watercress Sandwiches

1/3 cup finely chopped watercress
2 tablespoons mayonnaise
Dash of salt, pepper, and paprika
Whole watercress for garnishing

Mix watercress and mayonnaise into a paste.

Cut fresh bread into very thin slices and remove crust. Spread with watercress paste and roll. Optional: Insert sprig of fresh watercress at one end before rolling for garnish.
Makes 2 dozen mini-sandwiches.

Minced Chicken Sandwiches

One cup shredded white meat of chicken or turkey. Add just enough prepared whipped topping to bind chicken into a paste. Season with lemon juice, salt and pepper to taste. Spread between white bread and cut in squares. (Low in calories, too!)
Makes 5 dozen mini-sandwiches.

Toasted Mushroom Sandwiches

1 cup chopped mushrooms
1 tablespoon butter
1/4 teaspoon salt
3/4 cup condensed cream of mushroom soup (not diluted)
Dash of nutmeg

Sauté chopped mushrooms in a small skillet with butter until golden. Add salt. Remove from skillet and mix with soup and nutmeg. Preheat oven to 475° F. Spread on very thin slices of white bread (trimmed) and toast in oven for about 5 minutes or until brown. Cut criss-cross into four squares or triangles.
Makes 40 sandwiches.

Hot Toasted Cheese Rolls

Make the filling the day before the sandwiches are to be served. Chill overnight.

Equipment: Double boiler, egg beater

1 tablespoon flour
1/4 teaspoon Worcestershire sauce
1/4 teaspoon mustard
1/2 teaspoon salt
Dash of red pepper
1 cup milk
1 cup grated sharp American cheese
4 egg yolks, beaten
Dash of Tabasco sauce

1. Combine flour and seasonings except Tabasco. Add milk slowly to make a smooth paste and cook in double boiler until thickened.
2. Add cheese and stir until melted and sauce is smooth.
3. Beat yolks, add Tabasco, and pour part of the hot mixture into beaten egg yolk, then return egg mixture to double boiler.
4. Cook for a minute longer and remove from heat. Chill overnight.

On the day of the party warm cheese to room temperature for easy spreading on thin slices of fresh bread with crust removed. Roll cheese and bread and toast under broiler for a few minutes or until cheese melts and toast turns gold. Serve hot by passing on platters covered with paper lace doilies.
Makes 4 dozen rolls.

Cucumber Sandwiches

2 medium-sized cucumbers
2 teaspoons salt
Bottled mayonnaise with horseradish or 1 tablespoon horseradish mixed into
1 cup mayonnaise

1. Pare and slice cucumber very fine. Taste raw cucumber to see if it's bitter. Once in a while one does get a bitter cucumber, and it's best to buy an extra one just in case this should happen.
2. Sprinkle with 2 teaspoons salt and let stand for several hours in refrigerator. Drain water. Use very, very thin white bread, or cut regular slice in half horizontally. Spread with thin layer of horseradish-mayonnaise and cucumbers.
3. Cover with bread and gently press together.
4. Trim edge of bread and cut in half. Keep cool until serving.

Makes 40 sandwiches.

Merry-Go-Round Pie

This open faced merry-go-round sandwich truly appeals to the eye as well as the palate. It can be served at receptions and cocktail parties as well as teas. All ingredients are prepared ahead of time, just the assembling is left for the last hour. A genuine work of art—an assemblage!

For this you need a round 9-inch uncut rye bread, which you can order from the baker or find at your supermarket. Coax him to slice it for you through the very center, horizontally, in several slices. (If you have a chef's knife at home, you can manage it yourself.)

For 2 merry-go-round sandwiches (cut into 12 pie-shaped slices each), you need:

4 hard-cooked eggs
3 tablespoons mayonnaise
1/2 teaspoon salt
1/4 teaspoon dry mustard
1/8 tablespoon cayenne pepper
2 tablespoons sour cream
10 chopped black pitted olives
2 cans boned sardines
1 lemon
1/8 lb. butter
1 4-oz. jar red caviar

1. Prepare hard-cooked eggs. Mash yolks and mix with mayonnaise seasoned with salt, mustard and cayenne pepper.
2. Chop 2 of the egg whites and mix with sour cream, separately. Chop black olives, medium fine, separately. Mince sardines with juice of 1/2 lemon, separately.
3. Remove crust from sliced bread and spread with softened butter. Spread black olives in a dollar-sized circle in center of bread. (Optional: You may substitute black caviar for olives.)
4. Carefully spread egg yolk mixture in a ring around olives with a knife. Spread red caviar around yellow egg yolk mixture evenly. (Optional: You may substitute deviled ham for red caviar.)
5. Spread chopped egg whites around red caviar. Spread minced, boned sardines flavored with lemon juice around red caviar. Garnish platter with sprigs of parsley.
6. Place whole slice of round rye on platter and cut into 12 pie-shaped pieces with a very sharp knife, leaving the effect of the disc as a whole, decorated with rings of variegated colored spreads.

Hot Lobster Canapés

1 can (7-1/2 oz.) lobster
1/4 cup sherry wine
1/4 cup grated Parmesan cheese
1/3 cup bread crumbs softened with melted butter
Paprika

Shred lobster meat, add sherry and cheese. Spread on small rounds of bread in mound. Sprinkle with buttered crumbs and brown lightly in broiler for a few minutes. Sprinkle lightly with paprika.
Makes 4 dozen canapés.

Stuffed Cherry Tomatoes

Slit 1/3 down each cherry tomato and let a little juice flow. Then fill slit with your favorite dip of cottage cheese, cream cheese, pimento, etc. For cocktails use the saltier dips such as anchovy paste and cream cheese, etc. Stuffed cherry tomatoes are tasty and very decorative used as a garnish on platters, too, along with big bunches of parsley.

Iced Orange Tea

Any hot summer day, after a fast game of tennis, people like to drop by our house for a refreshing glass of iced tea while we re-hash the trials and triumphs of the morning's sets of mixed doubles.

Our iced orange tea recipe, garnished with a sprig of fresh mint from the garden, is also refreshing used as a summer punch with paper-thin sliced lemons and oranges floating on top, garnished with cloves and a slice of strawberry. The punch is ladled over ice in a glass. For an added kick, reduce amount of orange juice to half and add 1 cup of triple sec liqueur.

2 quarts water
1/2 cup loose leaf orange pekoe and pekoe tea
1/2 cup frozen orange juice concentrate
2 cups water
1/2 cup lemon juice
Garnishes

Bring fresh water to a rolling boil. Add tea and let brew for 5 minutes. Pour tea through a strainer into 3-quart pitcher. (Place a long-handled metal spoon in pitcher if it is glass to prevent cracking.)

Combine frozen orange juice concentrate with 2 cups water. Add orange juice and lemon juice to tea.

Serve in 8-ounce glasses half filled with ice and garnish with slices of lemon and orange, clove, mint, or strawberries. Let guests sweeten with sugar to taste.

Makes 16 glasses.

Iced Coffee

Whenever my husband and I cruised by car through Michigan in the summer, we stopped off at a roadside restaurant for refreshment and he always asked the waitress for a glass of iced coffee and she almost always said, "We don't serve that here," to which my husband gently replied, "Very well, just bring me a cup of hot coffee and a glass with ice." This she is both willing and relieved to do, and he proceeds to pour the hot coffee into a glass of ice, adding cream and sugar. *Voilà*—iced coffee!

With all the coffee drinking that's done in this country it's hard to understand why it's taken so long for iced coffee to become popular when it's so good! Iced coffee is just as easy to serve to a large group as hot coffee. It's best to make it extra strong, then let it cool before pouring so the ice in the glass doesn't melt too quickly. Sugar and cream or saccharin is up to the individual.

Coffee Kahlua

This Mexican coffee variation appeals to many. Just add 1 jigger of Kahlua (a delicious coffee liqueur) to each glass of iced coffee, then top with just a dab of whipped cream.

Presenting a Punch

Presentation is a punch's prerequisite! A hot punch served in a brightly gleaming silver bowl or a chilled punch served in a sparkling crystal bowl with a long-handled ladle presented on a round table with matching punch glasses has the sort of eye appeal that's bound to draw an enthusiastic crowd.

A friend of mine volunteered to serve cocktails at home to a large group of 250 out-of-town delegates before an annual dinner meeting. To help break the ice, literally and figuratively speaking, she served the ever-popular martini in a punch bowl! In the center of the bowl she put a large block of ice with a small depression on top for olives and for an added touch of color she surrounded the olives with a wreath of bright flowers. Truly a conversation piece! (Martini recipe in Chapter Four.)

Pineapple Tea Punch

People have asked me for this recipe more times than I can count! (By permission of Hawaiian Visitors Bureau.)

Equipment: Large punch bowl, medium-sized saucepan, sieve

2 cups boiling water
4 tablespoons tea leaves (black)

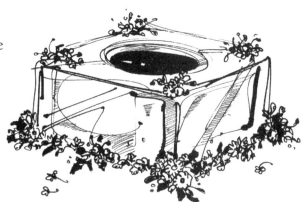

3 large lemons
2 cups sugar
4 cups cold water
1 teaspoon vanilla extract
1 teaspoon almond extract
2 bottles (28 oz. each) ginger ale
1 can pineapple tidbits (frozen)

Put pineapple tidbits in freezer the day before to be used later instead of ice!

Pour 2 cups of boiling water over tea leaves; cover and steep for 10 minutes. Wash lemons, extract juice, and keep rinds. Pour lemon juice into a medium-sized saucepan, add sugar, water, and lemon rinds and heat, stirring until sugar is dissolved.

Strain tea through sieve and add to mixture. When cool, stir in vanilla and almond extract. Refrigerate until serving time. When ready to serve, pour into punch bowl and add ginger ale. Instead of using any ice, add frozen tidbits of canned pineapple to punch.

Makes 30 cups.

Fresh Peach Punch

For a summer wedding

Equipment: Crystal punch bowl preferred

3 lbs. ripe peaches, sliced
1/4 cup sugar
1/4 cup brandy
1 fifth red wine (chilled)
1 fifth white wine (chilled)
1 bottle domestic champagne (chilled)

Add sugar and brandy to peaches and let stand 3 to 4 hours. Place in crystal punch bowl and pour over red wine and white wine. Keep cold. Add block of ice and just before serving, then add champagne.

Makes 24 servings.

Silver Champagne Punch

Equipment: Silver punch bowl preferred

3 magnums of domestic champagne (a magnum is 2 quarts)
1 quart Counoisier
Several dashes of bitters

Pour over molded ice ring and serve in silver punch bowl.
Makes 50 servings, 3 ounces each.

Chapter Four

Stop By for a Drink!

"Wine is light held together by water."

—Galileo

The Cocktail Party Ritual

A cocktail party can be as intimate as a throbbing violin or as noisy as a brass band. It can be as impromptu as "Drop by for a drink," or as formal as a written invitation. It can include no more than a handful, or a house full! The cocktail party at its best is as American as iced coffee, as tempting as a hot dog and as noisy as a ball game. You can be bored one minute and deeply engrossed the next. You can be too hot or cold, drink too much, eat too little, and go home too late. But the cocktail party ritual is as habit-forming as reading the Sunday paper, and though you may not care for today's headlines, you can't ignore them any more than you can ignore the next warm invitation for a small libation.

R.S.V.P.s

No matter whether you give a cocktail party for fun, or to raise funds, there are two points worth remembering when writing invitations that generally don't apply at other times. First, set the exact hour the party is expected to begin and end. This is a welcome bit of information every guest wants to know (and should abide by). For example: from

5:00 to 7:00, or 5:30 to 7:30, or 6:00 to 8:00, or 5:00 to 9:00 if you like! There are times you might not care if your friends want to stay and *s-t-a-y*, drinking their dinner, but then again don't feel it's necessary to urge people to stay just to be polite. When they say, "Well, we've got to be running along"—let them run!

The second point involves a recent trend for written invitations and that simply is writing the words "Regrets Only" instead of "R.S.V.P." Or, putting it positively, some hostesses prefer the phrase, "Acceptances Only." Either way, this grassroots movement has not been officially acknowledged in all etiquette books, but there's a good chance it may catch hold, simply because it cuts down on the deluge of phone calls which follows the mailing of a large batch of invitations. So perhaps we should be open to change whether we like it or not. (I would never be this casual for dinner invitations!) It's unfortunate that only a minority ever troubles itself to send written notes of acceptance or regrets—even though one has to pay a caterer for every guest. Manners, like language, undergo constant adjustment, bending with the stress and strain of our times. "It's me" is considered quite acceptable by the majority of linguists today because the grammatically proper "It is I" sounds artificial to our ears.

Getting back to invitations, there is another alternative, and that is simply eliminating the request for R.S.V.P.s entirely (which one can do for an Open House on occasion), but that does leave one hanging, doesn't it?

What? No Peanuts—or Pretzels?

Why, oh why, do some hostesses delay serving as much as a pretzel during the early cocktail hour until all the guests have arrived? This could mean a pretty long wait until the last straggler has made his appearance, so why penalize the punctual guest this way? At least set a bowl of nuts, pretzels, or olives for those who've perhaps made the supreme effort to be on time in spite of a flooded basement or a long-distance telephone call or a missing puppy!

Open House Cocktail Party

Our last cocktail party for over a hundred was the easiest, most successful, and therefore my favorite! The date: A Saturday in January. The time: 5:00 to 9:00. The occasion: To celebrate our newly remodeled kitchen.

In the past, we've always been cramped for space, but now we decided to feature our remodeled pride and joy by turning our square kitchen into a bar. For once, there's ample counter space for mixing drinks, for ice, liquor, mixes, glasses, etc.!

We filled the sink with crushed ice, then colored it green with food coloring, and plunged bottles of white wine in with the crushed ice. The effect was stunning! Running water was always handy and used glasses were quickly whisked out of sight and deposited in the dishwasher.

Fortunately, our new cove lighting under the hanging cabinets made glasses sparkle. Our oven fan conveniently drew out odors and a braided string of red onions hanging from our beamed ceiling added a nice touch of color. We were surprised and delighted to discover that our functional, attractive, spacious kitchen now served a dual purpose, as do many of the newer homes with their "great" rooms and kitchen-family-dining rooms.

A successful party has to breathe, to flow, and the vitality of a party, like physical well-being, often depends on good circulation. Guests like to move about freely, to wander over to the bar for more ice, or to stop by the hors d'oeuvres table for a snack, or to pause in front of a cozy fire. People don't like being trapped in corners for the entire evening. Avoid bottlenecks throughout the house, such as setting up a portable bar in the hallway. This space is better reserved solely for arriving and departing guests.

We've learned from experience when entertaining a large group that it's best to eliminate dainty chairs and tippy tables, and since we don't have a magnificent view through our windows at night, we always draw the draperies, giving our living room an intimate, congenial atmosphere. We build a crackling fire in the living room fireplace where alternating groups gather comfortably.

In the dining area, the hors d'oeuvres table is moved against the wall to give us additional room. On this occasion we used an arrangement of colorful fruit: whole apples and avocados, bunches of grapes, and some fruit cut in half, such as pineapple, limes, and pomegranates. We added assorted candles of various colors and sizes at one end of the table—big fat ones and short chunky ones.

When planning the menu for a cocktail party, it's simplest to divide foods into four basic groups: cheese, seafood, meat, and vegetables. These in turn are divided into two sub-groups: hot and cold. This done, we're off to a good running start! The paradox in planning, however, is, the more variety, the fancier, but sometimes the fancier the food— the less variety! For instance, one could offer nothing but the finest selection of imported cheeses from France, Holland, Denmark, Norway, Italy, etc., which could be served whole, sliced, cubed, or creamed with an assortment of rye bread and crackers. Or nothing but fresh seafood—shrimp, herring, crabmeat, salmon, oysters, and caviar!

Our Open House menu was chosen carefully because we didn't want to mess up the kitchen by cooking or broiling on the day of the party, nor did I wish to be on my feet all day, so everything was prepared the day before, leaving the kitchen (and me) bright and sparkling.

Open House Menu

Liederkranz ring mold
Hot cheese cookies
Imported Swiss cheese
Smoked Virginia ham
Marinade cubed beef over hibachi
Liver paté
Michigan smoked fish
Water crackers
Party rye
Fresh sweetened pineapple chunks on toothpicks dipped in powdered sugar
Mocha coffee

Liederkranz Ring Mold

Equipment: Small ring mold, bowl

5 packages (4 oz. each) Liederkranz cheese
1 cup domestic dry white wine
1-1/4 lbs. sweet butter, softened
1/3 cup brandy

1. Put cheese in a bowl and pour wine over to cover, and soak overnight.
2. In the morning, drain cheese, add sweet butter, and mash well together.
3. When well blended, add 1/3 cup brandy, mix and put in mold and chill in refrigerator.
4. To remove from ring mold before serving, place platter over ring mold and turn upside down. (If necessary, place hot wet towels on ring mold and shake platter and ring mold gently, until Liederkranz cheese falls free.) Serve hot.
Serves 20.

Hot Cheese Cookies

Equipment: Wax paper, large mixing bowl, cookie sheet, metal spatula

Cheese cookies can be made ahead and freeze very well. They're just as good when reheated and may be served hot or cold. We like to keep them warm on an electric hot tray, but they're gobbled up so quickly, it's not easy!

1 cup grated sharp cheddar cheese, room temperature
1 cup grated medium sharp cheddar cheese, room temperature
1 cup flour
1/2 cup butter, softened
1/4 teaspoon cayenne pepper

1. Put cheese in large mixing bowl and add flour, softened butter, and cayenne pepper. Mix really well by hand until mixture looks like dough. Divide into 2 balls.
2. Roll balls into 2 long rolls, each about 1-1/2 inches in diameter. Place rolled dough in wax paper overnight in refrigerator. (For quickie results, put in freezer for 2 hours instead.)
3. Preheat oven to 400° F. Remove dough from refrigerator when hard. Peel off wax paper and slice in 1/4-inch thickness. Lightly grease cookie sheet and place cookies 1/2-inch apart on cookie sheet. Bake for 12 minutes, or until cookies are pale gold. Repeat until all cookies are done.
4. *Gently* remove from cookie sheet with metal spatula. Serve hot.
Yield 4 dozen.

Smoked Virginia Ham

Three hundred years ago, aristocratic European families were captivated by the rich, succulent, sweet nutlike flavor of Virginia hams, and our guests are just as captivated today. It takes almost a year to smoke and age this meat to perfection, but the wait is well worth the result.

For a large cocktail party, I sometimes order one smoked ham (see Sources of Supply). This is delivered by mail, fully cooked, ready to serve hot or cold (we prefer it cold). A 10- or 15-pound ham, spiral cut and served with party rye, will go a long way at your next party.

Fun with Fire

To serve food piping hot at a cocktail party—or brunch or buffet supper—you need an accessory or two, such as a chafing dish, a fondue set, a hibachi charcoal burner, or an electric gadget. You couldn't possibly own, let alone store, all the different items available on today's market. We must decide which is the handiest accessory for us and then become proficient in our own delightful specialty. A friend of mine uses a portable electric roaster for making miniature hamburger hors d'oeuvres right in her living room. She orders petit buns (2 inches in diameter) from her bakery and you should see the line queue to the right! A "Sunday" carpenter built a table with aged bricks over stereo heaters that keeps his informal buffet suppers warm. And then there's the young couple who found a mini wood-burning stove that looks adorable in their early American setting. This conversation piece is used frequently to keep popcorn, hot cider, chestnuts, etc., warm.

Marinade for Cubed Beef

For our Open House, we decided to marinate 1-1/2-inch cubed filets overnight and let our guests charcoal-broil them over our hibachi stove placed on our antique cobbler's bench. There are portable electric grill pans available. Check Sources of Supply.

People are still asking for our marinade recipe, but of course we won't tell because I believe one should have a few specialties of the house. Besides they'd be disappointed if they knew our simple secret. All we did was buy a prepared Japanese sauce, Kikkoman Teriyaki marinade!

Fluffy Liver Paté

May be served on crackers or in a mold
Equipment: Chopping tool, electric mixer

2 lbs. fresh chicken livers
1 medium-sized onion, chopped fine

3/4 cup salad dressing (Miracle Whip)
1 tablespoon brandy
1 hard-cooked egg, chopped fine
Salt and pepper to taste

1. Boil chicken livers in covered saucepan, medium heat, 10 to 15 minutes. Remove from heat, drain and cool. Chop livers finely and add finely chopped onions to liver.
2. Put in medium-sized mixing bowl. Add salad dressing, brandy, chopped hard-cooked egg, salt, and pepper. Turn on electric mixer at medium speed for 5 minutes or until fluffy.
3. If you like to use a mold, butter it and fill with paté and place in refrigerator for several hours or overnight. Take out of refrigerator half hour before removing from mold. If necessary, place hot, wet towels on mold to help loosen paté. (There are attractive chicken-shaped molds on the market that are appropriate for chicken paté.)

Rainbow or Brook Trout

What bliss stuffing on fresh oysters at a New Orleans style oyster bar, or munching on San Francisco Bay crab, or savoring Maine lobster or gorging on Oregon salmon! But in our part of the country, we specialize in smoked lake trout and whitefish, and no cocktail party is complete without this local delicacy.

For a special treat we like to serve freshly caught rainbow or brook trout caught in our private trout stream. We like to poach the whole trout in pickle juice right out of the dill pickle jar, and then serve it cold as an hors d'oeuvre. We did a little experimenting and found we can achieve good results now using frozen trout and pickle juice, which means we can serve this treat all year 'round.

Equipment: Shallow baking pan

2 lbs. frozen trout
1-3/4 cups juice from a jar of kosher dill pickles
6 cloves

1. Preheat oven to 350° F. Place whole frozen trout, head and all, in a shallow pan uncovered and add pickle juice. After 15 minutes, when skin is tender, place 3 cloves through the skin of each fish. Baste occasionally. A large or 1 lb. frozen trout will be done in 40 to 50 minutes (fresh trout only takes about 10 to 15 minutes).
2. Cool and place fish whole on a platter and garnish with fresh parsley, chervil or watercress, and serve at room temperature.

Addenda: There's a bit of hocus-pocus connected with boning this delicacy which should be done before your guests. For this you'll need an extra bone plate.
1. With a sharp knife, sever the backbone vertically at head below gills and on tail section.
2. With a flat fish knife, or spatula, cut individual portions down to the backbone, but do not sever the backbone.

3. Lift the individual portions from the top layer of the fish and serve bits of fish on rounds of toast or crackers.
4. After the top layer has been served, the exposed backbone and ribs can be loosened easily and removed in one piece, leaving bottom layer for additional servings.

Hot Crabmeat Cocktail Spread and Other Seafood

Some supermarkets are well stocked with herring in sour cream, frozen shrimp, fresh lobster and crab. Shrimp, lobster, and crab may be served cold with a dip or heated in bite-sized chunks and served with a tangy sauce in a chafing dish. (A chafing dish is nothing more than a double boiler that's crashed society.)

When fresh seafood is not available, fill in with some of the excellent canned products on the market, including lobster, crabmeat, crab fingers, canned sardines, clams, oysters, and tuna. When one thinks of fish foods, one should also think of ice because shrimp, caviar, lobster, crabmeat, and oysters have greater eye-appeal when lavishly presented on plates or shells of seafood on a sparkling layer of crushed ice with wedges of lemon. A choice of tangy dips is guaranteed to make the most sanguine guest raise an eyebrow!

Hot Crabmeat Cocktail Spread

Equipment: Medium bowl, shallow ovenproof dish

8 oz. soft cream cheese
1 tablespoon milk
6-1/2 oz. drained, flaked crabmeat
2 tablespoons finely chopped onion
1/2 teaspoon prepared horseradish
1/4 teaspoon salt
Dash of pepper
1/3 cup sliced toasted almonds

In a medium-sized bowl, combine cream cheese and milk. Add crabmeat, onion, horseradish, salt and pepper. Blend well. Put in shallow ovenproof dish. Sprinkle with toasted almonds. Bake at 375° F. for 15 minutes. Serve with chips or crackers.
Makes 1-1/2 cups.

Fresh Pineapple Chunks

Refreshing fresh fruit of all kinds, but especially pineapple, I've found, is most welcome at cocktail parties. To improve the flavor of fresh pineapple chunks, boil 1/4 cup sugar with 1/2 cup water for 5 minutes and pour over chunks from one pineapple. Let stand for 1 hour in sugar water. Optional: Soak pineapple chunks in 1/4 cup Kirschwasser (cherry brandy).

More About Hors d'Oeuvres

The literal translation of the French word *hors d'oeuvre* is "outside of work," or   something extraordinary or unusual. For years, canapés and hors d'oeuvres made by professional chefs were elaborately garnished and beautifully designed jewel-like tidbits on which a great many hands spent a great many loving hours. As time marched on, soaring costs and scarcity of labor, plus the fact that these fancies were no longer so extraordinary or unusual to sophisticated palates, forced a new trend in cocktail party hors d'oeuvres—simplicity. We fell unwilling heir to the dip, the deviled egg, and the celery stuffed with cheese, but happily this day too is past and today's trend seems the most sane development we've encountered in the evolution of the hors d'oeuvre. Today's popular hors d'oeuvres live up to their name—they're extraordinarily tasty because we've drawn unusual ideas from all over the world and developed them into our own inventive cuisine. *Voilà!*

Nonplus-ultra: Scoop out a little of the inside of a large, ripe strawberry and fill with black caviar and serve chilled. Or buy large pitted green or black olives and stuff with Roqueford cheese.

Hot Chutney Cheese Hors d'Oeuvres

Equipment: Medium bowl, cookie sheet

For a quick hot chutney hors d'oeuvre, try my reliable standby recipe in your oven. Whenever I serve it, people ask me for the recipe. (Chutney is a delicious mixture of fruit and spices. It comes in a glass jar and is available in all grocery stores.)

2 tablespoons butter
1 cup grated strong cheddar cheese
1/2 cup chutney
1/2 teaspoon dry mustard

In medium-sized bowl, cream butter and cheese. Add chutney and mustard. Spread on toasted round of white bread. Bake on ungreased baking sheet at 450° F. for 5 minutes or until brown.
Makes 4 dozen.

Hot Hors d'Oeuvres Wrapped in Crisp Bacon

Equipment: Toothpicks, shallow baking pan

One can't discuss hors d'oeuvres without mentioning this specialty because it's so compatible with almost everything and may be prepared ahead then broiled in the oven at the last minute. And such variety!

Wrap any one of the following and secure with toothpicks. In a shallow baking pan broil in oven at 450° F. until bacon is crisp. (Timing varies depending on how lean or fat the bacon.)

- Pineapple chunks
- Large stuffed green olives
- Sautéed chicken livers, plain or with water chestnuts
- Prunes stuffed with almonds or walnuts, or chutney
- Dates stuffed with almonds and goat cheese

Canned Artichoke Bottoms

I've served these for years, but have recently noticed, like all good things, they are making a comeback in upscale catalogs.

Artichoke bottoms (not hearts) come in various sizes and are available in cans, usually 6 to 8 bottoms in each can. Serve cold. They may be marinated if you wish, after draining liquid from can. Fill bottoms with chopped crabmeat or your favorite seafood dip.

Small-sized artichoke bottoms can be eaten as finger food, but large-sized bottoms are best served on a plate and eaten with a small fork.

Sherry Cheese Paté

Equipment: Medium bowl, small serving platter

6 oz. cream cheese
1 cup sharp cheddar cheese, grated
1 tablespoon dry sherry
1/2 teaspoon curry powder
1/4 teaspoon salt

1/2 cup chutney, chopped
2 green onions, sliced thinly cross-wise

Soften cheeses, mix them thoroughly with sherry and seasonings. Spread about   1-inch thick on a serving platter. Chill. Just before serving, spread chutney over the top of the chilled cheese and sprinkle green onions over the chutney. Serve with sesame or wheat crackers.

Chinese Hard-Cooked Egg

Equipment: Medium and small saucepans

When I was a child I lived for four years with my parents in Shanghai, China, where my father was in the import-export business. Like everyone else at that time, we had several in help, including a Chinese cook named Fritz, who was an expert German cook. However, he also prepared meals for the Chinese staff, "Chinese fashion," and one of my favorite treats when I wandered into the kitchen was a Chinese hard-cooked egg.

Today we serve the same egg as an hors d'oeuvre and it's just as popular on this side of the world because of its salty good flavor.

4 eggs
3 tablespoons soy sauce
1 tablespoon of Italian olive oil

1. Place eggs in pan and cover with cold water. Bring to a boil, reduce heat, and allow to cook about 20 minutes.
2. Plunge the hard-cooked eggs in cold water for 5 minutes. Remove shells.
3. In a small saucepan, heat soy sauce and olive oil, then place eggs in sauce, basting them until they become a light mahogany color.
4. When cool, cut in half or quarters lengthwise with a sharp knife and serve—separately or as a garnish.

Caviar Sailboats

Sailing friends will be flattered when you salute them with this yachting hors d'oeuvre.

96

Equipment: Medium large saucepan, sieve, toothpicks

6 eggs
4 oz. jar of caviar
1 teaspoon lemon juice
1/2 teaspoon onion juice
12 toothpicks
12 strips of lemon or lime
1 bunch parsley

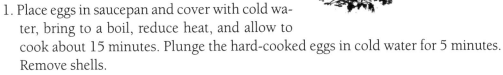

1. Place eggs in saucepan and cover with cold water, bring to a boil, reduce heat, and allow to cook about 15 minutes. Plunge the hard-cooked eggs in cold water for 5 minutes. Remove shells.
2. When cooled, cut in half lengthwise and remove yolk.
3. Fill center with caviar sprinkled with lemon and onion juice.
4. Press some egg yolk through sieve and sprinkle lightly over caviar.
5. Make a billowing sail by cutting lime or lemon rinds into 1/4-inch strips, and place toothpick through both ends, leaving one end of the toothpick longer than the other. Insert perpendicularly in egg for mast.
6. Place 12 sailboats on lush platter of parsley or watercress.

Raw Vegetable Bouquet

Equipment: Sharp knife, custard cup, toothpicks

It doesn't matter if your taste in art is 20th-century abstract expressionism or 17th-century still lifes, either way you'll have fun creating this arty centerpiece for your next summer cocktail table. It may add just the whimsical, pastoral touch you've been looking for.

Select a large white head of cauliflower. Cut a round hole in center, sink custard cup to be filled later with curry dip. Cut away about 2/3 of the buds intermittently in an even pattern. Place a toothpick in the vacancy and add carrot curls, radishes, miniature yellow and red tomatoes, raw cauliflower buds, bite-sized pieces of zucchini, accenting some of the empty spaces with sprigs of fresh parsley or mint. Garnish the base of the cauliflower with large curly-leaf cabbage leaves.

Serves 20 to 30 people.

97

Curry Dip and Vegetable Platter

Equipment: To serve on Lazy Susan or divided platter

1 cup mayonnaise
1 teaspoon Worcestershire sauce
1 tablespoon curry powder

In a small mixing bowl, mix mayonnaise, Worcestershire sauce, and curry powder until well blended. Refrigerate until ready to serve.

Addenda: There's a simpler, quicker, and effective alternate presentation, on a Lazy Susan, or on a round divided platter. Offer a variety of raw, tender, garden-fresh summer vegetables with a spicy curry dip placed in the center. Select vegetables when they are at their peak and arrange in alternate colors, such as orange baby carrots next to buds of white raw cauliflower, green broccoli or snap beans, and red cherry tomatoes beside strips of raw cucumbers or tender green pea pods; or strips of yellow squash next to small stalks of white celery or rings of green pepper; and red radish flowers next to whole mushrooms.

Raw Onion Trees

Equipment: Two styrofoam cones, toothpicks

Flank your vegetable bouquet with a pair of candles set in firm small cabbages, or for a more sensational effect, make a pair of edible onion trees. Here's how:

For two onion trees, buy two styrofoam cones about a foot high. Insert several dozen toothpicks into cone, then poke white spring onions into picks, starting at the top, letting green stalks hang down until cone is completely covered. Or, using the styrofoam cones, one can build a strawberry tree with toothpicks. Everyone plucks his own berry and dips it in a saucer of powdered sugar, whipped cream, sour cream, or melted chocolate.

Marinated Mushrooms

Equipment: Medium saucepan, small saucepan, strainer

Stop By for a Drink!

1 lb. fresh mushrooms
1 teaspoon salt
3 tablespoons lemon juice
1 cup vinegar
1 bay leaf
Pinch of freshly ground pepper
Pinch of thyme
2 shallots, cut fine
1/2 cup olive oil
1 tablespoon catsup
1 tablespoon chopped chervil (optional)

1. Boil mushrooms for 5 minutes in salt water and lemon juice. Drain water and dry mushrooms.
2. In a small saucepan boil vinegar, bay leaf, pepper, thyme, and shallots for 5 minutes. Cool and add olive oil, catsup, and mushrooms.
3. Marinate in refrigerator for at least 3 hours. Before serving, strain dressing and pour back over mushrooms. Sprinkle with fresh chervil if you have some in your herb garden.

Hot Potato Balls

"What I say is that, if a man really likes potatoes, he must be a pretty decent sort of fellow."

—A. A. Milne

Equipment: Scoop-shaped melon ball knife

Maybe this is the way some pretty important selections are made in Washington, D.C., these days, for I'm told these hot potato balls are served at some of the most sophisticated parties there!

Make raw potato balls by using the same scoop-shaped knife one uses to make melon balls. Drop in boiling salt water to cover and cook until they are tender but still firm, about 8 or 10 minutes. Drain. Add melted butter and serve hot, on toothpicks.

Figure 2 or 3 per person.

Hot Chutney Crescents

Equipment: Medium bowl, wooden spoon, wax paper or foil, 3" cookie cutter

The dough for this Far East hors d'oeuvre is prepared the day before and refrigerated overnight. Or crescents may be made ahead and kept frozen.

Or for short cut, use Pillsbury Quick Crescent Dinner Rolls. Unroll 1 can dinner roll dough, cutting into 3-inch rounds, and fill with chutney.

Makes 16 crescents.

1/2 cup butter
1 package (3 oz.) cream cheese
1 cup sifted flour
1/2 cup chutney

1. Start with butter and cream cheese at room temperature. In a medium-sized mixing bowl, cream together with a wooden spoon until smoothly blended. Add flour and mix thoroughly. Shape dough into a smooth ball, wrap in wax paper or aluminum foil, and chill overnight in refrigerator.
2. Remove from refrigerator and let stand at room temperature for 1/2 hour. Roll dough to 1/8-inch thickness. Cut with 3-inch cookie cutter. Place 1 teaspoon of cut-up chutney in center of each round. Fold over and press edges together. Bake on ungreased baking sheet at 375° F. for 15 minutes. Serve warm.

Makes 32 crescents.

Garlic Toast Hot Appetizers

Equipment: Small bowl, cookie sheet

1/4 cup mayonnaise
1/2 cup chopped green onion, stem and all
1/2 lb. bacon bits
24 garlic rounds

In a small bowl mix mayonnaise, onions, and bacon bits. Spread on toast rounds. Place on cookie sheet. Just before serving, preheat oven to 500° F. and place round in oven just long enough for spread to bubble.

Makes 24 appetizers.

Sweet 'n Sour Cocktail Franks

Equipment: Small saucepan, chafing dish, toothpicks

We've said it before: It's not always what you serve but how you serve it that counts! This is true in the case of the humble hot dog which, by any other name (Vienna cocktail frank), tastes just as sweet! Especially when cooked in the following sauce:

2 (5 oz.) cans Vienna cocktail franks
2 (10 oz.) jars currant jelly
1 (6 oz.) jar French's mustard

Simmer jelly and mustard for 2 hours. Add uncooked franks and continue cooking for another half hour. Transfer to chafing dish and serve bubbly hot with toothpicks.

Grilled Cocktail Wieners

Equipment: Can of sterno, toothpicks

Another amusing disguise for the pedestrian wiener is to serve either bite-sized bits or miniatures on toothpicks placed in a leafy red or green cabbage. (To achieve a rose petal effect, core bottom of cabbage and roll outside cabbage leaves around a pencil toward center vein. Remove pencil and repeat.)

Cut a round hole in the center of the cabbage and insert a can of sterno. If you like, cover sterno with a sheet of copper screening. (For a smooth edge turn under about 1 inch.)

Marinate wieners in your favorite barbecue sauce and serve on toothpicks. Insert toothpicks in cabbage. Guests grill their own wieners over flames. Serve with Dijon mustard.

Mini-Meatballs

Equipment: Large bowl, shallow baking pan, chafing dish

These mini-meatballs are extremely flavorful, juicy, and tender, and so easy to prepare in the oven in quantity before the party! Serve in a chafing dish.

2 lbs. fine ground round steak
2 eggs
3 slices whole wheat bread
1 lb. cottage cheese, small curd
1 cup yogurt
1 package dehydrated onion soup (Lipton's)
Dash of beau monde seasoning
1 cup catsup

1. Preheat oven to 250° F.
2. Combine everything but catsup; let stand for 20 minutes.
3. Roll meat into small balls about the size of a very large olive. Place in a large shallow pan and bake in oven for 1 hour.
4. Brown meatballs under broiler for 5 minutes, turning once. Put in chafing dish and cover with thin layer of catsup and serve with toothpicks.

Bar-B-Qued Beefsteak

Equipment: Roaster, 2 kitchen forks, wooden cutting board, chafing dish

There probably aren't too many people around any more who have had the pleasure of eating the piquant, juicy meat of an ox roasted in open pit, but if you ever have, it's a pleasure you never forget. There's only one slight drawback: It takes a half dozen strong men to dig the pit, rub the ox with salt and wrap him in parchment, muslin, etc., and serve the half a ton of barbecued meat to a crowd of 700 people!

Thanks to a friend who created this recipe of modest proportions, we're able to enjoy this flavorful hors d'oeuvre any time we're in the mood for a barbecued treat. Great for a tailgate party because it serves a crowd. Order 6 dozen tiny hamburger buns (2 or 2-1/2 inches diameter) from your bakery.

7 Ibs. round steak cut 2-1/2 to 3 inches thick
1/4 cup salt
1 bottle (1 lb. 2 oz.) prepared barbecue sauce

1. Rub salt into meat thoroughly. Place meat in a roaster with one quart of water.
2. Cover and bake at 350° F. for 3-1/2 hours. Remove from pan, reserving liquid.
3. With 2 kitchen forks, on a wooden cutting board shred meat into small pieces, mix shredded meat with most of the juice, leaving 1/2 cup to add to chafing dish during the evening to prevent meat from becoming dry. Add barbecue sauce and stir until well mixed.
4. Serve hot from chafing dish on warm hamburger buns.

Hors d'Oeuvre Addenda

Refer to following chapters for hors d'oeuvre recipes:

Chapter Three: Toasted Cheese Rolls, Toasted Mushroom Sandwiches, Stuffed Cherry Tomatoes, Hot Lobster Canapé, Merry-Go-Round Pie, Smoked Salmon

Chapter Five: Cheese Fondue, Baby Spareribs

Say "When" for Mixing Drinks

When it comes to the art of mixing drinks, there are several vocal but opposing schools of thought. Some people maintain the first drink should be good and strong—then go lightly on the rest. This misguided group claims that after the first drink, nobody knows the difference! The tragic mistake in this approach is that when someone is tense, hungry and tired, a stiff drink can turn one into a drunk stiff! (It's better to coat the tummy before the party at home, if you can, with a cup of hot creamed soup.)

Another group suggests mixing all drinks equally strong; they rationalize the bartender is relieved from the chore of constantly refilling glasses. Then there's a third group who feel all drinks should be on the light side, keeping everyone drinking pleasantly and steadily all evening.

When you're playing bartender, the best advice is to use your own good judgment, and that includes pouring the "one for the road" back in the bottle when necessary. If you engage a professional bartender, don't hesitate to tell him how you'd like your drinks measured before the party starts. He'll be glad to follow your instructions.

How Many Fifths?

No matter how often one entertains, there's always the question, "How many bottles of liquor do we need?" Using the following measurements as a guide, one is able to judge the number of drinks per person.

One case of liquor = 12 bottles
1/5 bottle = 1/5 of a gallon, or 7 ounces less than a quart
1/5 bottle liquor, using 1-oz. pony = 25 drinks
1/5 bottle liquor, using 1-1/2 oz. jigger = 18 drinks
   (The difference between a pony and a jigger is 1/2 an ounce.)
1/5 bottle champagne, using 3-oz. glasses = 7 drinks

The average guest will have two or three drinks, or figuring roughly one drink every 30 to 40 minutes.

For a large group it's a good idea to use smaller glasses (6 or 8 oz.) because people frequently set a glass down and forget where they put it. For this reason, you'll need about three glasses per person.

Experts on alcoholism advise us against forcing drinks, and who doesn't approve of that? Better to offer some non-alcoholic beverages and give people who are abstaining for whatever reason a glass to hold without comment or apology.

Instead of an open bar, there are times it's preferable to pass trays of prepared or mixed drinks from the pantry or kitchen. Drinks can be mixed ahead and kept chilled in a pitcher in the refrigerator. Just add ice and garnish when ready to serve. For a large group you'll need some extra professional help, but for a small group, before dinner, the host can easily handle this job himself.

The sky's the limit when it comes to stocking a bar with a variety of wines and liquor, but the basic list includes only two whiskeys: Scotch and either rye or bourbon. (A rye man won't be offended when you offer him bourbon, or vice versa, but Scotch drinkers always like Scotch.) Next on the list is gin. Buy London gin at better prices, because cheap gin is for hangovers. Vermouth, vodka, rum, sherry, and one or two after-dinner drinks if you wish, round out the complete list.

Before-Dinner Wines and Champagne

It's becoming more and more popular to serve a good grade of imported or domestic sherry (New York State grows wonderful grapes for sherries) or a Chardonnay, or a fine California wine as a cocktail before dinner.

For festive occasions, such as wedding receptions or special anniversaries, imported champagne may be your first choice served pure, chilled and bubbly. A domestic champagne makes a good cocktail. (For Champagne Punch, see Chapter Three.)

Champagne Cocktail

Pre-chill champagne glasses and wine. Place a medium-sized loaf of sugar in the glass and saturate with angostura bitters—about 2 dashes. Fill glass with thoroughly chilled champagne. Add a twist of lemon or orange peel.

Step-Saver Suggestions

When setting up an improvised bar indoors or out, drape a cloth around the edge of a large sturdy table, or aluminum folding table, that reaches all the way to the floor, behind which you can store extra liquor, lemons, limes, olives, napkins, glasses, soda water, ice buckets, empty bottles, and a wastebasket. In a small condo, if you are cramped for space, a sturdy ironing board may serve as a bar.

Keep a large tray handy for quick trips to the kitchen with used glasses and figure using about three times as many glasses as there are guests.

Bar Equipment and Supplies

Some people tape a time-saving list inside the liquor closet door that may read something like this:

Liquor

Bourbon or Rye; Scotch; Gin, Vodka, Vermouth; Rum, Sherry; Courvoisier, Kahlua, Crème de menthe

Soft Drinks

Cola drinks; root beer; ginger ale
Mixes
Soda water; quinine water; grape juice; tomato juice
Fruits, etc.
Lemons; cherries; olives; onions
Ice: crushed, cubed

Suggested Supplies

Ice bucket; tongs; bottle opener; corkscrew; lemon squeezer; strainer; water pitcher; long-handled bar spoon; steel paring knife; towel; glasses; coasters; cocktail shaker; bottle caps; jiggers; recipes.

A special word about ice. Ice bought at any metropolitan ice company is pure, whereas the ice from your own refrigerator may not be. Ice drinks up odors of a refrigerator as a sponge drinks up water.

Please see Chapter Eight for more about glassware.

What Every Young Bartender Should Know

There's a good story making the rounds at cocktail parties, so please stop me if you've heard this one!

A young Royal Mountie is having his gear checked by his instructor for his first solo into the hinterland. As they look over the gear, item by item, they come to the last small package.

"What's this?" inquires the Rookie.

"That's in case you get lost."

"But I have my compass."

"This is in case you *really* get lost, man," says the instructor, pointing to the contents of the package. "Here's a small bottle of gin, and here's some vermouth, and here's a bottle of olives. Mix yourself a martini and within two minutes someone will walk up to you and tell you that you didn't do it right!"

A Respectable Martini

Cocktail shakers have become collectibles, but a respectable martini still ought to be mixed in a shaker.

2 oz. imported gin
1 oz. Italian dry vermouth
Lemon peel
Stuffed olive or onion

Pre-chill glasses and shaker and the liquor, if you're fussy.

Fill shaker with cubed ice and add vodka and Italian dry vermouth. Stir quickly, but gently. Rub lemon peel around edge of glass before serving. Pour liquor into chilled martini cocktail glass and add stuffed olive or pearl onion.

Cosmopolitan Martini
A new popular drink

1/2 oz. Cointreau
1 oz. vodka
Juice of 1/2 a lime
Splash of cranberry juice for pink color

Pour all ingredients into a mixing glass or shaker that is half filled with ice. Shake and strain into a chilled martini glass.

Bloody Mary

Mix one part vodka with 2 or 3 parts tomato juice, according to taste. Add a dash of Worcestershire sauce and a dash of lemon to taste. Salt and pepper, a dash of Tabasco sauce, and ice complete the drink.

Bullshot

Three parts canned bouillon to one part vodka and ice. No seasoning.

Margarita

The margarita, a Mexican drink, has fast become a favorite summer drink throughout our country. It is made with tequila, and some brands are stronger than others so be careful. No ice is added to this drink and it is intended to be sipped very slowly from a cocktail glass frosted with salt! Yes, salt!

1-1/2 oz. tequila
1/2 oz. triple sec
1 teaspoon fresh lemon or lime or 1/2 oz. unsweetened lime juice

Wet 3 oz. or 3-1/2 oz. cocktail glass and chill in freezer. If you like, rub edge of glass with lemon. Dip rim into a saucer of table salt and serve.

Pineapple Swipes

This ancient Hawaiian libation might be called the granddaddy of all mixed drinks. All one needs for this novelty is a sun-ripened pineapple. Slice off the top with a long-bladed knife, carefully cut up the interior without puncturing the outer skin, add a cup of sugar and a cake of yeast. Replace the top and secure with toothpicks; let it set in the warm tropical sun for three lovely days.

At the end of this time, uncap the pineapple and sit yourself in the cool shade of a coconut tree and sip the smooth tropical nectar. It won't be long before you'll hear the song of a nightingale!

What, you say? No sun-ripened pineapple? No coconut tree? Then try this shortcut.

Beachboy Screwdriver

1 jigger vodka
1/2 cup pineapple juice

Pour vodka over ice cubes in highball glass. Add pineapple juice. Garnish with orchid, azalea, or gladioli blossom. For a frosted cocktail, mix in blender with ice for about 60 seconds at high speed.

Stop By for a Drink!

Broken Leg
Served hot

My favorite hot *après-ski* drink (originated by the Old Crow Distillery Co.) is called Broken Leg. It's easy to prepare, not too sweet and not too sour, but *so-o-o* smooth! (I have successfully prepared and served hot apple juice from an electric coffee maker.)

For each portion allow:

6 oz. apple juice
1 stick cinnamon
1 thin slice lemon
1 oz. bourbon, 80 proof

Heat apple juice. (I have used my electric coffee maker). Place cinnamon, lemon slice and bourbon in individual mugs. Add hot apple juice and enjoy, enjoy.

Planter's Punch

1 teaspoon sugar
1/2 oz. orange juice
1 oz. lime juice
1-1/2 oz. dark rum
Soda water
Garnish: orange slice and a cherry

Dissolve sugar in fruit juices. Add rum. Shake and pour into highball glass filled with crushed ice. Add soda water and garnish with orange slice and cherry. Serve with straw.

The Frozen Daiquiri

A good daiquiri is made with good rum!

1/2 teaspoon sugar
1/4 teaspoon lime juice, fresh
1 jigger light rum

Shake vigorously with plenty of finely crushed ice and strain into chilled cocktail glass. Or mix ice, sugar, lime juice and rum in blender. Garnish with sprig of mint.

Chapter Five

Casual Cocktail Buffets

"Where there's room in the heart, there's room in the house."
—Danish Proverb

The Cocktail Buffet: America's Contribution to Entertaining

A fun-loving couple from Cleveland sent out more than fifty cocktail buffet invitations in honor of their tenth wedding anniversary. They engaged a caterer and a couple of bartenders for the happy occasion, and as car after car pulled up in front of the circular driveway, guests were greeted by the welcome glow of flickering Hawaiian torches. At the entrance, an attendant in a white jacket opened the door wide and lively music drifted across the bright threshold. As the smiling hostess greeted her guests, one of the ladies gushed, "Why honey—you fussed!"

Now it's no secret to anyone who cares about these things that giving a successful party does take a certain amount of fussing, and hosting an outstanding party is not an effortless, unplanned, unbudgeted, haphazard happening! It's work, but the synergistic kind of work that can be a delightful challenge, a satisfying experience and a world of fun.

Four Seasons Cocktail Buffet

The advantage in giving a cocktail buffet rather than a sit-down dinner is that there is so little regimentation! Guests arrive early or late, drink as long as they like, eat when they're ready, sit down where they choose, leave when they wish, and the hostess couldn't care less.

Another advantage is that when people call the hostess to accept or decline an invitation, or procrastinate with "I'm not sure if we'll be in town on that date—we had better decline. May we have a rain check?," she can honestly reply, "We do want you to come— let us know when you can!" Or if someone says, "We can't be with you because we're having houseguests from out of town," she can sincerely follow up with, "Please come and bring your friends!" (The Bible tells us, "Be not forgetful to entertain strangers, for thereby some have entertained angels unawares" [Hebrews 13:2].)

I do enjoy giving cocktail buffets or suppers, and mine usually start small and grow like Topsy! My husband used to tease me about the time I suggested we invite a few people over for a drink on the 4th of July and we ended up with 85 for a cocktail buffet!

Post a Timetable

Before a party, I always prepare a written timetable along with the menu and post this schedule on a kitchen cabinet for a last-minute check, both for myself and any extra help that's engaged for the party. On the checklist I write the number of guests, the time cocktails and hors d'oeuvres are to be served, and when the hot things are to be put on the table, plus who's responsible for what.

When Buffet Service Began

See Chapter Eight for details.

Few people are aware of how and when buffet service originated. Believe it or not, Ben Franklin was the host responsible for this delightful innovation. When he was an ambassador to France (1776–1785), he was required to host a 4th of July party, to reciprocate the lavish hospitality of his royal hosts. Not only did he lack the funds, but he also lacked space, equipment, and staff! Thus he conceived the plan to invite more guests than could be seated. The food was set out on long tables and everyone helped themselves. Guests strolled through the French doors into the gardens carrying their own plates. Thus the buffet supper was born and became the rage of Paris.

Intimate Four Seasons Buffet Supper

Marinated mushrooms
Olives wrapped in crisp bacon
Stuffed pasta shells
Green spinach salad
Wine—Italian Chianti classico
French and Italian bread
The best chocolate cake
Decaffeinated coffee

The beauty of this menu is that the stuffed pasta shells and spinach salad can all be served together on one plate. This is especially nice if one decides to let guests sit wherever they choose. Offering large white dinner napkins is a thoughtful touch.

Stuffed Pasta Shells

I have made this dish two or three days ahead and kept it in my refrigerator, thus the flavors marry nicely together.

Equipment needed: Cuisinart, saucepan, garlic masher, 10" x 15" Pyrex dish

1. Tomato Sauce (keeps several days in the refrigerator)

1/4 cup extra virgin olive oil
4 plump garlic cloves put through masher
1/2 teaspoon red pepper flakes
Sea salt to taste

To prepare: Put in saucepan but do not turn on burner until all ingredients are already mixed together. Now turn on burner and cook for 1 minute or so until garlic is golden.

Then add:
1 28 oz. can crushed tomatoes
Stir and let simmer on low about 15 minutes or until thickened.

Stir in:
1 cup heavy cream
Cook 1 more minute.

2. Jumbo Shells, 12 oz. package. Cook, slightly *al dente.*

3. Filling for Shells

1/4 lb. Genoa salami
1/4 lb pastrami
1/4 lb. pepperoni
3 Italian sweet sausages (or 1-1/2 lbs.) that have been boiled 15 minutes and cooled;
    remove casing.
1/4 lb. provolone
1/4 lb. mozzarella
1-1/2 cups sour cream
1 cup small curd cottage cheese
1/4 cup Romano cheese

To prepare: Cut up meat and put it through the food processor but do not over-process, because you want texture. Then add cheese. Mix together and stuff cooked shells.
   Put some of the tomato sauce on the bottom of a large Pyrex dish then add stuffed shells in a single layer. Add more sauce and finally sprinkle on additional Romano cheese.
   Bake uncovered at 350° F. for 30 to 40 minutes or until bubbly. Let set before serving. Serves 12.

Spinach Salad

   The beauty of this salad is that the flavorful dressing adheres to the spinach and doesn't run into the thick tomato sauce. Therefore the red stuffed shells and green salad can be served together on one plate.

Equipment: Salad bowl, garlic masher

12 oz. bag of pre-washed baby spinach leaves
1 large garlic clove, mashed
2 teaspoons Dijon mustard
2 teaspoons red wine vinegar
2 tablespoons extra virgin olive oil
Fresh black pepper and salt to taste
Croutons, optional

Mix garlic, mustard, vinegar, and olive oil in bottom of bowl, and then add well-dried spinach on top and mix well. The dressing will stick to the spinach and not be runny.

This recipe serves six.

The Best Chocolate Cake

It took me twenty years to coax this chocolate cake recipe from my high school chum. I remembered eating it at her parents' round dinner table on Gough Street in San Francisco. Now whenever I serve it, my gourmet friends ask me for the recipe, which I will gladly share with you.

Equipment: Double boiler, stand-up mixer (optional), two 9" cake pans, large mixing bowl, wooden spoon

6 squares baker's unsweetened chocolate
1/2 cup water
2 cups sifted cake flour
1 teaspoon baking soda
1 teaspoon salt
1-1/2 teaspoons baking powder
2/3 cup butter, room temperature
2/3 cup firmly packed light brown sugar
1 cup granulated sugar
3 eggs
2 teaspoons pure vanilla extract
1 cup sour cream

1. In a double boiler, melt chocolate in water over very low heat, stirring until blended. Cool thoroughly.
2. Meanwhile, on a sheet of wax paper, measure and sift flour, soda, salt, and baking powder together.
3. In a large bowl, cream softened butter and sugars until light and fluffy. Add eggs one at a time, mixing well after each addition. Blend in vanilla.
4. To cooled chocolate add sour cream and mix well.
5. Alternate chocolate mix and flour mixture to the butter-egg mixture and beat well after each addition.
6. Line two 9" cake pans with wax paper and add batter.
7. Bake in moderate oven 350° F. for 35 or 40 minutes. Remove from oven and cool.

Chocolate Sour Cream Frosting

4-1/2 squares baker's unsweetened chocolate
3 tablespoons butter or margarine
1-1/8 cups sour cream
6-3/4 cups unsifted confectioner's sugar
1/2 teaspoon salt
2 teaspoons pure vanilla extract

1. In double boiler, melt chocolate and butter. Cool thoroughly.
2. In a large mixing bowl, blend sour cream, sugar, and salt. Gradually beat in chocolate. Add vanilla. If frosting is soft, chill until thick. Makes enough frosting for between layers, top, and sides.

Dobos Torte
May be made a day ahead or weeks before because it freezes beautifully

I learned how to make a Dobos torte from a Hungarian cook, who used to work at the embassy in Washington, D.C. The ingredients for making a Dobos torte are so economical compared to the prices charged by professional bakers, and the results are so   spectacular, it's hard to understand why more budget-minded people don't make this "nonplus ultra" dessert. One of the nice things about making a Dobos torte is that it can be done in two stages the day before. I usually bake the individual layers in the morning and make the chocolate icing in the evening, when things have quieted down around the house. The torte freezes beautifully. (I put it in a cardboard cake box and then wrap the box in freezer paper.) It is ready to serve whenever the spirit moves you. Just allow several hours' defrosting time.

Equipment: To make a Dobos torte you need two, three, or four 8" spring form pans (with removable bottoms), because it's speedier with several pans. The following recipe, using 8" pans, makes 6 layers.

If you double the recipe you can add more layers and/or use 9" or 10" pans. There's just one thing. Don't use pans of different sizes or your torte will droop on the sides when you put it all together.

Another point: Have all ingredients at room temperature.

Dough

1 cup flour
7 eggs, separated, room temperature
1/2 teaspoon salt
1 cup powdered sugar

1. Preheat oven to 375° F. Put two sheets of wax paper on counter. Sift pre-sifted flour once on wax paper, measure, then sift again 4 times.
2. In a large bowl beat egg yolks, salt, and sugar until thick.
3. In another large bowl, beat egg whites stiff but not dry.
4. Alternately fold in flour and egg whites with egg yolk mixture lightly until smooth but still fluffy.
5. Butter and flour only the bottoms of the cake pans.
6. With a rubber spatula spread dough evenly on cake pan 1/4-inch thick. Bake in moderate oven from 6 to 8 minutes. Dough should not turn brown but remain very pale yellow.
7. Remove cake at once from pan with a metal spatula and let cool. Repeat until all the dough is used. You should have 6 layers.

Filling and Icing

1/4 lb. sweet chocolate
1/4 lb. bitter chocolate
3 tablespoons water
3 eggs
1-1/2 cups powdered sugar
1/2 lb. butter
1 teaspoon vanilla

1. Melt chocolates with water in double boiler while stirring.
2. In a medium-sized bowl, mix eggs and sugar and add to chocolate. Stir constantly until thick. This takes quite a while.
3. Remove chocolate mixture from stove. While it is cooling, cream butter until light. Add vanilla to butter, then add chocolate mixture and beat until well blended.
4. Spread a thin layer of chocolate mixture on cake, place another layer of cake on chocolate mixture and repeat until cake is 6 layers high, leaving enough chocolate to cover both top and sides of cake.

Caution: Be sure to place layers very evenly one on top of the other. Allow torte to set a day before serving.

Addenda: A Dobos torte is always sliced thin because it is quite rich.

Makes 12 servings.

Sunday Night Suppers

The rosy afterglow of a Sunday evening get-together helps most people drive away those Monday blues. Young people, old people—in fact, most people—enjoy going to someone's home for a "gemutlich" Sunday evening supper. Since Sunday is such a relaxed, informal kind of play-day, it's a perfect time for single men and women to entertain family, friends, or other single men and women. It's the one day of the week when almost anything goes! One can invite a medley of ages, teenagers and parents; one can invite more men than women or more women than men; one can arrange word games for young and old after dinner; one can sing songs or play the guitar; one can play bingo or bridge; one can show travel movies or spin old collectors' discs; one can roast shish kabob or popcorn; one can play truth or consequences; one can play charades or backgammon or

Monopoly or hearts; one can dress up or down; one can have a lot of fun just being together in a congenial group!

A friend who lives alone and likes it frequently entertains on Sundays because she's discovered a Sunday supper invitation is accepted joyously and enthusiastically. Sunday may be a trying day for people who live alone or for couples whose grown children have moved away to college campuses, army bases, or suburbia. Once there weren't enough minutes in the day for doing all the things that a family tries to squeeze into those precious 24 hours of togetherness; now the hours drag and one can't wait for the stimulation of a work week.

My single friend entertains with a flair. Though her menus are always carefully budgeted, they're still imaginative. We all look forward to her little Sunday night suppers because, as she puts it, "I don't try to compete with fancy French restaurant food. My women friends feel it's a treat to enjoy some good home cooking in company—a meal they haven't had to plan or shop for." And the men love it because, "I always try to give them something hearty." She gives more than that.

Besides good food, there's always good discussion after dinner at her house, too. People who have known each other for years without ever exchanging more than superficialities suddenly become interesting and loquacious story tellers. How is this wonder accomplished? For one thing, she serves a buffet, then sets up three card tables in her compact living room, and after dinner she allows her guests to remain seated around the card tables for a relaxed, after-dinner cordial and light conversation.

"It's so much more comfortable this way for small group discussions. Sometimes people push a chair back and chat with the group at the next table, then break up into twos and threes again. I've found that when I remove the bridge tables and chairs, everyone ends up sitting around the living room in a large circle, and conversation becomes stilted and people have little to say."

When Boswell complained to his friend, Dr. Samuel Johnson, "of having dined at a splendid table without hearing one sentence of conversation worthy of being remembered," Boswell replied, "Sir, there seldom is any such conversation!"

"Why then meet at the table?" Boswell asked.

"Why, to eat and drink together and to promote kindness; and, Sir, this is better done when there is no solid conversation; for when there is, people differ in opinion, and get into bad humour, or some of the company who are not capable of such conversation are left out and feel themselves uneasy."

Things haven't changed that much since 1776!

Sunday Night Supper with a Green Theme

The theme for the table decoration reflects the menu. An arrangement of bells of Ireland accented with green zinnias is flanked by a pair of candles placed in clear glass hurricane chimney holders. Rough earthenware crockery bowls and platters are set on a pale blue denim tablecloth.

Bells of Ireland Menu

Appetizers
Green olives
Dilli-beans
Hot buttered potato balls (Chapter Four)
Senegalese soup
Hungarian green noodles and cabbage casserole
Corned beef on saddle of rye bread
Horseradish sauce
Cucumber
Salad pickles
Beer
Coffee
Boston cream cake

Senegalese Soup
Made with chicken broth

Equipment needed: Electric blender, sauté pan, sieve, saucepan

This smooth, delicate soup may be served hot or cold. It can be assembled quickly when using Swanson's canned chicken broth.

2 stalks finely chopped white celery
1 large sliced onion
3 medium sliced fresh apples
1 banana (optional)
1/2 lb. butter

2 tablespoons curry powder
1/3 cup flour
8 cups Swanson's chicken broth
1/4 teaspoon salt
1/4 teaspoon white pepper
Dash of cayenne pepper
2 cups light cream
1/2 cup white wine

1. Sauté celery, onions, apples, banana in butter in a sauté pan.
2. When apples are soft pour mixture into blender and purée. Return to saucepan and add curry powder, gradually mix in flour.
3. Add chicken broth and dry seasonings. Reduce heat and add cream. Do not allow to boil. Just before serving, add wine.

Makes 10-12 servings.

Addenda: Pieces of diced white meat of chicken or chutney are sometimes served on the side.

Hungarian Green Noodles and Cabbage Casserole

Equipment: Colander, frying pan with cover

I'll admit this sounds ordinary, but through alchemy the combination of these two standbys complement each other in such a way that an unusual party dish results.

1 medium-sized cabbage
2 oz. butter or 4 strips of bacon
1 medium-sized onion
1 teaspoon salt
2 small apples
3 tablespoons red wine
1 package (16 oz.) broad egg noodles

1. Slice cabbage medium fine. Rinse raw sliced cabbage with hot water through colander.
2. Melt butter or bacon strips in a large frying pan.

3. Slice onion very fine and sauté in frying pan until lightly brown. Add rinsed cabbage and simmer for 5 minutes. Add salt.
4. Peel and quarter apples, add them to cabbage, and simmer for 15 minutes. Cover frying pan and simmer for another 15 minutes.
5. Add 3 tablespoons of red wine and simmer for 5 minutes.
6. Before serving, cook noodles in boiling water as directed on package. Drain. Combine with cabbage and serve hot.
Makes 12 servings.

Fresh Corned Beef on Rye

Buy two fat (not lean) corned beef briskets, totaling about 7 pounds; remove any cellophane. If your local butcher or delicatessen cannot supply first-rate quality, do not hesitate to send away for them. Store them in your freezer until needed and defrost before using. (See Sources of Supply.)

Equipment: 8-quart covered stock pot, shallow baking pan, sauté pan

2 corned briskets of beef
2 unsliced rye breads
1/4 lb. (4 oz.) butter or margarine

1. Tie briskets separately with twine lengthwise very tightly and knot securely. Then tie each brisket crosswise twice. This holds the meat firmly together for carving.
2. Place in one large stock pot or two medium-sized pots and cover with cold water. Bring water to a rolling boil. Reduce heat and let simmer slowly for 3-1/2 to 4 hours or until meat is tender.
3. Remove from water and place in shallow pan in warm oven for 15 minutes. When ready to serve, cut and remove twine. Remove top bottom and side crust from breads. Melt butter in sauté pan, and sauté bread on both sides. Place warm bread on serving platter and place corned beef on top of rye bread.
When carving serve each person a slice of corned beef with a slice of rye. The juices of the meat flavors the bread. Garnish with parsley and be prepared to serve seconds!
Makes 12–14 servings.

Boston Cream Cake

Equipment: Large mixing bowl, sifter, egg beater, 9" cake pan, double boiler, spatula, cooling rack

4 eggs
1 cup sugar
4 tablespoons hot water
1 cup flour
1 teaspoon baking powder
1/8 teaspoon salt
1 teaspoon vanilla
1 lemon rind, grated

Preheat oven to 350° F. Separate eggs. Beat egg yolks in a large mixing bowl, add sugar and continue mixing until thick and lemon-colored. Add water. Sift flour, baking powder, and salt and add to egg yolks. Beat egg whites until stiff and add vanilla and grated lemon rind. Pour into cake pan and bake in oven for 20 minutes. Remove from oven and turn pan over. You may need to coax the cake from the pan with a spatula. Place on cooling rack.

Custard Filling

3 egg yolks
2 tablespoons flour
1 tablespoon cornstarch
1/2 cup powdered sugar
2 cups half-and-half cream
2 tablespoons butter
1 teaspoon vanilla
1 cup whipped cream

Cook everything except whipped cream in double boiler, stirring occasionally until thick. Cool. Fold in whipped cream. Cut the two layers in half horizontally and spread with custard filling. Sprinkle top with powdered sugar or cover with chocolate frosting.

Chocolate Frosting

1/4 cup brown sugar
1/4 cup water
1 tablespoon butter
1 square bitter chocolate
1 cup powdered sugar
1/2 teaspoon vanilla

Boil brown sugar, water, and butter; while stirring add chocolate. When melted, remove from range. Add powdered sugar and vanilla; beat with egg beater until smooth.
Makes 10 servings.

Après-Ski Party (and Other Impromptu Get-Togethers)

One of the most delightful "happenings" occurs when people join you at the spur-of-the-moment for potluck meals.

Does the thought of company for potluck appall you? It certainly will if you maintain that the whole house has to be spic-and-span—but if hanging out a fresh guest towel will do, then you'll have all the time and energy needed to enjoy the companionship of people.

Living in a summer and winter resort as we do, unexpected company (that doesn't mean unwelcome company!) is almost a weekly occurrence. Admittedly there are times one wishes one could repeat the "miracle of the loaves" (unhappily no one can tell us how to make two pork chops into four), but there are ways of stretching dinner by adding an extra course, opening an extra can, or defrosting an extra cut of meat.

During ski season we often meet friends on the slopes and invite them home for potluck; this usually means charcoaling hamburgers or steaks, knowing full well that our freezer is well stocked with additional casseroles, French bread, and dessert. This is the fun time to recount tall tales of thrills, chills, and spills on the various slopes.

The first thing we do when we return home is to take out the meat from the deep-freeze, along with a casserole, homemade Bundt cake, and a loaf of sourdough bread. We quickly spread a bright green cloth on our dining room table for our buffet and arrange the silverware and napkins for self-service. Our large soup tureen is placed at one end of the table to be filled with crab bisque—a hot, filling soup that really hits the spot after a salubrious day on the snow—or *in* the snow, as the case may be!

Casual Cocktail Buffets

While we're bathing and changing into comfortable après-ski outfits, our dinner is defrosting. Soon the doorbell starts ringing and everyone gathers around the fire, sipping soup, while the inevitable kibitzer has his fun directing the precise grilling of his steak: How raw is rare? How pink is medium? A few guests can be conned into cutting up raw vegetables. After the hot soup course, warm plates are set out, along with some good homemade relishes and warm bread, sliced thick and served in straw baskets. Our simple menu is quite filling, but if one is lucky enough to have a casserole of Cheese Magic in the freezer (which I serve instead of potatoes), this après-ski menu will guarantee a blue ribbon!

Après-Ski Menu

Cocktail—Hot Broken Leg (Chapter Four)
Crab bisque and crackers
Homemade corn relish, pickles, olives, carrots
Charcoal-grilled steak
Sourdough bread (bought)
Cheese Magic casserole
Imported beer
Bundt cake (Chapter Two)
Café Royal

Quick Crab Bisque

With apologies to the purist, this is the time to open a few cans.

Equipment needed: Double boiler

1 can (10-1/2 oz.) condensed tomato soup
1 can (10-1/2 oz.) creamed pea soup
2 empty soup cans filled with milk (or, 1-2/3 cups milk)
1 can (7 oz.) crabmeat
1 tablespoon sherry
1 pint whipped cream topping (low-calorie)

1. Mix soups and milk in large double boiler and bring to boil. Drain crabmeat and remove bones and add to soup.
2. Just before serving, pour in a tablespoon of sherry. Warm soup tureen and soup plates in oven.
3. When ready to serve, pour hot soup in tureen and serve in individual soup plates, topped with whipped cream topping.

Makes 6 servings.

Homemade Corn Relish
Keeps a long time in the refrigerator

    1 can (12 oz.) whole kernel corn
    1 teaspoon mustard seed
    1/2 teaspoon dry mustard
    1/4 teaspoon salt
    1/4 teaspoon pepper
    1/3 cup cider vinegar
    1 tablespoon salad oil
    2 tablespoons light brown sugar
    1/2 cup chopped onion
    2 cans pimentos, drained and chopped
    1/4 cup chopped green pepper

1. Drain liquid from corn into small saucepan. Stir in mustard seed, mustard, salt, pepper, vinegar, oil and brown sugar. Bring to a full boil.
2. In a medium bowl mix together corn, onion, pimento, and green pepper.
3. Pour hot liquid over corn mixture. Toss lightly until well mixed. Refrigerate covered several hours before serving.

Makes 2-1/2 cups.

Cheese Magic Casserole
From freezer to oven to table

Not a soufflé—not a pudding—but a kind of magical delight that I serve instead of potatoes, it brings rave reviews from critics. Make it the day before or freeze it for any performance.

Equipment needed: An attractive serving dish that you can transfer from freezer to oven to table

8 slices white bread, buttered
1/4 lb. butter for casserole
1-1/2 lbs. sharp cheddar cheese, grated
6 eggs
1 finely minced green onion
1/2 teaspoon dry mustard
1/2 teaspoon beau monde seasoning (Spice Island)
1/2 teaspoon salt
1/4 teaspoon paprika
1/8 teaspoon cracked black pepper
Dash of cayenne
2-1/2 cups half-and-half cream
1 rounded teaspoon brown sugar
1/2 teaspoon Worcestershire sauce

Remove crust from bread and butter well. Dice into about 1/4-inch squares. Generously butter 2-quart casserole, arrange bread on bottom, lay generous layer of grated cheese on top, then more bread and second half of remaining cheese. Beat eggs and add minced green onions, dry seasonings, half-and-half, then brown sugar and Worcestershire sauce. Pour over bread and let stand 24 hours in refrigerator. Two hours before baking, remove from refrigerator and let stand at room temperature. Preheat oven to 300° F. Set casserole in a shallow pan of water with heavy paper on bottom. Bake for 1-1/2 hours.
Makes 12 servings.

Café Royal

After the last sigh of "I'm so full!" and while everyone is still languishing before the fire, it's time to nudge the group gently by offering them a flaming surprise. For this witchery, turn the lights low, bring in a tray with a pot of hot strong coffee, cups, saucers, and some fine brandy along with a dish of cubed sugar for Café Royal.

All you need is a steady hand to first warm the spoon by holding it over the hot coffee for about a half a minute, then place a cube of sugar in the spoon, add a little brandy and ask one of your guests to take a match and light the brandy for you. As the brandy flames, lower the spoon gently into the coffee just below the surface. This will ignite the surface of the coffee. Swish the spoon gently back and forth in the cup until the flame dies out. An added twist of lemon is optional. Give this a trial run first so you will be at ease during this performance.

The Backyard Barbecue

This little rhyme was composed by Felix Jewell, a jewel of a professional chef whose backyard barbecues were never like the one he describes:

The charcoal smoked
The steak was burned
The corn was raw
The host concerned
The meal was late
The children whined
Mosquitoes swarmed
And amply dined
The night was cold
The moon obscured
And, I the guest was bar-b-cured!

Cooking outdoors can be a delight or disaster! Little things like a shift in the prevailing wind can fill the garden with smoke instead of sunshine. A broiling sun can melt the chilled consommé, because, contrary to general opinion, jellied dishes are not good for summer buffets unless they are kept chilled over ice. Aromatic good food can attract a horde of insects, but citronella candles help keep them at bay.

When all goes well, the following menu is one of my favorites.

A Favorite Barbecue Menu

Mint juleps
Raw vegetable bouquet (Chapter Four)
Barbecued chicken

Cole slaw
Red Fox tomato pudding
Corn on the cob (in boiling water needs less than 5 minutes!)
Dilli casserole bread
Cheese pie with fresh strawberries
Coffee

Barbecued Chicken Timed to Perfection

Equipment: Gas or charcoal grill, shallow pan, brush

Perhaps the biggest bugaboo in barbecuing is timing. I learned the hard way, when grilling chicken, that either my chicken or my guests suffered (and one always led to the other!). Sometimes the broilers were still raw when we were ready to eat; other times we dallied over cocktails and the chickens were overdone. Here's a solution that never misses!

Marinate broilers or small frying chickens in your favorite Italian dressing; let stand in shallow pan several hours. Drain. Place in a low preheated oven (325° F.) uncovered and precook for about 45 minutes. Light charcoal fire. About 15 minutes before you are ready to eat, your guests will be impressed when you finish browning the chicken to perfection by brushing them with melted butter over the charcoal grill.

Red Fox Tomato Pudding

There used to be a remarkable eating place in what is now affectionately called "Hemingway Country" in Northern Michigan. Just down the road from the Red Fox Inn in Horton Bay was the scene of one of Ernest Hemingway's earliest short stories, "Up In Michigan." While living in Paris he reminisces, "Horton Bay, the town, was only five houses on the main road between Boyne City and Charlevoix. There was the general store and post office with a high false front and maybe a wagon hitched out in front. . . ."

Nothing much has changed since Hemingway first married Hadley Richardson in a white frame church just shouting distance down the road from the Red Fox Inn. Any stranger driving by today never notices that simple white farmhouse because there are no bright signs commemorating its excellence.

But the cognoscentes who used to arrive by jet and Lincoln Continental on nostalgic pilgrimages from far-off New York, Chicago, and New Orleans to savor Mrs. Fox's country-fresh chicken dinners with dumplings and gravy, freshly picked tender young corn on the cob, crisp cole slaw salad, hot cheese rolls, homemade pickle relish, and strawberry jam will always remember the experience.

How many family birthdays and anniversaries we've celebrated in that same original and unpretentious setting! How many times we've walked up the uneven painted steps to wait on the narrow screen porch with the slanting floor where one can have a drink before dinner—if you brought your own liquor! And how many discussions have been waged as to who's best able to duplicate the tomato pudding. There are those who say it's best made with tomato purée—and Mrs. Dwight Eisenhower belonged to this school. Not only did Mrs. Eisenhower frequently serve the President's favorite dish during their term in the White House, but in a letter to me she recalls the first time she tasted it—at Mrs. George Humphrey's plantation in Georgia. Good recipes travel far!

An equally staunch group of gourmets maintain that tomato pudding is best prepared with whole tomatoes because the presence of seeds adds to the flavor and texture of the pudding.

Fortunately, I possess the original recipe as given to Mrs. Fox. It can be prepared in two stages, or as well in the quicker puréed version which I like. Which recipe do you like best? The proof of the pudding lies in the eating!

Tomato Pudding
Served as a vegetable

Equipment: Medium saucepan, baking dish

1 can (12 oz.) cooked tomatoes
1/2 cup dark brown sugar (packed)
1/4 cup melted butter
1/4 teaspoon salt
1 cup dry white bread cut into 1-inch squares
1/3 cup bread crumbs

1. Drain tomatoes.
2. In a saucepan put tomatoes, add sugar, butter, salt, dry bread.
3. Cook slowly on top of stove for 2-1/2 hours. Remove from stove and put in baking dish.
4. Sprinkle with bread crumbs and bake uncovered for 30 minutes at 375° F.
Makes 6 servings.

Tomato Pudding Purée
Served as a vegetable

Equipment: Saucepan and baking dish

2 10-oz. cans Hunt's tomato purée
2 cups dark brown sugar
1/2 teaspoon salt
2 cups fresh white bread cut into 1-inch squares
1 cup melted butter

1. In a saucepan put purée, sugar and salt. Heat to boil and reduce to simmer for 5 minutes. Place bread squares in casserole and pour melted butter over bread.
2. Add hot tomato mixture and bake covered for 30 minutes in moderate oven at 375° F. Stir before serving.
Makes 6 servings.

Dilli Casserole Bread

Equipment: Large mixing bowl, rubber spatula, 8" round baking dish

1 package active dry yeast or 1 cake compressed yeast
1/4 cup really warm water
1 cup creamed cottage cheese, heated to lukewarm
2 tablespoons sugar
2 tablespoons finely chopped onion
1 tablespoon butter
2 tablespoons dill seed
Dash of salt
1/4 teaspoon baking soda
1 unbeaten egg
2-1/4 to 2-1/2 cups sifted flour
1 teaspoon lemon pepper (optional)

1. Soften yeast—not in lukewarm, but really warm, almost hot water. In a large mixing bowl combine warm cottage cheese, sugar, onion, butter, seed, salt, soda, egg, and

    softened yeast.

2. Slowly add flour to form a stiff dough, beating well after each addition.
3. Cover, let rise until double in size, about 50 to 60 minutes.
4. With a rubber spatula gently transfer dough into well-greased 8" round oven-proof baking dish. Let rise again in well-warmed place until light, 30 to 50 minutes.
5. Preheat oven to 350° F. Bake for 40 to 50 minutes, until golden brown.
6. Let dilli bread cool slowly in warm oven with door open. Brush with soft butter and sprinkle with lemon pepper. Serve warm. (Freezes well.)

Makes 12 servings.

Cheese Pie

Equipment: Food processor is a must, 10" Pyrex pie dish, medium bowl

There are cheesecakes made in a spring form and cheese pies made in a pie dish, and you may have your favorite—but this recipe is my favorite! Why? One reason is because the very first time I tried it—perfection! It's even better made the day before we plan to serve it. I do not recommend freezing. It's good served with fresh strawberries in the summer.

Crust

18 graham crackers, broken up
1 tablespoon sugar
3/4 stick butter (scant 1/2 cup) softened at room temperature

In your food processor put crackers, sugar, softened butter and pulse until blended. Remove and press mixture into bottom and sides of pie pan.

Filling

1 lb. cottage cheese (or 2 cups)
2 eggs
1/2 cup sugar
1/2 teaspoon vanilla
Dash cinnamon

1. In your food processor put cottage cheese, eggs, sugar, vanilla, and cinnamon and pulse until smoothly blended.
2. Transfer ingredients to crusted pie pan.
3. Place in preheated 375° F. oven for 20 minutes, then increase the temperature to 475° F., and add topping.

Topping

1 pint sour cream (or 2 cups)
2 teaspoons sugar
1/2 teaspoon vanilla

1. In a medium-sized bowl, mix together sour cream, sugar, and vanilla, and spread over the pre-baked mixture.
2. Return to 475° F. oven for 5 minutes or until set.
3. Cool, then chill. Serve with fresh berries.
Makes 12 servings.

Hiawatha Cookout

One of the most unusual parties I ever attended was given in August by a bachelor whose tiny summer cottage is no larger than a small condo. It opens up through sliding doors into a charming, well-cared-for garden completely enclosed by a six-foot fence, giving a feeling of great intimacy and complete privacy.

On this balmy summer evening, tall hurricane lights flickered among the shrubs and, as if by signal, a silvery moon rose over the bay. Bob had set up outdoors two folding tables for ten with folding chairs. The tables were covered with red and white checkered tablecloths. We noticed some activity in the corner and when we strolled over to inquire, we saw an enormous pit, approximately three feet wide, six feet long, and two feet deep, aglow with several layers of charcoal. Across the pit was a heavy metal mesh on which was stretched half a young pig, sizzling merrily. Well, this certainly wasn't going to be an ordinary dinner, though we should have known from the unusual invitation we received made from a scrap of leather with the wording hand-pricked by needle!

In the dusk of the evening we noticed in another corner of the garden three saplings. They were braced and tied together at the top, from which an enormous black kettle was suspended by a long metal chain. Under the kettle a brisk fire was burning, but before we could wonder, Bob greeted us dressed as a Native American in full regalia—beads, feathers, deerskin dress, and moccasins, carrying a huge basket of freshly picked corn. Into the kettle of boiling water went the corn and the lovely aroma made our mouths water. But not for long, because soon we were handed a plate and guided to a buffet table. Here the salad bar was a picture—a gastronomical delight.

First there was a large bowl of crisp, fresh iceberg lettuce and another bowl of curly endive, accompanied by smaller bowls of sliced tomato and onion rings, sliced eggs, watercress, chopped celery, chopped green peppers, sliced cucumbers, sliced avocado, radishes and pickles, and a handsome pitcher of herb salad dressing. What fun we had concocting the salad of our choice!

I don't know if I'll ever get around to the roast pig with the Indian outfit, but what a grand idea this salad bar is for a summer luncheon. My economical heart jumped with joy when I realized no more soggy leftover salads to be reluctantly tossed away. Darned clever, these bachelors.

When we finished our last ear of corn, Bob passed steaming hot washcloths, neatly folded in a wooden bowl, for our sticky fingers. We nibbled on fresh fruit and cheese while lingering over hot black Java until we heard the soft notes of a piano, and gradually we drifted along with the rest of the guests back into the cottage, where some hummed old melodies around the piano and others stretched in front of the fireplace, which was banked just low enough to take the dampness out of the cool night air.

On the leisurely drive home that evening, I thought how lucky for us that Bob did not have a push-button automatic kitchen. For if he had, his originality and ingenuity would never have been challenged to create such a memorable evening for us in the land of Hiawatha. You will find below a menu inspired by Bob's party. Substitute spareribs or pork for the roast pig, but don't forget the salad bar and the steaming washcloths.

134

Hiawatha Cookout Menu

Make-your-own salad bar (see above)
Fresh corn on the cob
Bar-B-Qued spareribs or Sweet 'n sour pork chops
Corn meal sticks
Fresh fruit and berries with assorted cheeses and crackers
Coffee

Bar-B-Qued Spareribs

Equipment: Baking dish, chafing dish

Order 3 pounds baby-back spareribs and ask your butcher to cut the whole rib in 2-inch strips. Cut between ribs with scissors into individual pieces and place in a baking dish.

Sauce

2 tablespoons molasses
1 teaspoon Tabasco sauce
2 teaspoons vinegar or lemon juice
2 tablespoons prepared mustard
1 tablespoon soy sauce (or Kikkoman Hawaiian teriyaki sauce)

1. In a small bowl place molasses, add Tabasco, blend well.
2. Stir in vinegar (or lemon juice), mustard, and soy sauce. Brush over spareribs several times during baking.
3. Bake in moderate oven 350° F. about 2 hours and transfer to chafing dish.
Makes 12 servings.

Sweet 'n Sour Pork Chops

My mother collected Oriental recipes from missionary friends who lived deep in the interior of China. In those days, that meant four weeks by rickshaw, wheelbarrow, and sedan chair from Shanghai. Porky the pig, a favorite in the Orient, landed in America long before the Mayflower; in fact, he was brought to the New World by Columbus and has flourished here ever since. This recipe is a summer treat in any part of the world.

Equipment: Baking pan

12 pork chops
2 cans (13-1/2 oz. each) or fresh pineapple chunks
2 cans (11 oz. each) or fresh mandarin oranges
12 dried cherries
1 cup vinegar
1 cup light molasses
1 teaspoon salt
1/2 teaspoon ginger
1 teaspoon soy sauce
1 cup pineapple-orange syrup
2 teaspoons water
4 teaspoons cornstarch
6 tablespoons diced green pepper

1. Cover chops with foil and place on rack in baking pan and bake in moderate oven at 325° F., for about an hour or until well done.
2. Drain pineapple, oranges, and cherries; reserve 1 cup syrup. Combine vinegar, molasses, salt, ginger, soy sauce, and syrup in saucepan.
3. Blend cornstarch with 2 teaspoons cold water until smooth, and add to molasses mixture.
4. Add green pepper. Place over medium heat and bring to boil, then stir and reduce heat to simmer for 5 minutes.
5. Add pineapple, oranges, and cherries. Simmer for several minutes. Remove chops from oven and place on warm serving platter. Pour sauce over chops and serve.
Makes 12 servings.

Holiday Aftermaths

During the bright social holiday season, we ought to be prepared—like a real scout—for impromptu entertaining. It's fun to be able to say when you're in a Mardi Gras mood at a friend's cocktail party, "Why not come over to our house for a bite later?," knowing there's a kettle of turkey gumbo waiting to be warmed up at home. My New Orleans chums introduced the hearty gumbo to us and it's become a family standby ever since. It's the perfect way to turn turkey scraps and carcass into a dish fit for a king.

Turkey Gumbo
New Orleans style without okra

Equipment: Large stock pot, strainer, ice cream scoop (optional)

1 turkey carcass
2 stalks celery with greens
1 large onion
1 teaspoon salt
1/2 teaspoon pepper
1 level tablespoon shortening (Crisco, etc.)
1/3 cup chopped onion
2 tablespoons flour
1 or 2 teaspoons filé powder (as thickener, available among spices)
1 cup raw long-grain rice, cooked according to package directions

1. Remove nice chunks of dark and white meat from carcass to use later.
2. To make the broth, take a large kettle and cover carcass with 3 quarts cold water. Add celery, onion, salt, pepper. Bring to boil then reduce heat and let simmer slowly for 2 hours. Strain.
3. Make roux by using a very large frying pan and heating shortening, mixing with chopped onion and flour. Add broth to roux, stirring constantly until thick. Add small chunks of turkey meat.
4. At the last minute, add filé powder, but do NOT boil soup any longer.
5. Serve gumbo in soup bowl. Scoop rice into balls using an ice cream scoop if you have one, and place in center of gumbo.
Makes about 10 servings.

Tamale Pie

The meat and bean mix may be prepared the day before and stored in the refrigerator or frozen. Cornmeal batter may be added before baking.

The flavorful tamale pie is a dish which guests enjoy, winter and summer. Served with avocado and grapefruit salad, and a light custard or flan, its fiesta quality is unmistakable.

Equipment: Large-sized skillet, 2-1/2 quart baking dish

1 lb. chopped beef
1 tablespoon oil or shortening
1/2 cup chopped onion
1/2 cup chopped green pepper
2 cans (15 oz. each) tomato sauce
2 cloves garlic, minced or pressed
1 tablespoon chili powder
2 flakes red pepper, crushed
1 can (1 lb., 12 oz.) kidney beans
1 package Jiffy corn muffin mix (8-1/2 oz.)
1 egg
1/3 cup milk

1. Preheat oven to 400° F.
2. Brown the meat in a large skillet in shortening. Add onions, pepper, tomato sauce, garlic, chili powder, and red pepper and cook over low heat for about 30 minutes.
3. Stir occasionally. Add beans and remove from heat.
4. Prepare cornmeal muffin batter according to directions on package with egg and milk.
5. Pour meat and beans into 2 1/2-quart baking dish, cover top with cornmeal batter and bake for about 40 minutes or until top is brown. Optional: Make extra cornmeal muffins to serve on the side. Serve piping hot.
Makes 8 servings.

Lima Beans and Pear Casserole

Another uncomplicated holiday buffet centers around a cooked ham which is served with lima beans and pear casserole, and Camembert salad a la Rothschild—both are refreshing changes from the usual dishes served with ham. The recipes follow.

Equipment: Large bowl and saucepan, 2-quart baking dish

2 lbs. dried lima beans
1/2 teaspoon salt
2 cans (1 lb., 13 oz. each) Bartlett pear halves
1 cup melted butter
1 cup brown sugar
1/2 teaspoon powdered cinnamon
1/2 teaspoon clove or allspice
1 cup vinegar

1. In a large bowl soak lima beans overnight in cold water. (They swell up to triple.)
2. In a large saucepan, cover lima beans with salt water and cook about 30 minutes or until really tender. (Much depends on the freshness of the beans.) Drain.
3. Alternate lima beans with layers of pears in a 2-quart baking dish; add some juice.
4. Add melted butter, sugar, vinegar, cinnamon, and clove and bake in 300° F. oven for 2 hours. Very tasty when reheated.

Makes 12 servings.

Camembert Salad a la Rothschild

For buffet supper parties, the Camembert salad a la Rothschild is a refreshing change from the usual tossed salad and may be served either with the entree or, the way Californians prefer, as a first course.

2 heads Boston lettuce
8 oz. Camembert cheese (room temperature)
2/3 cup chutney
1 cup French dressing
2 teaspoons paprika added to French dressing

Cut cheese and chutney with scissors into bite-sized pieces. Add dressing and toss gently.
Makes 12 servings.

New Year's Eve

The question "What are you doing on New Year's?" almost always draws a spirited response. It seems to me that the people who argue the loudest about staying home alone seldom do. The people who try convincing anyone who'll listen that New Year's Eve is just like any other night end up at the zero hour tooting their paper horns the loudest. The people who feel they can't bear to stay in town looking at the same old faces run to resorts where they run into the same old faces. And even the people who make the least fuss over this emotionally charged holiday find that, no matter how you look at it, New Year's Eve can be a problem. If you go out, it's terribly expensive. If you stay home, whom will you invite? If you're invited out, who's going to be there? If you go, do you have to stay? If you leave, where will you go?

One way to overcome the dilemma is to plan a group party where each person or couple assumes part of the responsibility. It's best to keep the group small, nine couples would be ideal; according to a University of Michigan research study, people function best in groups of sixes (nine couples compose three groups of sixes).

Assign each couple to bring a truly exotic dish (one might pick a nationality menu with a corresponding party theme). The cost of the liquor is then equally divided and the group either engages extra help to serve and clean up or uses attractive disposable paper goods.

Then too, it's best not to sit down to a big meal all at once because then everyone gets sleepy and wants to go home. Instead stretch out each course through the evening, starting with cocktails and substantial hot hors d'oeuvres served up to about eleven o'clock; move on to a very light entree or roast such as cold filets and a marinated vegetable salad platter, beautifully arranged in sections, and served in the living room, and wind up around two o'clock with coffee and sweets.

At other times, a successful variation of the above gourmet dinner is to make nine teams, splitting each couple in the process. Assign each team a job in preparing the meal. It's always surprising how many men enjoy demonstrating their skill with the skillet and it gives everyone something to do—but not too much! The host provides the supplies and has everything handy in the kitchen, including one or more cookbooks or typed directions for reference. It's a good idea to set up a time schedule on a blackboard which might look like this:

7:30 Team 1: Mix and serve cocktails.
7:30 Team 2: Prepare hors d'oeuvres.
8:00 Team 3: Start charcoal fire and grill steaks when ready. (Or use broiler later.)
8:00 Team 4: Bake potatoes; set the table.
8:15 Team 5: Make ice cream in electric ice cream freezer.
        (Hostess prepares ice cream base the day before.)
8:30 Team 6: Prepare salad and dressing.
8:45 Team 7: Warm rolls and make coffee.
9:00 Team 8: Host and hostess announce dinner is ready!
9:00 Team 9: Serve dinner to guests.

Fondue Fun

In February, especially on weekends, a persistent *rat-tat-tat* humming sound breaks the stillness of our moonlit nights on the quiet outskirts of Charlevoix in Northern Michigan. It's the sound of snowmobiles as they cut through wooded trails and snake their way over white hills and valleys, across open cornfields, and along frosted Lake Michigan beaches. Not only in Northern Michigan, but all over the United States, snowmobile enthusiasts are skidoo-ing merrily in twos and fours over the rough terrain and manmade trails. Their numbers seem to multiply as fast as the rabbits who scurry nimbly out of their way.

My Swiss neighbors invited us to a cheese fondue supper (*fondue* is a French word that means "to mix together"), and the evening turned out to be a real mixer of not only cheese and wine but also of good food and fellowship.

Long before we sat down at a gemutlich round table in front of a fire, we were intrigued by the preparations that were underway in the kitchen where cheese was melting in a *caquelon*, as the Swiss call their fondue pot. These pots are made of earthenware with flat bottoms and hollow handles.

Our hostess explained that only the earthenware *caquelons* (no copper or metal will do) can develop a heavenly crust which forms on the bottom of the fondue dish and tastes like crisp toasted cheese—so good and chewy! We could hardly contain ourselves until the fortuitous moment when the *caquelon* was transferred to the dining table and placed over an alcohol burner and we were seated in a cozy circle just dipping away until there wasn't another lick of cheese or a crust of bread. Not until the flames in our grate fire had died very low did we reluctantly leave the table and bid our *adieus*.

The Swiss consider fondue almost a meal in itself and they usually serve only a little smoked ham or sausage afterward, followed by fresh fruit, such as apples or pears.

Our hostess was more generous, and, here's our fondue dinner menu:

Fondue Fun Menu

Spinach salad with anchovies
Cheese fondue
Hickory smoked Danish ham
Cubed French bread
Fresh fruits, pears, apples, black and white grapes and nuts
    (Grapes may be frosted by dipping them when wet in superfine XX granulated
    sugar; chill in refrigerator.)
Crispy lace cookies (see Chapter Three)
Kirsch
Tea or coffee

Cheese Fondue

Equipment: Cheese fondue pot

People who know about this insist that imported Swiss cheese must be used because American Swiss cheese is not sufficiently matured to make a proper fondue. If one uses cheddar, be sure it is very mild, such as the Canadian cheddar.

1/2 lb. imported Swiss cheese (Emmentaler)
1/2 lb. Gruyère or mild cheddar
4 teaspoons flour
1 clove garlic
2 cups dry white wine (Neuchatel, Riesling, or Chablis)
1/4 cup Kirschwasser (no substitute)
2 teaspoons cornstarch
Dash of nutmeg, salt, and pepper
(Methyl alcohol for burner)

1. Trim edges of cheese. Cut cheese in 1/2-inch cubes and dredge lightly with flour by shaking them in a paper bag. Rub pot with garlic. Pour wine in pot and heat very slowly until air bubbles rise but do not boil. Add a handful of cheese cubes and stir with a wooden spoon in a figure 8 waiting until each handful is melted before adding more cheese. Keep stirring (about 15 minutes) until all cheese is smooth and fondue is thickened and bubbling slightly. Now add Kirschwasser (if the fondue is thinner than you'd like it, stir 2 teaspoons cornstarch into the Kirschwasser— but not into the fondue or it will be lumpy!). Fondue may be cooked on the stove and then transferred to the alcohol burner on the table if one wishes. Add nutmeg, salt, and pepper.
2. Cut very crusty French bread into bite-sized pieces, wrap in foil, and heat in oven until warm.
3. Each person uses a long fondue fork for dipping bread into cheese.
4. Be sure to warn everyone not to touch the bottom of the pot when dipping because one of the rituals of the fondue bit is to allow a crust to form on the bottom of the dish. This begins as soon as one stops stirring and when there is sufficient heat causing the cheese to bubble. When you feel the crust forming, you can very carefully lift the nice brown crust off the bottom with a fork without breaking it and serve it to your guests.

Serves 4 persons for dinner; 12 for cocktails.

If the crust is disturbed during the dipping it will come up into the fondue in little crusty pieces and spoil the looks of the fondue and the crust itself. The consistency of cheese fondue is similar to chocolate syrup and it's much milder and more delicate in taste than Welsh rarebit.

Addenda: This is one recipe that's better not doubled because it takes the cheese too long to melt. Instead use 2 *caquelons* or fondue pots.

As An Hor d'Oeuvre

Cheese fondue served as an hors d'oeuvre is delicious with added crabmeat mixed with the fondue, then spread on toasted rounds or served with torn, toasted bits of sourdough bread.

Spinach Salad

Equipment: Small mixing bowl, medium-sized saucepan, egg beater or wire whisk

1 package fresh spinach
1/2 lb. crisp bacon bits
1 small Bermuda onion, sliced thin
6 radishes, sliced thin
1/2 cup vinegar
1/2 cup water
1/2 cup sugar
1/2 teaspoon salt
1 egg, well beaten
3 hard-cooked eggs, sliced
2 cans anchovies

1. Wash spinach thoroughly and dry with a towel. (Remember that our delicious salad dressing won't cling to wet spinach!) Put spinach in salad bowl and add bacon bits, onion and radishes.
2. In a small mixing bowl, beat one whole egg with egg beater or wire whisk
3. In a medium-sized saucepan, pour vinegar, water, sugar, salt, and beaten egg, and bring to a boil.
4. Let cool and pour over tossed salad ingredients. Garnish with sliced hard-cooked eggs and anchovies.
Makes 8 servings.

With Fresh Fruit

Fresh, chilled winter pears, either the Anjou, Bosc, or Comice, are wonderfully compatible with cheese fondue, either as a dipper or dessert. A pear cutter (available at any hardware store) is handy for slicing the juicy, fresh pears into thick, even wedges. Or provide your guests with dessert knives.

A perfect dessert for this continental supper is a colorful platter of pears, apples, grapes, dried raisins, or cherries and nuts.

Chapter Six

Large and Small Dinner Parties
with a Flair

"All human history attests
That happiness for man—the hungry sinner
Since Eve ate apples,
Much depends on dinner."

—Lord Byron

Stretching One's House

"Oh, I wish we could give a lovely dinner party—but where to put everyone? There isn't enough room! It's impossible! I just can't begin to manage!" Does this sound like you? Or do you agree with poet William Allingham, who rhymed, "Solitude is very sad, but too much company is twice as bad!"

If so, your problem is not unique. Jacqueline Kennedy faced the same problem during the Kennedy term in the White House. She ingeniously doubled the seating arrangement for state dinners, making it possible to invite twice the number of guests! She also was responsible for introducing the friendlier round tables instead of long tables. No fairy godmother stretched the White House formal dining room, nor will she wave her magic wand and turn your efficient condominium into a king-sized palace, or your cozy Cape Cod cottage into a rambling castle, but there are calculated ways of s-t-r-e-t-c-h-i-n-g your home so that you can comfortably double or even triple the number of guests.

I once attended a large party in Chicago where the host stretched his house by renting a van and used it as a "coat closet." When guests entered the front door, an attendant checked their coats for them. We don't have to go to such extremes, but how do we stretch a condo or even a mansion?

First, let's mentally clear all furniture from the room. (Yes, there are some people who actually do put their furniture in storage for a couple of days when giving a gala ball at home, but that doesn't concern us here.) Let's pretend we're designing a set from scratch. Walk around your imaginary bare stage and do a little creative play acting. Let's see, guests enter here—or do they? Sometimes traffic patterns can be changed to advantage by using an alternate entrance or by setting up portable coat racks for hats and coats. The bar should be located against a long wall because this is where the hard-core group likes to congregate (and sometimes it's a good idea to set up an auxiliary bar). Shall we move the couch over a little and turn the table the other way? Let's dispose of that dainty chair and tippy table and avoid accidents.

Buffets, Lap Food, or Platters?

What about the dining area? Shall we plan a pumped-up cocktail party or a pared-down dinner buffet? Is it going to be self-serve, or will there be enough room for a sit-down dinner with waitstaff passing platters? Hmm—maybe we should not set any places at all but only serve lap food—no knives required. Some people like to bring a filled dinner plate from the kitchen to the table when they are serving six or eight guests, and if you can handle this graciously, so be it. I prefer letting people help themselves at a buffet, because it gives them a choice of how much to take from tempting dishes that they might normally avoid.

For sit-down dinners, we have the choice of extending our dinner table by adding a card table or folding aluminum table on one end. In order to make it match the width of the dinner table, I had a carpenter make a plywood top for the card table to equal the width of the dinner table. Covered with a cloth, one would never know that the dinner table was patched. A friend of mine from Washington solved the problem by simply stretching her dining room table to accommodate twelve instead of ten by simply exchanging her commodious dining room chairs for a set of twelve rented, smaller gilt chairs.

I once doubled the space in a dining room for a series of buffet dinner parties by setting up an eight-foot plywood board on two wooden horses across a small credenza along a long wall. Over this we spread a large white damask cloth that hung almost to the floor, completely covering both the credenza and wooden horses. This spacious sideboard gave us plenty of room for plates, hot trays, covered vegetable dishes and platters. We could easily seat ten at the dining room table and eight at a folding table in the adjoining family room. On informal occasions with young people, everyone helped themselves to second servings from our improvised sideboard, but for more formal dinners, waitresses passed second helpings on platters and cleared the table for dessert and coffee.

Or we can completely clear the dining area for just serving cocktails, and then set up either a long table or several card tables in the living room or family room for a cozy, sit-down dinner.

Spacing and Seating for Large, Tented Affairs

For tented affairs, we can rent round folding tables—they come in two sizes to accommodate either eight or ten persons. Twelve round tables for eight will seat 96 people. Caterers plan on ten square feet per person for buffet dinners, twelve square feet per person for sit-down dinners, and six square feet per person for cocktails.

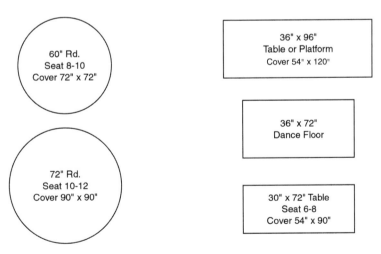

"Cover" means tablecloth

147

Allow ten square feet for every 60" round table that seats eight people, and allow twelve square feet for every 72" round table that seats ten people. This guideline provides adequate room for chairs and for serving by waitstaff.

A 30" x 96" rectangular table seats ten people comfortably, and a 30" x 72" rectangular table seats eight people comfortably.

If it becomes necessary at the last minute to subtract or add one or two people, this may be done more easily if you plan well from the beginning. Seat only seven people at each table for eight and only nine people at each table for ten; then you may add a guest without extreme crowding or subtract a guest without creating a large gap.

Tents and Dance Floors

A 40-square-foot tent accommodates 16 round tables to seat 128 people. An 18-square-foot dance floor will accommodate 38 couples if you allow three square feet per couple.

Garages and Porches, Etc.

Party consultants have a dozen clever tricks up their sleeves and know how to stretch a house by taking advantage of an enclosed porch or hallway where one can store an extra card table that is completely set for dinner to be whisked out only when everyone is ready to sit down. Only the water glasses need filling.

Turning a garage into a serving pantry has also become routine for large catered parties. It's a handy plan that saves hundreds of steps.

But that's nothing compared to the ingenuity of two condominium dwellers who solve the kitchen space race by developing a mutual assistance pact that would shame most U.N. delegates. Both condos are located just across the hall from one another and whenever one couple entertains, the other takes charge of the clean-up.

This reciprocal system is so refined through practice that all the used dishes are stacked on a card table in the tiny kitchen and in minutes Mr. and Mrs. Neighbor step in, whisk the table away, dishes and all, to be returned clean and dry.

Who Needs Place Cards?

Place cards are a convenience when there are more than six guests, because no one likes to stand around while the hostess hesitates, "John please sit here. No, I think you'd better sit over there—no, I was right in the first place, do sit over here!"

Place cards were first introduced for "Service a la Russe" in 1810 and they peaked about 1870 after Russian service became popular throughout the dining world. (More about Russian service in Chapter Nine.)

For large, chichi dinner parties there is a seating chart prepared for all guests at the entrance of the dining room. Guests pick up a small envelope with their name written on it in fine script. Inside the envelope is a card with the table number giving assigned seating. Names are written out formally on the envelope, "Mr. and Mrs. John Heartwell," and the table number is written on a card inside. At the assigned table, guests will find individual place cards, one for "Mr. John Heartwell" and one for "Mrs. John Heartwell." Husbands and wives may or may not be seated at the same table, but it makes for better table conversation not to seat couples next to each other.

Place cards are a boon to thoughtful hosts because instead of allowing people who see a lot of each other to gyrate in the same direction and end up in the same tight little groups, place cards give guests the pleasure of meeting a few new people.

There's another ploy a friend of mine cleverly employs at her most successful parties. When she sees a couple engrossed in conversation during the cocktail hour, she manages to draw the lady aside and whisper, "John's your dinner partner, so save your chit-chat for later, darling!" A thousand blessings on her perceptive head!

Place cards can be creative fun at informal luncheons or dinners. My mother once invited a group of friends for lunch after recuperating from an operation and with her wit used her "Get-Well" cards as place cards. This idea prompted me that winter to save postcards from traveling friends, which I used as place cards for a delightful welcome-home party. What memories these little cards evoked! "Remember that cute little place—what was it called?" "That's where we had dinner with that charming couple from Australia!" and so forth.

When you don't care where guests are seated, it may be fun to pass out a different flower to each guest. The matching flower then is on the napkin at the table to signal where one is to sit.

You can also collect baby pictures of each guest in advance, or you can cut pictures from magazines highlighting each person's hobby, profession, or idiosyncrasy, and let them find their seats. You can take Polaroid pictures of arriving guests and use them as place cards; you can write a couplet or a ditty. For theme parties you can sketch matchstick figures or paint holiday designs on each place card; you can glue a tiny flower or piece of cloth that carries out the party theme on a plain, white folded card; you can use place card holders made of plastic, ceramic, wood or shells—yes, even rocks! You can also combine place cards with little favors.

Who Sits Where?

When planning your seating arrangements, remember that the gentleman guest of honor is always seated at the hostess' right, and a lady guest of honor is seated to the host's right. After this, scatter lively talkers and sober listeners with studied indifference, but never invite people knowingly who are not on good terms. They'll have a miserable time ducking each other!

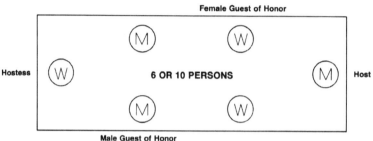

Alternating men and women at the dinner table was first popular in the late 18th century when separate dining rooms became fashionable—instead of the multifunctional great hall of previous centuries. Along with the separate dining rooms, the new custom of alternating men and women at the dinner table was referred to as "promiscuous seating."

When seating an even number of men and women at the table, notice that whenever there are four or any number divided by four—such as eight, twelve, sixteen, etc.—it works out mathematically that a man sits at the head and foot of the table. When there are six, ten, fourteen, it works out that a man sits at the head and a woman at the foot of the table.

There's no hard-and-fast rule that the host and hostess must be at the head and foot of the table. At the Belgian Embassy in Washington, D.C., a former ambassador and his wife often sat opposite each other at the center of the table.

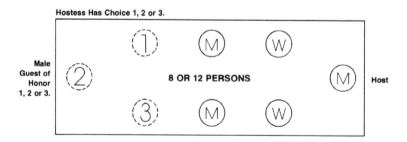

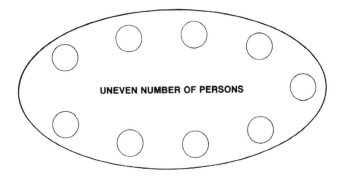

If you hire help, place yourself facing the serving pantry door so you may signal the waiter without turning around.

Serving Family- or English-Style at Home

There are occasions when one likes to skip the casual, cookout style of entertaining, and follow the more civilized family- or English-style of service, possibly for a holiday sit-down dinner at home, where good humor flows freely. Not long ago, I received a comforting thank-you note from a young man who admitted that, having experienced a pleasant, well-served meal during Thanksgiving in my home many years ago, he was motivated to persevere in his studies at college, so that when he graduated, he would be able to attain such a pleasant lifestyle—which he happily achieved.

When serving English-style, guests are invited to be seated at the dining room table where the salad, butter, and butter plates are in place and water glasses are filled, candles lit. Then the platter of meat, bowls of vegetables and potatoes are set down in front of the host and he fills each guest's dinner plate by asking, "Do you prefer dark or light meat?" or some such question. He serves the vegetables and potatoes as well, then passes the filled plate to his guest. Only rolls need to be passed.

At dessert time the hostess has previously placed cups, saucers, dessert plates, cake server, knife, creamer and sugar nearby on a tray. She first clears the main course (first trip to the kitchen sink) and returns with the dessert cups and plates to the dinner table. She then presents a lovely dessert, and lets one of her guests do the honors of cutting the cake or pie, leaving her free to sit down and pour coffee at her usual place.

Sometimes the host might prefer to invite everyone to seat themselves in front of the fire for a demitasse of coffee, dessert and brandy, or a sweet combination of coffee, brandy, and whipped cream—Irish coffee.

Irish Coffee

Fill a parfait glass or an old-fashioned glass with strong coffee, stir well with a lump of sugar. Add a jigger of scotch, bourbon or Irish whiskey. Top with a dash of whipped cream and serve hot.

What to Do About Delays and Latecomers?

Speaking of delay, they say there's nothing new under the sun. I'd like to share with you the amusing comments on the manners and mores in English society when dinner was delayed. It comes from a delightful little etiquette book printed in 1834:

> If, by any unforeseen accident, any fortuitous circumstance, the moment of dining be put off for only one hour, just look at your guests, and twig what long faces they make; see how the most animated conversation languishes, how blue everyone looks, how all zygomatic muscles are paralysed, in short, how every eye appears mechanically turned toward the dining-room! Is the obstacle removed? The master of the hotel, a napkin under his arm, comes to announce that all is ready and served up; the words act like a charm—they have a magical aspect which restores to each his serenity, his gaiety, and wit. An appetite is read in every eye, hilarity in every heart; and the tumultous impatience with which each runs to take possession of his plate, is a manifest and certain sign of the unanimity of wishes and the correspondence of sensations. Nature then resumes all her rights: and at that moment of the day, the flatterer himself suffer his thought to be read in every feature of his countenance. The longing looks, the smacking of lips, the anxious expectation, which are every where visible, paint the conflict of the belly-gerent powers, eager for the attack.

The other side of the coin—when guests keep the host waiting—was a problem even in Dr. Samuel Johnson's day. It was Boswell who said,

> One of the company not being come at the appointed hour, I proposed, as usual upon such occasions, to order dinner to be served, adding, "Ought six people be kept waiting for one?" "Why, yes," answered Johnson, with a delicate humanity, "if the one will suffer more by your not sitting down, than the six will do by waiting."

Dinner Menu with Cornish Game Hen

Hot cheese cookies
Cornish game hen
Mixture of white and wild rice
Sorbet
Wines (a light Merlot or Pinot Noir)
Dinner rolls
Mousse au chocolat
Decaffeinated coffee
Mints

Cornish Game Hens

There's an amusing story that goes with this—my very own recipe—and I will share it with you here and now. Last winter I invited eight friends for a sit-down dinner and served this Cornish game hen menu because it is a little out of the ordinary, yet easy for me, a time-challenged person, to prepare. My guests were enthusiastic all during the meal, and after dinner they asked for the recipe, but I pleasantly declined by saying, "I am planning to serve this dish again this season and I think I would rather keep it to myself a while longer." The next day the butcher called to tell me he had been asked several times for the recipe. Fast forward and repeat requests again and again! Finally the phone rang and I was asked to donate the recipe for a charity auction benefit. Several of my friends wanted to bid against each other! Still with ornery hesitation, I declined. Sorry, if people want it this badly—!

Now at last, I have decided to share this special treat with my long-time, devoted readers.

Cornish Game Hen Recipe

Cornish game hens are smaller than chickens and although I serve one half to each guest, for hearty eaters you might care to allot a whole hen per person, or offer second helpings. You don't need to serve a salad or any vegetables with this dish, but if you like, a fruit sorbet would be nice. Serve with a mixture of white and wild rice. (Please do not use minute rice!)

Equipment: 10" x 15" Pyrex dish, garlic press, medium saucepan

4 or 5 Cornish game hens

Ask your butcher to hand-cut 4 Cornish game hens in half, and have him save the livers for you. (They will be good for breakfast with scrambled eggs.)   If hens are frozen, have him defrost them before splitting in half.

2 tablespoons butter, dash of salt and pepper
2 bottles Kikkoman teriyaki sauce
Fresh ginger root (or use ginger paste sold in jars in Oriental specialty stores)
1-1/2 cups orange juice
2 cups currants or raisins
1-1/4 cups chutney
1/2 teaspoon cinnamon
1/2 teaspoon curry powder
Dash of thyme
1 banana, sliced
1/2 cup split blanched almonds
1 small can mandarin oranges, whole
Chopped parsley
Several green onions, sliced fine
4 strips of crumbled crisp bacon
1/2 cup coconut chips

1. Place hens skin side up in a greased, shallow baking dish. Cut fresh ginger root into 1/4-inch pieces, and using a garlic press, squirt a dash of juice on each half-hen. This takes the most time, but is worth it! Pour teriyaki sauce over hens and mari-

nate overnight.
2. Bake hens at 450° F. for 15 minutes or until golden brown.
3. Meanwhile in a saucepot combine orange juice, currants, chutney, almonds, cinnamon, curry power, and thyme and simmer on top of the stove for about 10 minutes to blend flavors.
4. After first 15 minutes, pour orange sauce, etc., over hens.
5. Reduce heat to 350° F. and bake 1 hour longer or until tender. Baste occasionally.
6. Transfer hens to serving platter and garnish top with sliced banana, mandarin oranges, chopped parsley, sliced green onions, crumbled crisp bacon, and coconut chips.
7. In a separate sauce dish, serve the orange sauce that the hens were baked in.
Makes 8 or 10 servings.

Mousse Au Chocolat

This may be prepared in the morning or the day before. It's almost too rich for encores.

My do-it-yourself dinner parties always include a dessert that doesn't need assembling at the last minute. For instance, I'd never fool with ice cream and hot fudge sauce and cookies. Just think of all the time and steps involved: removing the ice cream from refrigerator; scooping it into individual sauce dishes; heating the chocolate and pouring the sauce over the ice cream; placing the sauce dishes on a plate then on a tray and adding the cookies; and carrying the tray in to the dinner table. Much better to reduce these five steps to two by opening the refrigerator and carrying a cake, pudding, or pie to the dinner guests.

Equipment: Double boiler, small bowl, egg beater, serving dish or individual sherbet glasses

1/4 lb. bitter chocolate
1/4 lb. semi-sweet chocolate
3/4 cup powdered sugar
1/4 cup water
5 eggs
1 teaspoon vanilla
Whipped cream (optional)

1. In a double boiler, melt together chocolates, sugar, and water. Carefully stir until smooth and velvety and thoroughly blended.
2. Remove top of double boiler from heat and set in a pan of cold water. Stir occasionally until mixture is cool.
3. Separate eggs. Beat yolks well in a small bowl. Add vanilla and blend with chocolate mixture, which should be semi-fluid. (If too firm, add 4 or 5 tablespoons tepid milk.) Beat egg whites until stiff and fold into chocolate mixture gently, but thoroughly.
4. Chill for 6 to 8 hours.

Fills a 9" x 12" serving dish, or may be poured into individual sherbet glasses. Decorate with whipped cream if you like.

Makes 10 servings.

Progressive Parties

There's nothing political in planning a progressive party—it's just a convenient way for two or three or more couples to entertain elegantly, especially when they live within easy walking or a short driving distance from each other. Try to pick a fair weather month; walking from house to house when flowers are in bloom or the leaves are turning is a lark, but in foul weather, pulling galoshes or snow boots off and on all evening is a drag!

A progressive party, like a well-structured play, is divided into two, three, or more acts. The first act opens with cocktails and hors d'oeuvres followed by intermission, when guests proceed to the next house for the second act, where entrée and dessert are served, or a third act could wind up with dessert and dancing in another location.

The advantages here are obvious: Each hostess is responsible for only one course, instead of providing an entire meal plus entertainment. However, there are pitfalls. With a progressive party there must be perfect cooperation and teamwork between hostesses to keep the entire group moving smoothly on schedule from one home on to the next. When it's time to leave it might be wise to dim the lights momentarily as is done in theater lobbies, or to ring a bell announcing that it's time for the next act to begin.

Progressive parties can be tied into fundraising home tours. Friends of mine planned a progressive fundraiser in a condominium complex in Florida. One can feature ethnic themes so that each house has related party decorations and food. Or the theme can reach back to American history: a 17th-century pioneer party, an 18th-century colonial party; a 19th-century Victorian party; or a modern, digital-age party.

Split the Expenses and Double the Fun!

I find party-giving a lot less worrisome when we share the fun of planning and doing, along with the advantage of splitting expenses with a friend or another couple. Many people find that co-hosting a party is also advantageous for newcomers in a community, who may not be familiar with all the local "ins and outs," as well as for local hosts whose space, budget, and guest list are not in balance.

Planning

Once the selection of a congenial co-host or hosts has been made, there are two choices: 1) The proposed party can begin and end at the same address; or 2) The progressive party can move from one house to another—as described above.

In either case, preparations, party chores, and party clean-up, as well as expenses, should be shared equally.

Preparation

If the party is to be given solely at our house, we have a greater responsibility in getting ready, and consequently our co-hosts should assume extra chores, such as ordering flowers, writing place cards, arranging games after dinner, and/or addressing invitations.

Just Another Word about Invitations!

When a party is co-hosted, it's better to send written invitations. Too many beautiful friendships have been strained when guests have been invited over the phone or a little too casually without it being made crystal clear that the party is being co-hosted. Only one return address is necessary, because it's simpler for one person to keep track of all acceptances and regrets.

Party Themes

Creating a mood, an atmosphere, is a key to giving a party with character and individuality. Will it be a bright bash, a swing and sway, or a harvest-moon mood? Now is the time to coordinate a timely or amusing party theme by choosing appropriate invitations, decorations, music, entertainment, and menu. (See Chapter Nine on party themes.)

Budget

In order to prevent any future unpleasantness, it's best to decide now if the party will be geared to beer-on-tap or champagne standards. Whatever you decide, always serve the best quality, whether it is apple cider, ale, or whiskey.

When dividing financial responsibilities, some people like to keep a duplicate list and an accurate record of every penny spent, i.e., 1 lb. butter, 1 pt. cream, 1 tablecloth laundered, etc., while others are quite content to be extremely casual and say, "We'll supply the liquor and food, and you take care of the orchestra and flowers," or some such thing. A third group falls somewhere between these two. Leafing through my party diary, my notes look something like this:

Date_____ Co-hosts_____ How Many?_____

Place_____ Occasion_____

LIQUOR
   2 cases $XXX.xx
FOOD
   Bakery
        Cake
        100 rolls
        4 rye breads   X.xx
   Butcher
        2 hams, 2 turkeys
        2 lbs. chicken livers   XX.xx
   Grocery
        3 dips, cheeses, coffee, etc.   XX.xx

CATERER

    Mrs. Caterer   2 casseroles

    2 waitresses   XX.xx

BARTENDERS

    Mike & Bill   Ice   XX.xx

RENTAL EQUIPMENT

    Bar, chairs, dishes, glasses, silverware   XX.xx

MUSIC

    University Band, 3 pieces, 9 P.M. to 1 A.M.   XXX.xx

MISC.

    Candles, candy, laundry, flowers, etc.   XX.xx

                                  TOTAL $XXX.xx

                              Our Share $XXX.xx

A memorandum from our co-hosts says, "Although there was more drinking than we anticipated, the cost is still about 50% less than if we had held the party at the club."

Progressive Party, Act One

Showmanship means "hooking" an audience with a solid opening scene, and good showmanship is as fruitful in the social world as it is in the theatrical one. The beat of music, live or recorded, is an added boon that helps get a swinging party off the ground quickly. The artistic host, who is only responsible for the cocktail hour, has a superb opportunity to "hook" his guests with a marvelous display of hors d'oeuvres (see Chapter Four) and a glamorous drink to suit the occasion. Of course, it's impossible to list here all the exotic drinks. Almost any fair-sized book on mixed drinks contains hundreds of recipes. We have mentioned only a few popular mixed drinks in Chapter Four and several basic punches in Chapter Three. But there are many unusual chilled summer drinks to choose from: shrubs, coolers, collins, fizzes or punches; or hot winter toddies, grogs or nogs.

Throw caution to the winds and enchant your guests with a specialty of the house by using an unusual container or garnish. You might decide to frost the rim of a glass with sugar for daiquiris or salt for margaritas. Use cups, mugs, or tankards made of china, pewter, or glass.

4343943334

Finally, the *piece de resistance* is a decorative perky garnish on your "specialty" made of a sprig of fresh mint, a few leaves of borage, sweet woodruff, lemon balm, or scented geranium. One may use fresh strawberries or slices of pineapple, lemon, lime or orange. One may use olives, pickled onions—or fresh flower blossoms, as they do in Hawaii.

Act Two

The hosts at the second home know that a sound first act does not guarantee the success of a play. Holding the audience in their seats depends greatly on the second act, and for a successful progressive dinner it's best to plan a menu that will "hold" in the oven, too. An overdone roast beef or a limp soufflé is an avoidable tragedy!

Instead, an excellent choice for a cocktail supper might be Indian curried shrimp or *rijsttafel* (rice table) with assorted condiments, because: 1) it's something different, and 2) there's no need to fear that the food will melt or wilt or dry out. Everything is cooked and arranged ahead of time, leaving a carefree hostess to enjoy the cocktail hour.

Reluctant to serve a curried dish? Afraid too many people won't enjoy it? Better stick to the old tried and true? Oh, no! It's perfectly astonishing how popular curried foods are even among the uninitiated. I've seen them return again and again for second and third helpings. (But, for the rare guest whose diet is strictly limited, you can have on hand some fried or roast chicken or stewed breast of chicken or some such thing.)

Instead of rolls, I like to serve pappadam (also spelled poppadum, puppodum). These are available at many specialty food stores, or they can order them for you. Follow the directions on the package and fry each thin pappadam, one at a time, in hot oil, then drain on a paper towel. They can be made several hours ahead. They fry up very quickly and turn out crisp, looking like giant potato chips. Your guests will be very impressed when you serve them as something new in a large basket.

This Far East menu has another advantage because exotic Indian dishes are so easy to display with a flair. Use an inexpensive Indian paisley tablecloth, add brass candle holders, and at one end of the table, borrow if you must, two brass or china bowls. Fill one with curried shrimp and the other with rice sprinkled with parsley. Invest in a dozen inexpensive Oriental bowls. (They can be used again for outdoor barbecues, filled with mustard, catsup, pickles, relishes, and other condiments.) Each bowl holds nuts, coconut, etc. Place the small bowls in a semi-circle around a basket of golden crescent rolls or Papadums and introduce your guests to a new taste thrill. Suggest they try a sampling of whatever condiment appeals, but chutney, of course, is essential.

There are many curried dishes to choose from in addition to shrimp, such as lamb or veal, chicken, turkey, duck, capons.

Act Two
Menu for 32

Shrimp curry
Fried chicken
Rice with parsley
Assorted accompaniments
Wine (Gewurtztraminer)
Crescent rolls or Papadums
Tea
Coffee
Boston cream cake

Accompaniments:
A grouping of individual 8-ounce bowls of: seedless raisins or currants; sweet pickles diced; slivered almonds; grated coconut; grated orange rind; chopped black olives; grated egg yolk; chopped bacon; chopped egg white; chopped peanuts.

Larger bowls of pineapple chunks and chutney (4 bottles). Plan on refilling these bowls.

Shrimp Curry
This may be prepared a day ahead.

Curry powder: Although many of us know what curry powder looks, smells and tastes like, few know what it actually is—anywhere from a blend of five to fifty spices capable of almost infinite variation, including black and white pepper, cayenne, chili, cinnamon, nutmeg, cloves, allspice, poppy seeds, fenugreek, cardamom, coriander, fennel, cumin, turmeric, ginger, and saffron. Compare three or four of the better-known brands before settling on just any old curry powder.

Equipment: 12-quart stock pot, large saucepan

12 lbs. shrimp
1 cup finely chopped onion
3 cups butter
3 cups flour
8 tablespoons curry powder
12 cups (3 quarts) coconut milk, canned (see following recipe) or dilute
   2 cups powdered coconut in 3 quarts milk
4 teaspoons ground ginger
2/3 cup lemon juice
4 tablespoons salt

1. Buy frozen, shelled and de-veined shrimp.
2. Sauté onion in butter in 12-quart stock pot for 5 minutes. Stir in flour and curry powder. Add coconut milk and cook over low heat until thickened, stirring constantly. (Coconut milk is very sensitive to high heat.)
3. Add shrimp, ginger, lemon juice, and salt. Simmer uncovered for 30 minutes, stirring frequently. Place in refrigerator.
4. Reheat just before serving. Add plain milk if required.

Act Three

Heads will turn when hosts in the third and last home offer a flaming dessert as the grand finale. It's a dramatic and delicious climax for a progressive cocktail supper and is sure to win the enthusiastic applause of every party-goer. Here's a golden opportunity to use, rent or borrow a lovely chafing dish (an electric frypan or a copper skillet over a hot plate will do nicely) and, taking a leaf from the great French restauranteurs, to perform a bit of *legerdemain* for guests.

Arrange everything needed in advance on a separate table or hostess cart and never yield to the temptation ever to ignite a flaming dessert in the kitchen or to carry it in like a birthday cake, because the flame rarely lasts until you reach the dining room. Besides, mixing the sauce and pouring the brandy and lighting the flame is all so much a part of the total performance—it should be done onstage and not in the wings!

There are two simple keys to success when serving any flaming dessert or coffee.

1. Dim the lights low to achieve the greatest visual effect. (Unplug the electric skillet too, for safety.)
2. Have everything hot, including the spoon with which you ignite the brandy.

Crêpes Suzette

Preparing Crêpes Suzette may sound fearful to some, but once you've prepared this tasty dish you'll want to serve it often, for if you can swing a golf club, tennis racket, or hammer, you can swing an omelet pan! Remember, a crêpe is nothing more than a thin pancake composed of a batter made with eggs, flour, and milk and poured sparingly into a frying pan and fried on both sides. Simple?

Crêpes can be made weeks before and frozen between sheets of wax paper and wrapped in freezer wrap. All one need do on the morning of the party is to make the sauce and add it to the crêpes, which are then rolled or folded into quarters. Before serving, place them in the oven at 350° F. to warm.

There are many variations of crêpe batter and fillings besides the one recommended here. Alsatian crepes are filled with raspberry jelly, sprinkled with sugar and glazed with raspberry jelly and placed in a hot oven. (For breakfast, any fresh fruit—strawberries, bananas, apricots, blueberries, etc.—may be served with crêpes without the liquor.)

As a luncheon dish, eliminate the sugar in the batter and fill crêpes with a variety of cheeses such as cream cheese, cottage cheese, or sour cream.

But let's get back to Crêpes Suzette, which is so elegant served as dessert or at midnight on New Year's Eve.

Equipment: Large bowl, medium-sized bowl, egg beater, omelet pan, double boiler, chafing dish

2 level cups sifted flour
2 tablespoons sugar
6 eggs, beaten
1 cup clarified butter or polyunsaturated vegetable oil
　　(Most of this is used to brown the crêpes in the pan)
1 quart milk
3 or 4 drops vanilla flavoring

1. Make batter: In a large bowl, combine flour and sugar.
2. Beat eggs in a separate, medium-sized bowl and add 6 tablespoons of clarified, unsalted butter or oil. (To clarify butter: In a small container, melt unsalted butter over low heat without stirring. Let simmer for 10 or 15 minutes. Do not allow to sizzle. Strain butter, skimming off foam from remaining clear yellow liquid.)
3. Add milk and vanilla. Pour liquid into flour, gradually mixing until batter is smooth, using wire whisk or egg beater. Let batter stand for at least one hour. Add milk as batter thickens.
4. Heat a 5- or 6-inch omelet pan or iron skillet and melt 1 teaspoon of clarified butter. Measure a tablespoon or so of batter into pan with a small circular motion. This spreads the batter and makes the crêpes very thin. Tilt pan to spread crêpes. If there are holes in the crêpes, cover with a drop or so of batter. When they are golden, turn crêpes over and brown quickly on second side. If crêpes are to be sauced later, cover with wax paper to prevent drying. They may be frozen between sheets of wax paper.

Makes 28 crêpes.

Sauces

1/2 lb. butter
2 egg yolks
1 cup powdered sugar
1 cup grated orange rind
1/2 cup orange juice
1 jigger Curaçao

1. The sauce may be prepared in the morning. Melt butter in double boiler, add egg yolks, sugar, orange rind and juice and stir, cooking slowly until mixture thickens. Add Curaçao and stir. Remove from stove.
2. Remove crêpes from freezer and thaw. Spread sauce lightly over crêpes and roll or fold in quarters. If you prefer rolling crêpes, slice off the tips to give them a more uniform appearance. Arrange neatly in ovenproof dish and pour rest of sauce over crêpes. Warm for short time in 350° F. oven until ready to flambé.

The Flambé

When it's time to serve, place platter with crêpes on cart, next to warm individual dessert plates. In a heated chafing dish pour in 1/2 cup 80-proof brandy. When warm, not boiling, light with a match. Appoint an assistant to help you by placing two or three crêpes on an individual dessert plate, while you spoon flaming brandy over them.

When flame dies down—*voilà!* Crêpes Suzette!

My Favorite Christmas Dinner

When a dozen skis and poles, like matchsticks, are piled up on the front porch; when the stereo belts out the same pop tune over and over; when a borrowed high chair sits in the corner; when the dog barks at the substitute postman; when the cat paws blue and gold pine cones on the Christmas tree; when the ample house shrinks to half its size, then it's my favorite time of the year—Christmas vacation!

Traditionally we celebrate Christmas Eve dinner with at least twelve to twenty close friends and relatives whose age range may be anywhere from one to 81. The climax of the months of shopping, gift wrapping, labeling, and whispering occurs after dinner when a bell is rung announcing Santa's arrival and all the lights in the world seem to glow in the eyes of the smallest believer.

Our seating and menu is also traditional, but this year when we had 18 guests, we made two innovations. First, we set up two tables of nine, one in the dining room for the adults, and one in the adjoining study for the young people. Then we set up identical buffet tables in each room, so instead of one enormous turkey, we prepared two medium-sized ones along with duplicate platters of vegetables, sweet potatoes, etc. We appointed a junior host and hostess to look after the young folks, a plan which succeeded even beyond our wildest dreams, because one of the three-year-olds announced, "Mother, you can't come in here—we're having our own party!," leaving us gleefully free to enjoy a leisurely, uninterrupted meal!

Holiday Dinner Menu

Cold smoked salmon
Baby Swiss cheese
Crackers

Roast turkey with chestnut dressing, pan gravy
Cranberry sauce
Sweet potatoes with marshmallows Cockaigne
Spinach soufflé
Cloverleaf rolls
Rum fruit savarin ring
Christmas cookies
Nuts
Mocha coffee

Roast Turkey

Equipment: Roasting pan with rack, large bowl, sauté pan, small saucepan, aluminum foil, muslin cloth (optional)

Forgive me if I sound like a TV commercial, but for the juiciest, most delicious turkey you'll ever enjoy, put the dressing under the skin of the breast instead of in the cavity. You see, the tender breast meat is usually done before the tougher legs, and when you stuff the turkey under the skin it helps to correct this imbalance. If you first coax away the skin around the neck of the turkey, the rest separates very easily. My mother first learned this trick from a Hungarian countess, and now all my grown children from coast to coast prepare their turkeys this way for their Thanksgiving and Christmas dinners.

Fresh or Frozen?

A fresh turkey is better, of course, but not always available. For frozen turkeys, allow 2 hours per pound for defrosting in refrigerator.

Chestnut Dressing

You may prepare the stuffing ahead, but always wait to stuff the bird until just before roasting. Use your own favorite stuffing or our favorite chestnut dressing, which is made as follows for an 8- to 10-pound turkey.

1 lb. can chestnut stuffing (domestic or imported)
4 cups toasted bread cubes

1/4 cup water or stock
1/4 cup chopped onions
2 tablespoons butter or margarine

1. Place chestnut dressing in a large mixing bowl, add bread crumbs and liquid. In a sauté pan, sauté onions in butter and mix chestnuts, bread cubes, and water together lightly.
2. Rub turkey inside and out with salt. To stuff turkey, use a spoon or your hand to loosen skin from flesh (you'll meet with a little resistance just at first) and gradually work your hand across the entire turkey breast all the way to the neck. Now take a handful of stuffing at a time and spread under loosened skin until it is evenly distributed in a flat layer. (Remember the dressing will expand some.) The crop cavity as well as the loose skin of the neck may also be stuffed. If there's any stuffing left, put this in the cavity of the turkey.
3. Close both openings with small skewers, or sew skin together with a darning needle threaded with white string. Tie a heavy knot on the end of a long piece of string and wrap crisscross around turkey, taking care to tie wings and drumsticks close to the body. Secure the end of the string with knot on top.

Turkey Paste

1/4 lb. butter
2 tablespoons honey
3 tablespoons paprika

1. In a small saucepan, melt butter, add honey and paprika and rub over turkey.
2. Cover turkey lightly with aluminum foil. Remove foil a half hour before, so it may brown.

A "no basting" trick: If you cover turkey with a muslin cloth soaked in butter instead of using foil, you don't need to baste it. Remove cloth a half hour before serving so turkey may brown.

Roasting Time

Preheat oven to 450° F. Place the turkey on a rack in an uncovered pan, breast side up and immediately reduce oven heat to 325° F. Baste if needed occasionally.

Figure 25 minutes to a pound for a stuffed bird weighing 12 pounds. For a turkey over 18 pounds, reduce the oven to 300° F. and allow 20 minutes per pound.

To make stock, see Pan Gravy.

Delicious Pan Gravy

This must be made in the roasting pan and not in a separate skillet! Remove turkey from pan and keep bird warm on platter by covering with foil. Pour off all but 2 table-spoons of drippings and place roasting pan on stove over low flame. Add 1 tablespoon flour and stir until thickened. Add either a 10-1/2 oz. can of chicken consommé or 1 cup turkey stock. (This is made in a saucepan. Fill with 2 quarts of cold water, add turkey giblets, wing tips, neck bone, 1 sliced onion, 2 stalks of celery with tops, and several sprigs of parsley. Bring to boil and let simmer for 2 hours. Strain.) Add salt, pepper and stir over low flame for 5 minutes. Optional: You may strain the gravy before serving in your gravy boat.

Sweet Potatoes with Marshmallows Cockaigne

Equipment: Electric mixer or potato masher

In France, Cockaigne is an imaginary country of idleness and luxury—"Schlaraffenland" in Germany.

We always serve a sweet potato casserole topped with marshmallows for our Thanks-giving and Christmas dinner because most children, as well as adults, demand it! If one cares to bother, instead of serving the sweet potatoes in a baking dish, make individual baskets by taking an orange and cutting two wedges from the top half, leaving a little handle. Then remove the meat, and zig-zag or scallop the edge of the basket with a sharp knife. Add the following filling and top with half a marshmallow on each side of the handle. Warm in oven until the marshmallow begins to melt but does not brown.

12 large fresh sweet potatoes (or canned)
3/4 cup orange juice
3/4 cup brown or granulated sugar
2/3 cup melted butter
Dash of nutmeg (optional)
12 marshmallows

1. Cook unpeeled sweet potatoes in a large stock pot of boiling water with lid on until tender or for about 25 minutes. Peel while still warm.
2. Preheat oven to 325° F. Mash potatoes with a potato masher or in an electric mixer. Add orange juice, sugar, and butter, and beat until they are very light.
3. Place in 2-quart baking dish; warm in oven for 15 minutes. Just before serving, place marshmallows on top about 1/2-inch apart.
4. Turn oven on broil for a minute or until marshmallows are lightly browned.

Makes 12 servings.

Spinach Soufflé and Vegetables in General

Of all the foods that set a meal apart, it's the garden-variety vegetable that lifts a menu from the simple good dinner to a classic meal of elegance and charm.

The proper timing of cooked vegetables is so important that, from my party-going experience, unless one has an expert staff in the kitchen, too many vegetables, such as fresh asparagus, peas, and sometimes even snap beans, are usually overcooked, limp, or shrivelled. I must confess that, during the busy holiday season with numerous houseguests under our roof, I frequently resort to the shortcut of buying frozen spinach soufflés. Thus, I have no last-minute timing to worry about, and I am able to free space in my refrigerator, which is at a premium during the holidays. After they have been heated, two or three packages of frozen spinach soufflé can be transferred to an attractive serving bowl.

I am not above buying frozen peas and green beans when fresh are not available. However, I almost always use a shorter cooking time and less water than the package calls for. Then the vegetables stay crisp, moist, and retain their color.

Vegetables served in cases called "farçies," such as green peppers, cucumbers, blanched onions, or *petit pois* served on artichoke bottoms are generally most appealing on the home dinner plate. I never try to compete with the current restaurant fashion to create a towering assemblage on my dinner plate. On the contrary, like all Virgos, I prefer to have things neatly arranged and to know exactly what I'm eating!

Rum Fruit Savarin Rings

This recipe makes three rings and they may be prepared ahead or frozen. These have been served in the White House and are popular year round.

Defrost one ring and allow rum syrup to soak in the day before. Only fruit and whipped cream filling need be added before serving.

Use three 9" ring molds with curved bottoms. I am assuming that you will freeze two rings for later use (so handy to have in your freezer!) and am giving you the rum syrup and fruit filling for only one ring, which is enough for ten servings. These are popular to serve year 'round with fresh fruit.

Equipment: Electric stand mixer, 3 round-bottom ring molds, medium saucepan, a large and medium bowl, large round serving platter

Dough for Three Rings

1 cake fresh yeast
1/2 cup lukewarm milk
4 cups sifted flour
1 tablespoon sugar
1/2 teaspoon salt
9 eggs
1/2 lb. melted butter

1. In a cup crumble fresh yeast in really warm milk and stir until dissolved. In a large electric mixing bowl, pour sifted flour, sugar and salt. Add yeast mixture. In a separate bowl, beat whole eggs and add to dry ingredients. Turn on electric mixer at low speed for 10 minutes. Pour melted butter on top of batter but do not stir! Cover with a towel and keep away from drafts and let rise for 1 hour.
2. Then beat buttered dough again in the mixer at low speed for two minutes. Generously butter and flour three ring molds and pour 1/3 batter into each mold. Let rise until double.
3. Bake in 400° F. oven for 15 minutes, then reduce heat to 350° F. and bake 10 minutes more. Let cake cool in ring molds before removing. Freeze two if desired.

Rum Syrup for One Ring

2 cups sugar
3 cups water
1 orange rind, coarsely chopped
1/2 cup light rum

1. In a medium saucepan, boil sugar, water and orange rind for 15 minutes on top of stove. Add rum and remove immediately from stove.
2. Baste savarin ring repeatedly with boiling syrup until soft and puffy. Let cool slowly.

Fruit Filling for One Ring

1 pint whipping cream
1/2 cup milk
1/2 package vanilla instant pudding mix
1/4 cup light rum
2 cups fresh strawberries, or peaches, mixed with apricots, blueberries or raspberries

1. In a medium bowl, whip cream.
2. In a large bowl combine milk and vanilla instant pudding mix and add rum.
3. Before pudding sets, fold in most of the whipped cream, reserving some for decoration. Finally fold in fresh fruits, also reserving a few for decoration. Place rum-soaked savarin ring on round serving platter with curved side up. Fill the center with fruit-rum-pudding mix and decorate the top with whipped cream and whole berries.

One ring makes 10 servings.

Chapter Seven

Dial "C" for Caterer

"Life is service. The one who progresses is the one who gives his fellow beings a little more—a little better service."

—E. M. Statler

There's a dwindling number of glittery people who have the staff—and the Lowestoft—to serve several dozen illustrious guests at a formal sit-down dinner. The "I-never-cater" group is decreasing, while elegant entertaining is increasing. People who want to dine well—but don't want to cook—are dialing the numbers of reputable caterers to close the small remaining gap left between the automated, live-in kitchen and a spangly dinner party.

A caterer may mean anything from a woman who's a fine cook and owns a mini-van, who will prepare and serve a dinner for eight in your own home—to a large, professional catering service with mobile kitchens, who will wholly prepare and serve a gourmet dinner for several hundred under a heated tent, or for several thousand in a banquet hall.

And one doesn't need to wait for that once-in-a-lifetime occasion—for a 50th birthday or 25th wedding anniversary. Most any caterer will deliver hot hors d'oeuvres and a casserole or whatever you feel like ordering to give your special dinner party that necessary lift.

How does one go about finding a caterer? The best way, of course, is to sample the "cates." (Why did such a lovely, solid word ever go out of fashion?) When invited out, notice if the affair is being catered and if you're impressed, ask your hostess, when you call to thank her the next day, if she'll share with you the name of her caterer. A caterer may be recommended by word of mouth or you may do a bit of snooping on your own. I once found an efficient home caterer through a church bake sale; but if you're looking for a large, professional catering service, check the yellow pages of your phone book, and then shop around and compare what each has to offer in the way of menus, prices, and services, what parties they have catered, how long they have been established. Some caterers serve primarily industry (annual banquets, meetings, conferences, etc.), while others specialize in home functions (weddings, anniversaries, engagements, confirmations, and the like), and some do both.

On one of my earlier Hawaiian trips, I longed to reciprocate the famous island hospitality with a cocktail party of my own for about 20 people, so I turned to the phone book and fortunately selected a gourmet catering company. They delivered ice, glasses, platters, and chafing dishes filled with seven kinds of hot and cold pupus (the Hawaiian name for hors d'oeuvres). The cold marinated shrimp on frilly picks were served in half a scooped-out pineapple shell and, instead of bouquets of parsley, each platter was garnished with fresh orchid blossoms.

Of course, with a bartender the party would have cost more, but one of my quiet friends was delighted to have something to keep him busy mixing and serving drinks.

On another occasion, when our yacht was docked at the Brazilian Docks in Palm Beach, the dock master put us in touch with a pleasant caterer, who arrived on board in his white jacket carrying a black bundle under his arm, in which he had a supply of assorted chef's knives. He disappeared below and in a very short time he reappeared topside, not with platters of ordinary chips and dips for our dockside cocktail party, but with a flower garden of dainty garnishes shaped out of radishes, carrots, tomatoes, parsnips, cucumbers, parsley and watercress. Were we impressed!

The Old Team Spirit

Some caterers will supply everything, including fine linens, china, crystal, extra chairs and tables, and even the floral centerpieces with matching blossoms floating in crystal finger bowls. While others supply only the food and personnel, but they have access to, and experience working with, other members of the "Special Events" party team. This includes people knowledgeable in the art of calligraphy who will address invitations, musicians, acousticians, florists, photographers, lighting experts, parking personnel, and marquee suppliers.

A good caterer will:

• Welcome your suggestions and help develop your party so that it reflects your own taste and personality.

• Use your own recipes and keep them confidential.

• Supply you with bonded, trained waiters, waitresses, and bartenders.

• Free you from all responsibilities during and after the party. (I have known them to turn out the lights—after you've retired!)

Contracts with Caterers and Party Consultants

An experienced party consultant, who embraces and masterminds the entire design theme for a wedding, anniversary, birthday or any special occasion, will ask for a party-planning conference as described in the following letter:

Briefly given a date, the number of guests, a possible theme—if the host or hostess has one in mind, or the purpose of the party, and an estimated budget—we then develop a plan—whether it be a party, wedding or whatever, and submit this to the client together with the total charges involved. Upon receiving   approval, we then execute every detail. The decor, food, help, music or entertainment is booked, invitations are sent—the host and hostess need only be at the door to greet their guests—and pay the bill. We design and build all the special 'sets' that may be called for—sculpt ice or any number of other things—in short, anything a party might require, we do, including flower arranging or whatever.

After the conference, all arrangements are confirmed in writing, usually in triplicate: one copy is sent to the customer, one copy is retained by the party consultant, and the third copy is passed on to the person in charge on the party premises. Worksheets are sent to the catering kitchen where much of the food is prepared in advance, with additional copies sent along for reference by the cook who is later assigned on the party premises.

Things can go awry if you don't get confirmations in writing, especially when a function is planned in a hotel, restaurant, or club. The person in charge of arrangements can make lavish promises, but when the time comes, he is no longer around to fulfill them! Worse yet, you may be surprised with hidden charges. For instance, if you bring your own wedding cake, some places will charge a service charge for cutting and serving the cake. One also needs to know exactly when one is allowed to begin decorating a room and the exact time one must leave the room. Often a room is booked for more than one affair that day, which can cause problems.

A caterer who frequently caters year in and year out to the same people, in the same group, in the same places, finds it challenging to stamp each party with individuality. For this reason a seasoned caterer is obviously receptive to suggestions, including new recipes and original menus from his customers, so feel free to discuss your ideas openly.

A conference with party consultants should be as honest and above-board as any conference between you and your lawyer or your priest. Trust their judgment based on years of experience. Tell them exactly what your budget is, what your facilities are, and how many people you plan to invite, and they will tell you if it's possible and how it can best be done.

On the other side of the coin, I asked an experienced Chicago caterer what qualifications a dream customer ought to have. This was the reply: "One who knows nothing and trusts you—and has the wherewithal to do what's necessary—or an old-timer, who knows what he or she wants and can tell you!"

Novel Ideas

An innovative touch that surprised and delighted me after a formal dinner dance given on a Lake Forest estate in Illinois was to find a chef stationed near the exit on the terrace happily passing out freshly fried doughnut holes! At first we couldn't believe our eyes—was it the moonlight? No, there he was in his tall, white chef's hat, standing over his portable grills, dropping batter as fast as he could and bringing out golden bits of fluff, that we gobbled up with childish glee.

Another touch of individuality that's made a king-sized impression with the Cotillion Crowd is to serve hot onion soup in mugs while everyone's waiting for the attendant to bring the car around. Well, Chicago is windy, isn't it?

Seriously—I love this idea and can't wait to try it for those long, drawn-out cocktail parties, when one secretly wonders if one shouldn't have served something, after all, besides just drinks and hors d'oeuvres. Sending your guests off with a solid cup of hot soup is a neat way to help them bridge the gap between your place and wherever they're headed.

Public Places

What imagination some customers have! The latest trend, for philanthropic organizations, at least, is to hold meetings in out-of-the-ordinary places. The Chicago Horticultural Society, for instance, gave a party around blossoming azaleas in the conservatory at Lincoln Park. Seating was a problem, ingeniously solved with little tables of three under a veritable forest of flowering trees and shrubs. An excellent book, called *Places*, by Hanelore Hahn, is a directory of public places for private events and private places for public functions, covering ten major cities with 2,000 listings. (See Sources of Supply.)

Not lacking in pizzazz was a fundraising dinner held in the Lion House of the Lincoln Park Zoo. Such exotic locales, of course, present special problems to caterers, who face near-disaster with equanimity "every other day." The never-to-be-repeated blooper was a catered luncheon planned in a submarine docked at the city pier. When it came time for the cook to go down the hatch, she was much too broad in the beam and couldn't quite make it! It took several frantic telephone calls to book another cook with the proper measurements in the hips. Problem solved!

Help! Help! Help!

One question always asked is, "How much help do we need and how many guests can we handle?" Not enough help can be disastrous, but too much help can create confusion and inefficiency. One of my pet peeves is attending parties where there is too much help and very little service, because the staff is gathered in the kitchen having a ball of their own, and each one thinks someone else is taking care of the guests. At our big parties at home, to keep me from running around, I always ask one waitress to be stationed near me so that I can signal her to wipe up a spilled drink, or to call a guest to the phone, or to ask the cook to replenish a platter. The ideal amount of help is when each person has a definite assignment, knows what his job is, and is kept occupied but not frenzied. At a formal dinner today, if you expect excellent service, a waiter is required for every eight guests. One bartender will adequately handle 30 to 50 guests. (Later, some bartenders may double as waiters.)

For a formal buffet dinner at home, with cautious planning of the menu, I feel the ratio may be stretched to one waiter or waitress for every eight to ten guests. Their job in essence is to serve cocktails, offer second helpings, replenish water and wine, clear the table and the buffet, serve dessert and coffee, and finally load the dishwasher and clean up in the kitchen. This leaves the host and hostess free to enjoy the company of their guests and not be faced with kitchen drudgery after the party. The next day it's my job to put things away where they belong.

Caterers have pet peeves too, especially when they have to deal with a suspicious woman who thinks everyone is trying to take her for a ride. This true story concerns a doctor's wife, who engaged a cateress to cook and serve dinner at 7:30 for 12 guests. She was to prepare hors d'oeuvres, soup, duck l'orange, vegetables, wild rice, gravy, dessert, and coffee.

The caterer suggested she arrive at two o'clock in the afternoon bringing a prepared dessert with her, but the doctor's wife (who was paying by the hour) said she thought that was too early—four o'clock would be time enough because there would be other help there to get things started. When the caterer arrived at four o'clock, there was no other help around! Quickly and desperately she called a friend to give her a hand, and between the two of them they managed to cook and serve a lovely dinner, but she only went to that house twice—the first and the last time!

Most caterers know that people at buffets eat in frightening, horrendous quantities, and since the last six people at a benefit usually are the chairman of the board, the president, and the party chairman, with their spouses, when they look at the buffet table for the first time, if it isn't full and beautiful, they are sure to be disappointed.

It's not easy to outguess people's appetites. Caterers have told me, "If you underestimate you're a bum. If you overestimate, you charge too much. If you hit it right on the nose, you're skimpy!" Too bad, isn't it?

Let's Talk About Caterer's Recipes

Over a period of many years I have consulted with gourmet chefs and top caterers in New York, Chicago, Detroit, Washington, D.C., Palm Beach, Beverly Hills, Honolulu, London, Hamburg, and other major cities. Hearing this, you are probably under the impression that I have a collection of recipes firsthand from these experts that reaches from here to the ceiling! Yes and no.

Yes, I do have recipes, but no, they are not useful in the average kitchen, either because the directions are too sketchy, amounts too large, or the procedures impracticable in the home. So I'd rather not waste your butter and eggs by passing them on.

One of my best friends coaxed a recipe for a glamorous chocolate cake from her favorite caterer only to give up after wasting a day and costly ingredients. Why didn't the cake turn out? There are several good reasons:

1) Specialties of the house are treasured like gold—do you blame caterers for not passing them out?

2) Even the best-intentioned professional cooks might leave out a step, just because they assume everyone knows certain things—but, of course, everyone doesn't!

178

3) Some ingredients are unknown or unavailable to the average housewife; or

4) The equipment in the professional kitchen is so completely different that it's impossible to give accurate timing directions for baking, beating, grilling or reheating dishes. So let's leave the specialties to the specialist and turn to a good basic home cookbook for our party recipes.

Many people like to prepare a specialty of their own, even for the largest parties, when a caterer is called in to do most of the cooking. If you do prepare one homemade specialty, give it an important place on the menu—an excellent hors d'oeuvre or a showy dessert are focus points. You may have to increase the recipe to serve a large crowd. Fortunately, I've never had any difficulty in doubling, tripling, or quadrupling recipes, because I always take the precaution of writing the increased amounts of ingredients on a separate sheet of paper before starting to cook. It's safer to do your arithmetic in advance, not while you are measuring ingredients.

Why Uniforms?

When I'm invited to a casual party, I'd rather reach out my hand and introduce myself to one of the guests, instead of to one of the staff who is dressed in a T-shirt and blue jeans. This has happened to my friends and to me more than once, which is embarrassing to everyone! It follows then that the staff ought to at least arrive in a white shirt and black pants or wear a white apron. The same holds true for bartenders. For example, one can purchase a red bartender's vest at a uniform shop, which often comes in handy when hiring a college student.

Do ask anyone you hire, therefore, to tell you what they are planning to wear. Today's generation, as reflected in David Brooks' delightful book, *Bo-Bo's in Paradise* ("Bo-Bo" stands for "Bourgois-Bohemian"), is described as "liking loose manners, and members of today's affluent class may be suspicious of refinement. They like to think of themselves as natural, warm, honest, comfortable and sincere." But let's not include confusing! There are times one needs to strike a thoughtful balance, and for staff to wear uniforms is one of them.

The Liquor

At private clubs, hotels, etc., you will probably be told what the customary corkage charge is. There are various ways this can be figured. One way is to charge per person, which strikes a balance between those who drink and those who do not. The advantage of this system is that no one needs to count bottles at the end of the evening.

Some caterers, on the other hand, charge per bottle, and at the end of the evening you are charged for all opened and all empty bottles. The least popular method—because recording drinks is time-consuming—is to charge per drink at the bar.

You can choose the type of liquor you wish to serve—house brand, call brand, or premium brand. Remember that the bottle price should include the fee for the bartender, mixes, and glassware. (See Chapter Four.)

Tipping

People often ask how much they should tip and who should be tipped. (You recall that the word "tips" is an abbreviation of "To Insure Prompt Service.") As an example, let's discuss a function given at a hotel or club, where one expects good service. Unless there is a built-in service charge, the general rule is to tip various members of the staff 20%, which might include the *maitre d'*, the chef, and perhaps the bartender, in addition to the 20% of the bill that goes to the waitstaff. Then there are the valet parking and coat room attendants to consider. Musicians are always tipped when they play an extra half hour or more. Photographers are usually not tipped, and florists are optional. There ought not to be a "tip cup" anywhere at a private party. As a general guideline, anyone who performs a service or a kindness above and beyond the call of duty ought to be thanked with a thoughtful tip. If you have question regarding the custom of tipping in your area or at your club, the hotel or club manager will be glad to advise you.

Deciding the Right Time, the Right Place

When selecting a meeting room or hall, there are several important things to remember. Some rooms are easier to decorate than others. For instance, for luncheon meetings, I prefer a room with windows, while in the evening one doesn't require natural daylight. Instead, check the draperies for color and pattern. Rooms with mirrors and chandeliers, of course, are usually desirable at night because they reflect color and sparkle.

As a general rule, it's safe to say when decorating that one can create a striking effect by following the principle of a three-ring circus and concentrating on three focal areas: 1) the entrance; 2) the tables (speakers' table, buffet table and dining tables); 3) the orchestra or bar.

In addition, the room should be checked for the following conveniences. Is there easy access to the kitchen? Is there a platform for the speakers' table? Are there outlets for mikes and lights? What are the fire laws regarding the use of candles and flammable materials? (One may have to clear the latter with the fire department who have been known to station a fireman to standby on special occasions.) And finally, is there convenient parking for guests?

Total Testing

Even when you have a professional caterer taking care of every detail, it would be sensible for you to have a "run-through" before any exceptionally large party. Some hosts don't realize until the last minute that their kitchen facilities are inadequate, the borrowed pan is too big for the stove, the electrical wiring is inadequate for all the cooking equipment plugged into it, etc. (I had to rent a generator for one of my brunches, when we used three waffle irons at once.) Be sure that you test the working order of any stored, infrequently used articles.

For special occasions, when dining out at a club, fine hotel, or restaurant, it's not unusual for the punctilious host or committee chairperson to request a dress rehearsal dinner, where several dishes are carefully tasted, including wines, and the meal is appraised in toto for color, texture, and appearance.

Souvenir Menus

The earliest known menu was designed by Michelangelo in 1530. While traveling from Milan to Florence, he gave his servants detailed instructions describing exactly how the meal was to be served and in what order. More recently we have examples of a restaurant scene painted by such great artists as Picasso (Waiter Setting the Table), and menus by Georges Dufy in watercolor (The Liberation of Paris 1944), another by Gaugin (Colonial Satire), and one by Renoir (Juggling Chefs). Painting restaurant menus was one way to help the down-and-out artists pay for a meal.

Much attention has been given not only to restaurant menus, but also to menus used at private dinner parties, where a small printed menu is placed at both ends of the table, or by each place setting, so that guests can pace themselves from one course to the next.

I have frequently used souvenir menus to take the place of favors at weddings, anniversaries, birthdays, and even fundraisers. Artists enjoy the challenge of creating elaborate borders that reflect the theme of the occasion—floral, nautical, or patriotic. The original menu can be hand-colored and then photocopied in quantity. A menu can also be designed on a computer as well. One can roll up the souvenir menu and tie it with a colorful bow and place it beside the plate for each guest to take home. Some people have framed them as a memento of the occasion. To go one step further, it's fun to make up suitable names for the courses or items listed on the menu to suit the occasion or party theme. For example one could create an Anniversary Appetizer, or a Big Apple Dessert. The following Symphony Menu is a good example of how to develop a musical theme.

Symphony Gala

The world-class Detroit Symphony Orchestra, conducted by Finnish conductor Leif Segestam, left on a 12-city European tour in October 2001. Earlier, a major $500,000 fundraiser with an unusual twist was planned for the orchestra's Gala on opening night. First, an elegant meal was served before the concert to 500 major contributors. Tables were set with silver centerpieces and white flowers. A fantastic dessert table, enhanced with giant ice sculptures of musical instruments, was set up for minor contributors at a lively "afterglow" with dance music. Here Chairman of the Symphony Board Peter Cummings was noticed dancing with his lovely wife, Julie, who was wearing an eye-catching red designer dress. There were several testings of the elegant dinner menu, and fortunately I was able to coax the final menu of this gala event out of my dear friends and neighbors, the Cummings.

First Plate	Principal Plate	Finale
An Elaborate Seafood Palette	Sliced Rack of Veal with Morel Sauce	Mozart Gateau with Musical Notes
Jumbo Shrimp/Galatine of Lobster	Potatoes Dauphine/Asparagus Yellow Tomato Ratatouille & Baby Beets	Chocolate Mousse with Passion Fruit
Jumbo Lump Crab		Tri-color Tuille & Chocolate Sauce
Jacquesson Brut *Perfection* Rosé Champagne	1998 Ferrari-Carano Chardonnay 1996 Franciscan *Magnificat* Meritage	Coffee

The "afterglow" centerpiece consisted of fresh fruits and berries displayed among musical ice carvings. On the sweet table were assorted dessert cheeses, a variety of tortes, cheesecakes, flans, bombes, miniature French pastries, warm apple pie with caramel sauce, cherry cobbler with vanilla ice cream, chocolate-dipped pretzels, crème brûlée, bananas Foster, handmade truffles in bowls of chocolate, and assorted chocolate-dipped fruits.

Planning a Year in Advance

They told me that perfect party planning began a year in advance for a benefit party with His Royal Highness, Prince Philip, Duke of Edinburgh, as the guest of honor. The black-tie dinner, held in the Conrad Hilton Hotel in Chicago, was the flawless culmination of innumerable meetings and conferences on both sides of the Atlantic, but for most women like myself, our plans didn't begin until three seconds after we held the engraved invitation in our hot little hands.

What to wear? We were instructed to wear long gloves and gowns. Who's going? One thousand beautiful people. Do I need to curtsy? No, indeed. Where do we sit? At tables for eight. Will he speak to me? Yes, ah—yes, really!

Party For Prince Philip

Prince Philip spoke to everyone as he circled the room during the brief cocktail hour before dinner, asking the gentlemen, "What do you do?" while the ladies murmured, "Isn't he handsome!," "I thought he was taller!," "He's six feet tall!," "He seems so friendly."

After a private cocktail party, we were guided to designated elevators leading to the Grand Ballroom. Here, 125 tables were set with two-foot-tall centerpieces, decorated with a total of 5,000 fresh roses and 2,500 twinkling votive lights, entwined with 250 yards of Mediterranean-blue velvet ribbon. Truly impressive!

Before entering the ballroom, every gentleman received a small envelope with his name on it, and typed in the enclosed card, the table number for himself and his lady, while a chart nearby gave the location of the table numbers. A heavily embossed, gold-tasseled souvenir program with the menu lay at each place (don't you love to know what you are going to be served?), along with a white handwritten place card, accented with a gilt crown.

We were guided through the princely program by His Royal Highness' personal toast-master, dressed in a hunting pink tailcoat.

Formal Dinner Menu for Prince Philip

Clear Green Turtle Amontillado
Golden Cheese Straws
Relishes

Filet of Pike Sauté Véronique
Aux Fleurons

Jouvet Pouilly-Fuissé

Roast Baron of Beef

Sauce Perigueux
Petite Chateau Potatoes
Fresh Asparagus Tips Polonaise

Barton & Guestier Pommard

Hearts of Palm and Avocado on Bibb Lettuce
Oil and Lemon Juice Dressing

Chocolate Mocha Mousse Suprême
Petits Fours
Lady Fingers
Macaroons

Coffee

Le Bal Moderne

Once in a lifetime, perhaps, dream and reality blend in a charming mystical way to create enchantment, and such was the case on the memorable evening of the Bal Moderne, a forerunner of more recent special events.

Take a dream castle—or substitute the Great Hall of the Detroit Art Institute with its arched frescoed ceilings, its walls hung with 16th-century Flemish tapestries, its numerous Gothic entrances guarded by invisible knights in visible suits of armor. Add forty round tables for ten, covered with celadon green cloths and a gossamer overskirt of silver lamé, each with a 2-1/2-foot translucent cherub centerpiece gaily lighted from within by amethyst, amber, sky blue, and jade bulbs; turn a professional designer loose to decorate the adjoining marble-floored Rivera Court for cocktails and dancing among boxwood hedges topped with papier-maché white doves; add eight-foot magnolia trees and flood the scene with candlelight from twelve-branch candelabras—and you're off to a pretty good start.

But, still not enough for the benefit ball in behalf of the Friends of Modern Art. Serve the finest vintage wines and delicacies to 400 knights in white ties and their perfumed ladies; add the magic touch of a big band's dance music; invite Tony Martin to serenade the queens of Detroit's "wheeling" society dressed by top couturiers in ball gowns designed to complement the Futurist paintings on exhibit. Ah! Then you have a winning combination—an enchanting candlelight setting, a glittering gathering, a gourmet dinner with impressive gifts to boot, and swinging music.

Months of hectic planning preceded the spectacular success of the Bal Moderne, which was not only the highlight of Detroit's winter season but, according to Cleveland Amory, who was there too, "a statelier event than any New York ball this season." Thirty-three committee members divided the responsibility into 14 subcommittees as follows: advisory, dinner, entertainment, decorations, tickets, reservations, invitations, publicity, picture, gift, bar, lighting and P.A. system, general services, and table seating.

Today's Ultimate Private Party

People who recently attended this unbelievable private party will talk about it for years to come. I may never again attend such a "Gatsby-like" function, nor may you ever host such an event, but perhaps you may gather an idea or two from reading about it from start to finish.

The invitation—A black and white invitation that simply stated in large letters on top "Black Tie," followed by the name of the hosts, "Cocktails and Dinner," the date, the time (7:30) and place, with an R.S.V.P. on the lower left-hand corner. However, taped to the *back* of every invitation was a photograph taken of *you*, the guest, attending a previous party given by the host several years earlier. Well, of course, this made a big impression! How could one miss such an affair?

The setting—A private mansion in Winnetka, Ill., on the shores of Lake Michigan. As we approached the driveway, a valet attendant, *brandishing a neon wand*, waved us through the stone gate, where we gave the car to the valet parking attendant. Before mounting the steps, a photographer took our picture. In the front hall, our coats were checked by uniformed staff and we were offered a fluted glass of champagne—before even greeting our host!

Mingling—Two hundred fifty guests in black tie mingled elbow to elbow in the large reception room under a soaring cathedral ceiling. Guests marveled at the dramatic setting. Men and women admired huge bouquets of white flowers throughout the house. Since there were no draperies obstructing the view of Lake Michigan, votive lights flickered on all window sills. Tall fireplaces with real logs burned cheerfully in every room.

Hors d'oeuvres—The caterer told me there were 40 uniformed staff, some with walkie-talkies. The only way you could tell the waiters apart from the guests was because the waiters wore a red carnation in the lapel of their tuxedos! There was a permanent bar in almost every room with a wine steward or bartender the entire evening! Waitstaff constantly passed tempting trays of bite-sized hors d'oeuvres, such as thick slices of cucumber filled with crabmeat paté.

Stations—In a small parlor off the living room was one of numerous stations. On a large round table with an enormous white floral arrangement stood a large iced silver bowl of black caviar, and a choice of iced shrimp, lobster, and crab fingers. In an adjoining room, all the furniture had been removed, turning it into a spacious ballroom. Here, a five-piece orchestra played dance music until the last guest departed.

Seating—Many people were ascending the double staircase and I was urged to "take a look." What I saw upstairs was most surprising. In every one of the many spacious bedrooms, white marble bathrooms, exercise room, and paneled library were small white tables and chairs for four. Each table was covered with a white, floor-length tablecloth and on the center of the table was a white flower arrangement. A bartender was stationed in the upstairs library and we were offered iced black caviar from a huge silver bowl. A large ice sculpture held an array of wine bottles.

Buffet Supper—About 9 or 9:30, a buffet supper was served in the downstairs dining room. Salads, vegetable platters, and pasta were served in silver bowls, filets of beef were sliced by a chef, and fresh rolls offered in wicker baskets. Everyone picked up their own plates and sat wherever they pleased, upstairs or down.

Dessert—While people were still eating, I noticed the staff assembling a dessert table in the reception room. On one side of this huge flower arrangement were cookies and lemon bars and on the other side, the staff had set up a "help yourself"—with their help, of course—ice cream soda bar, with vanilla, chocolate, and strawberry ice cream, a variety of sauces, nuts and whipped cream. It was surprising how many people could not resist this sweet temptation!

Finale—To sum it up, 250 guests spent a delightful evening, freely socializing, merrily eating, moderately drinking, and smoothly dancing. You might guess that would be enough in the entertaining department, wouldn't you? Well, not for my friend, Keith Rudman. Much to my surprise, after several weeks, the mail brought a card matching the original invitation. We were thanked for "sharing the evening" and enclosed were several photographs taken of us with friends, documenting that unforgettable affair. As if anyone could ever forget!

Menu for a Formal, Seated Wedding Dinner
Gilbert-Duca Wedding for 250 guests
Genesee Valley Club, Rochester, New York

Appetizer
Chou Froid Stuffed Quail with Foie Gras
Watercress with Apple and Red Onion Chutney

Salad
Boston Bibb Florets with Avocado and Hearts of Palm
Balsamic Vinaigrette

Wine Beaujoulais Village   **Entrée**
Macoin Village   Wood Fired Filet Mignon
and Crispy Shrimp Cake
Roasted Mushroom Potatoes
Garden Vegetable Bundle

Champagne   **Dessert**
Blue and White Wedgewood
Wedding Cake
Coffee and Sweets

Menu for an Elegant Wedding Reception for 1,000 Guests
Not a sit-down dinner

Miniature charcoal-broiled tenderloin steak on tiny buns
Stuffed mushroom caps
Water chestnuts and bacon with soy sauce and brown sugar
Hot cheese soufflé with chutney
Crabmeat canapé au gratin
Sliced chicken finger sandwich (some on whole wheat)
Fresh shrimp canapé
Rolled cream cheese with sprig of watercress
Tiny puff shells filled with lobster salad
Bridal decorated mints
Fondant-dipped almonds
Giant salted nuts

Chapter Eight

Let's Set the Table with Style

"The world was my oyster, but I used the wrong fork."
—Oscar Wilde

Occasionally restauranteurs call to ask, "Which way does the blade of the knife go?" Wine salesmen ask me, "On which side of the water glass does the wine glass belong?" Everyone asks me, "Where do the dinner fork and the salad fork belong?"

When we sit down to eat we automatically pick up our fork on the left side of the plate and our knife on the right. It's something we don't need to think about when we're hungry, tired, or happy and excited. But setting the table is not automatic and we often take it for granted—until it's our turn to figure out where to put more than one fork!

Forks were once considered a luxury, so please, let's not take this simple little tool for granted. It has a long, distinguished, and yes, even controversial history!

The Two-Pronged Fork and Pasta

We can thank Marco Polo, the Venetian traveler, for introducing noodles to the Italian Court after his return from China in the 13th century. The Chinese were the first to invent noodles in the 1st century A.D., and they always used chopsticks, eating from a deep bowl.

The Italians, however, preferred using a tiny, two-pronged fork. (You may see an original fork at the Museo Poldi Pezzoli in Milan.)

By the middle of the 15th century, there were forces working like yeast in the booming Italian economy. New Oriental spices arrived daily from the east, while new foods like tomatoes arrived from the New World to the west. Thus the combination of noodles, spices, and tomatoes was the origin of the great Italian cuisine as we enjoy it today.

When Italian Princess Catherine de Medici married Henry II de Lorraine, King of France, it was her direct influence that brought the high art of fine dining to the French Court. Gradually, silverware became more and more fashionable and was put to general use at the Palace of Versailles during the long 75-year reign of the two French kings, Louis XIV and Louis the XV, and the rest of European royalty gladly followed the stylish trend. So, you can clearly see that the general use of knives and forks was never a grass roots movement! Instead it took several centuries for the use of round-tipped knives and four-pronged forks to trickle down to us from the royal courts of Europe.

It took a great many more years for the use of forks to be accepted by the general public. One reason for the delay was that some members of the clergy were known to preach vehemently from the pulpit against the use of the sinful fork, which they considered a tool of the devil! They claimed we should "eat with our ten God-given fingers" instead! It's no surprise then to learn that the British navy used to forbid not only the use of forks, but also knives, because their use was considered to be "prejudicial to discipline and manliness."

Later, on the other hand, during the Victorian era, silversmiths went slightly overboard by designing not only three- and four-pronged dinner forks, but luncheon forks, salad forks, fish forks, oyster forks, dessert forks, fruit forks, lemon forks, pickle or olive forks, cold meat and carving forks.

Forks Belong Where?

Forks belong next to the dinner plate, NOT under the dinner plate, and NOT on top of the napkin! Etiquette recommends that the first thing a person is supposed to do when sitting down at the table, is to put the napkin on one's lap. Right? Yes I know, many trendy magazines and catalogs show the fork on top of the napkin. However the real reason for this—and I've seen it happen with my own eyes—is that a photographer tries to scrunch the table setting as close together as possible in his view finder. He doesn't want to put the folded napkin on top of the dinner plate because he's paid to advertise the chinaware!

Consequently whoever sets the table at home follows this incorrect style, and it's not easy trying to convince everyone at this stage of the game that the proper place for the fork is not on top of the napkin, but next to the dinner plate.

Where does the salad fork belong? That depends when you serve the salad! Remember, we use our utensils from the outside in toward the dinner plate. Therefore if you serve the salad before the entrée, the salad fork goes to the left of the dinner fork. If, on the other hand, you serve the salad after the entrée, the salad fork belongs between the dinner fork and dinner plate. What about the oyster fork? Ahh, just like conjugating French verbs, here's the exception. This tiny fork always is placed on the extreme right, and the tines of the fork may rest on the bowl of a spoon at an angle. (Don't ask me why.)

As for the dessert fork, again you have choices:

1) It may be placed on the left, next to the dinner plate.

2) In Europe it is often placed horizontally above the plate, and this practice has been recently adopted in the United States. It is also advantageous when there isn't enough room to spread all the silverware out on the table.

3) The dessert fork and spoon may be brought in together with the dessert plate.

4) When only dessert is served and there is no knife being used, both the dessert fork and spoon are placed to the right.

Much Ado About Knives

King Charlemagne (742–814 A.D.) deserves full credit for encouraging his subjects not to eat with their fingers, but instead to spear meat and vegetables with the pointed tip of a hunting knife. It wasn't until the Middle Ages that knives came into general use as eating utensils by the public.

Today we may use a large variety of knives, including dinner knives, steak knives, luncheon knives, fish knives, fruit knives, cheese knives, butter knives, carving knives, and cake knives. Some knives, such as steak knives, are still pointed at the tip, but most dinner knives are rounded at the tip.

For this we can thank Cardinal Richelieu (1585–1642), the first minister of France, who became irritated when he dined with a friend who continually picked his teeth with the pointed blade of the knife. Consquently he persuaded King Louis XIII to order "that from this day forth—all knives shall be rounded at the tip." You will notice that round-tipped knives are still fashionable in both Europe and America today.

Meat Carvers' Guild

During the Middle Ages, when guilds for professional meat carvers had clout, the Meat Carvers' Guild of Venice tightened up its working conditions and announced that hereafter each carver would not perform for more than six guests!

Knives Belong Where?

Dinner knives are always placed to the right of the dinner plate with the blade facing in toward the plate. When more than one knife is used, such as a fish knife and a dinner knife, the knife used in the first course is on the outside. The butter knife is placed on the butter plate either vertically, diagonally, or horizontally.

> I eat my peas with honey,
> I've done it all my life.
> It makes the peas taste funny,
> But it keeps them on the knife.
> —Ogden Nash

Shells, Spoons, Love and Ladles

> "The louder he talked of his honor, the faster we counted our spoons."
> —Ralph Waldo Emerson
> "Eating with a spoon instead of your fingers is like making love through an interpreter!"
> —A former Shah of Iran

The history of the spoon goes as far back as time immemorial. Anthropologists tell us that the earliest spoon was probably a shell stuck into the end of a stick, and you may have noticed that the shell design is still frequently used on much of our silverware today.

In America, people in 1700 were using pewter spoons and eating off pewterware instead of china. Since then, the useful spoon has come a long way in popularity. Some of us may have inherited silver soup spoons, little cream or bouillon spoons, cereal spoons, coffee and tea spoons, demitasse spoons, dessert spoons, ice cream spoons, grapefruit spoons, iced tea spoons, berry spoons, sugar spoons, Bon Bon spoons, in addition to tablespoons and ladles. Believe it or not, the ladle for serving soup was first introduced by the Duc de Montaussier in the year 1695, and for this he was was publicly ridiculed!

Under the English reign of the Tudors and Stuarts it was customary to give a set of twelve Apostle spoons as a christening gift, and that was the beginning of the custom of selling flatware in sets of twelve.

Spoons Belong Where?

The soup spoon is placed on the right, outside of the knife. When a beverage spoon is added it belongs next to the soup spoon, also on the outside. As we mentioned before, the coffee spoon may be placed on the outside to the right, or horizontally above the dinner plate, or brought in on an empty dessert plate with the dessert fork.

Proper Place Settings

There is only one important rule to remember when it comes to setting the table, and that is:

We eat from the left and drink from the right.

This means that the glassware is placed above the tip of the knife on the right, and the salad, butter plate, and vegetable dish are always placed on the left.

Delicate Glassware Called "Transparent Silver"

Delicate drinking glasses were not available until the 13th and 14th centuries, with the rise of skilled Venetian glassmakers. Venetian drinking glasses were much sought after in all European courts and still are today.

In England, for example, Queen Elizabeth (1533–1603) was responsible for encouraging the importation of the lead crystal industry that gave employment to many of her subjects. In France, Louis XVI revitalized that country's glass-making industry when two glass manufacturers, St. Louis and Baccarat, produced the first aristocratic lead crystal which, as you know, is still on the market today.

193

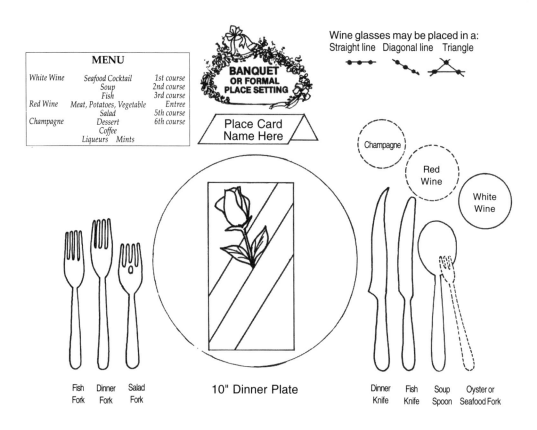

Wine glasses may be placed in a:
Straight line   Diagonal line   Triangle

MENU

White Wine	Seafood Cocktail	1st course
	Soup	2nd course
	Fish	3rd course
Red Wine	Meat, Potatoes, Vegetable	Entree
	Salad	5th course
Champagne	Dessert	6th course
	Coffee	
	Liqueurs Mints	

BANQUET OR FORMAL PLACE SETTING

Place Card Name Here

Champagne

Red Wine

White Wine

| Fish Fork | Dinner Fork | Salad Fork | | 10" Dinner Plate | | Dinner Knife | Fish Knife | Soup Spoon | Oyster or Seafood Fork |

Ordinary glassware is usually machine-blown into a mold and shaped by compressed air. For this reason, every piece is exactly alike. Fine crystal, which was once referred to as "transparent silver," is always hand-blown, and no two pieces are exactly alike. Tapping a crystal glass with your fingernail makes it ring clear as a bell.

The word "tumbler" came into use because these glasses were wide-based, without a stem. This design prevented them from tipping over when they were used in swaying coaches. The flat bottomed tumbler is mostly used today for water, milk, iced tea, orange juice.

Stemware refers to glasses of all sizes which consist of a bowl, stem, and base. These are used as white wine, red wine, brandy, cognac, cordial, martini, hi-ball, cocktail, sherry, beer, parfait, and sherbet glasses. On the other hand, people nowadays are using any glass they feel like using for whatever they choose. To simplify matters, both red and white wines are often served in what is called an "all-purpose" glass.

Glasses Belong Where?

Let's start with the water glass: When no other beverage is served, place the glass above the tip of the knife. When more glasses are added for white wine, red wine, etc., the water glass moves inside to the left. Wine glasses are placed sequentially, starting from the outside in according to the menu, light wines first, followed by heavier red wines.

Glasses may be arranged in a triangle, a straight line, or a diagonal line.

Glass Finger Bowls

Although rarely seen today except in fine restaurants—when they serve lobster or at the White House for a state dinner—finger bowls are usually made of glass and are half filled with warm water. Sometimes a thin wedge of lemon, a tiny leaf, or a blossom is floated in the water.

Traditionally the waitstaff places a finger bowl on a dessert plate, with a doily underneath, and a fork and spoon on either side, and then places this in front of a guest. The guest then removes the finger bowl and doily from the plate and puts it above the dessert plate. He then puts the dessert fork to the left and the spoon to the right of his plate. When using the finger bowl, he dips the tips of his fingers in the water, one hand at a time. He may touch his lips lightly with his moistened fingers and then dry them on a napkin. An option is for the waiter to simply place the finger bowl above the fork to the left of the diner. The dessert is then passed to the guest, who serves himself.

Placemats, Tableclothes, Napkins—and "The Naked Mahogany"

Table linen and laces came into vogue during the reigns of Henry IV and Louis VI, when separate dining rooms first became fashionable, along with their breakfronts and sideboards. Then it was customary to change tablecloths and napkins after every course. (The demand for more home cookbooks with recipes for smaller dinner parties was on the increase as well.)

As for table manners, the general public still needed to be cautioned by leaders like George Washington, who advised, "Cleanse not your teeth with a tablecloth, napkin, fork or knife."

Today, our choices are unlimited when it comes to setting our table. (We may even choose not to use any cloth or mats at all, but present our guests with what the writer Nathaniel Hawthorne once dubbed "the naked mahogany.") We may select from a wide range of materials, including handwoven fabric to straw, glass, or mirror. I have even seen clever "theme" placemats designed on the computer! We may use what is called a "runner" down the middle of our table or along both sides of the table. We may use a white or colored damask, chintz, a gay cotton print, an organdy, linen or lace tablecloth to match our decorating scheme.

Setting the Tone

The tablecover, probably more than any other item, sets the tone for the entire meal. A checked tablecloth conjures up picnics or farm suppers. A paisley pattern complements a Middle East ethnic menu. A white damask or lace cloth that you see through projects a formal dinner. I have found that people are very careful not to spill food or drink on fine damask or embroidered tablecloths. Consequently they don't need to be laundered every time they are used. If there is a tiny spot, it can easily be removed by hand with a little soap and water before folding the cloth away.

Tablecloths that match the menu enhance any meal. For a curried menu, I like to use a crewel Indian print or a Persian hand-loomed blocked print. Both are quite reasonable. Or you can make a dainty net overlay for a sweet table as described in Chapter Three under Champagne Teas. You can make use of felt, lace, organdy, satin, cotton, and denim. You can use bright patterns in prints, checks, and stripes. Cloths can be trimmed with rickrack, French ribbon, fringe and frogs with the trim made into coordinated napkin rings. Cloths can be appliquéd. No matter how formal or informal the party may be, an appropriate cloth adds a solid impact to the total decorating scheme! I find that I use these party cloths over and over again with my favorite menus, and hopefully you will too!

Even on a limited budget, the possibilities for creating a pretty table setting are limitless. You can use such inexpensive, yet amusing ideas for placemats, by spreading out a Chinese or Japanese newspaper for an Oriental supper, or taping sheets from old comic books together for a children's party, or as we mentioned earlier, using sheet music for a musical theme.

Placemats come in round, oval, and rectangular shapes and may be used for both formal or informal occasions depending on whether they are lace or quilted. For some placemats, such as fine linen, I like to use felt underliners, but not with lace mats because we are supposed to see through lace.

Tinting those old white linen cloths is another option. Select any shade of popular package dye you like on the market and follow the directions. First wet your linen and remove it from the washing machine. Then mix the dye thoroughly with hot water in your washing machine. Then put your cloth in the machine, follow package directions, and presto! It will emerge beautifully tinted. Don't hesitate to dye embroidered linen because it doesn't matter if the embroidery takes on a darker or lighter shade; in fact, it's prettier that way.

Finally, for big private or corporate parties a large variety of attractive matching tablecloths, skirting and napkins may be rented through a party rental store.

What Size Tablecloth and Napkin?

Tablecloths look best when they drop about 10 to 15 inches from the edge of the table on all sides. It should lay squarely on the table with the middle crease running up the center. Any wrinkles may be smoothed out or ironed out on the table.

The bigger the napkin, the better! Breakfast and luncheon napkins are usually about 17 inches square, whereas the formal damask dinner napkin is usually at least 22 inches square. Cocktail or hors d'oeuvre napkins may run 5" x 8" or thereabouts.

Popular Paper Napkins

When and when not to use paper napkins may be questionable at times. As a general rule, when entertaining outdoors, thick paper napkins are perfectly OK for all but the most formal entertaining. They may also be used indoors when there is a large group for a buffet, a serve-yourself luncheon or dinner if they are of good quality. But they should not be used when the table is set for a sit-down company dinner.

Heavy-duty, monogrammed 17-inch paper napkins are available, as well as some with artistic designs. Matching dessert napkins come in 13-inch, and smaller 10-inch cocktail napkins are available in a variety of colors and designs.

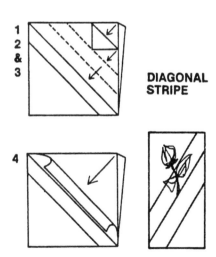

DIAGONAL STRIPE

Proper Napkin Placement and Napkin Folds

At home, the proper place for a folded napkin is to the *left* of the fork, or it may be placed on top of the dinner plate. It is never placed in a water glass as is done in restaurants, because here the busboy fills one's glass *after* a guest is seated. In the home, the water glass ought to be filled *before* the guest is seated.

For monogrammed napkins, the napkin is folded with the initals on the outside, facing the guest.

My favorite napkin fold is illlustrated [previous page]. I like this fold because one can insert a flower, a place card or a favor there in the fold:

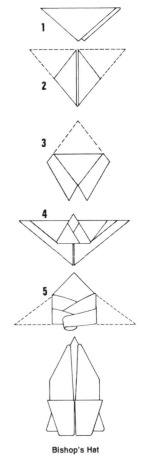

1. Fold napkin into half-, then quarter-size. Leave corners open at upper right.
2. Turn down one upper right corner for two inches.
3. Fold over again twice to create a diagonal fold across napkin.
4. Next turn down second upper right corner and fold into another diagonal stripe.
5. Fold left and right side under napkin.
6. Place vertically on table, enclose souvenir, name card, or flower into diagonal fold.

If you are looking for some height on your table, the Bishop's Hat napkin fold is very elegant [right].

1. Fold napkin into a triangle with center points facing down.
2. Then fold right and left point to a point in the center.
3. Fold top corner down to about 1 inch from bottom.
4. Turn folded point back up again.
5. Turn napkin over. Fold right and left points across, tucking one point inside the other.

Napkin stands by folding bottom point under for balance. By turning upper corners down, you end up with a "Fleur de Lis" fold.

Bishop's Hat

Porcelain Plates and Chinaware Rivalry

When Marco Polo traveled to China, he was impressed by the beautiful vessels from which the Chinese ate. He named the material porcelain, after the delicate shell, "porcelana." Porcelain dishes are still called "china" because the Chinese invented the process in the 5th century, and kept it secret for 1200 years.

Porcelain was such a highly sought-after product in Europe that, in 1706, King Augustus II ordered his alchemist, Bottger, to stop trying to make gold, but instead to turn his attention to making porcelain. The King figured correctly that with this knowledge he could fill his treasury with gold. Three years later, Böttger succeeded in making a fine grade of porcelain (the secret ingredient was kaolin, a fine white clay mixed with quartz and feldspar) and thus the King's renowned Meissen Factory was firmly established and ran successfully as a royal monopoly. Unfortunately the Meissen factory could only keep the process secret for ten short years. (Today Meissen is commonly called Dresden.)

The French King, Louis XV (1715–1774) eagerly entered the chinaware competition when he moved the small Vinçennes manufactory to Sévres in 1756. This land was owned by his mistress, Madame de Pompadour, and it was her mother who pointed out to her, "Sex and food—that's the way to hold a man!"

The Sévres factory kept the King's treasury filled by selling complete sets of china, consisting of thousands of breakfast, luncheon, and dinner plates, to many of his royal cousins scattered all over Europe. Spanish, Portugese, Russian, Austrian, and English royalty tried to emulate the trendy French Court's etiquette of fine dining, which by now had peaked. The privilege of watching the King eat was considered great theater and putting on a royal dinner was a performance that reached a high degree of splendor.

After seeing the historic exhibition, "Versailles and the Royal Tables of Europe," at the Musée National des Chateaux de Versailles et de Trianon, in 1994, I can readily understand how the china industry grew to be as big an industry then as our computer industry is today.

Still, politics as well as business influenced the sale of chinaware. After the American Revolution, English china fell out of favor in the United States and instead French Sévres dinnerware became very popular, because the French, as you will recall, were our strong allies during war. Thus Sévres china is still very much in vogue today.

There is a wide selection of not only French and English but other fine European chinaware on the market today. In addition to porcelain, there is bone china, which, like porcelain, also wears well without chipping or cracking. Bone china has a high percentage of bone ash that imparts whiteness, strength, and clearer translucency. Everyday china, such as hard-fired, nonporous stoneware, wears fairly well, but earthenware or pottery, which is thick and porous, easily chips or cracks. Melamine is a generic term for everyday plastic or non-ceramic dinnerware and, fortunately, this material is very hard, as well as chip- and break-resistant.

Care of Fine China

Fine china ought to be stacked carefully when it is put away and a felt pad or paper doily is needed between each plate to prevent scratching. When purchasing your china, ask if it is dishwasher-safe and microwave-safe. Fine decorative china, especially if it is trimmed with gold, silver, or platinum, should be hand-washed.

When washing by hand, line the sink with a cushioning rubber mat or towel, and immerse only one piece at a time. Then place wet china on a dishtowel to dry.

Never use scouring powder or any abrasives on fine china, crystal, or silver. If two tumblers or bowls stick together, place cold water in the inner one and stand both in warm water to loosen them quickly.

A Standard Place Setting

A standard place setting consists of five pieces: a dinner plate, dessert or salad plate, bread-and-butter plate, cup, and saucer.

Open Stock means that manufacturers and retailers have agreed to keep the pattern available for a definite number of years or for an unlimited time.

Trademarks or signatures of well-known manufacturers, such as crowns or crossed swords etc., are present on all fine china, i.e., Dresden, Sévres, Spode, Derby, Rosenthal, Flora Danica, etc., as well as on some pottery such as Staffordshire. There are numerous books on the market where one can readily identify these symbols.

A Handle on Cups

Chinese cups never had handles as our cups do today. It was customary in the Middle Ages, as a sign of generosity to fill the handleless cup and deep saucers to overflowing. Thus we recall the origin of the words in the 23rd Psalm, "My cup runneth over."

Sam Pepys wrote in his diary in 1660, "Today I had a drink which I have never drunk before, tea—served in a china vessel—". But it wasn't until the 18th century that cups with both handles and saucers gained in popularity.

The two-handled "loving cup," designed long ago for weddings, was passed around the table to toast the bride and groom.

I wish I were a china cup
From which you drink your tea.
For then I know at every sup
You'd give a kiss to me!
*   —Anonymous*

When to Serve Coffee

Cups ought never be on the dinner table when guests are first seated, as we often see in coffee shops. The correct time to serve coffee is after dessert has been served. Coffee may be served either at the dinner table or guests may be invited to move into the living room for after-dinner coffee or a demitasse.

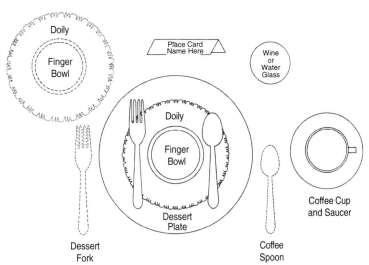

What About Chargers?

Your mother may have referred to a charger as a service plate or place plate and these are used only for formal dining just for show, and no one eats off these plates. A typical charger is a plate usually a bit larger than the standard dinner plate. It could be made of lacquer, metal, or porcelain and is on the table just for the sake of appearances when guests are first seated. Since no one eats off these plates, they don't always need to be

201

washed, just a quick wipe will do. There is usually a fancy doily on top of the charger. Dinner plates are placed on top of the doily. The charger remains on the table for the first course (soup) or two (appetizer). However, when I serve buffet, I let guests set their dinner plate on my gold lacquer chargers, and don't remove them until dessert is served.

Centerpieces

I was surprised to learn that flower arrangements as we know them today didn't become fashionable until the 19th century. It was stylish during the Middle Ages for royalty to use pieces of sculpture as centerpieces. In many museums you will find examples of centerpieces, such as the gorgeous Conch Shell centerpiece in the Kunstliche Museum, Vienna. Later popular centerpieces consisted of china figurines, tall candelabras, and epergnes filled with fruit, flowers, and nuts.

When I am in a practical and economical mood, I often resort to arranging a centerpiece composed of things I already have around the house: two blossoming violet plants set in a favorite bowl, an arrangement of exotic shells from my collection, or a container filled with pine cones, accented with a sprig of leaves with berries from the garden. Sometimes I add objects, like a carved duck, or turkey feathers at Thanksgiving, or a merry-go-round toy at Christmas. I have learned that small children calm down when there are candles on the table, so a choice of candles both short and tall are a must after dark. Sometimes it's fun to use a large bowl of grapes, when they are at their peak, as a centerpiece, or a colorful arrangement of fruits, such as red apples, yellow tangerines, green limes, or whatever strikes your fancy. Sometimes the menu is inspiring. For example, when serving pasta, one could use a still life arrangement of red and yellow tomatoes with green zuccini on a straw mat. Letting your imagination soar is the heart and soul of entertaining.

Several Ways to Serve an Informal and Formal Meal

Who is served first? In America the hostess is often served first on the theory that guests can follow her actions, which may help to put them at ease. But in Europe the guest of honor is often served first. The choice is yours to make.

When the hosts carves at home, if it can be done skillfully, the turkey or roast may be carved at the table or sideboard, but if one prefers, there is no reason not to do the carving in the kitchen, and then bring the sliced meat in on a platter for passing.

The following rules were designed to give the guest as little disturbance as possible and with minimal risk of accidents or spills Therefore the traditional rule is to serve the dinner plate from the left and remove the plate from the right by the staff. It is more convenient for the butter plate and salad plate to be removed from the left, rather than reaching across a guest. However, unfortunately, nowadays you will find many servers in hotels and restaurants do not strictly observe this rule due to the lack of trained staff.

All beverages ought to be served from the right. When pouring water, the glass ought not be lifted off the table, and it should only be filled 1 inch from the top and not to overflowing. Wine glasses ought only to be filled half or three-quarters full. It is becoming customary to have a bottle of red wine and white wine on the table during the meal. Water is poured before guests are seated, but wine is poured after everyone is seated—and the appropriate wine, lighter white wines with the first course, and heavier red wines with the second course.

No one should begin clearing the table until *everyone* has finished eating. To do otherwise is to rush slow eaters.

When clearing the table and before the dessert is served, *everything* is removed except the centerpiece, candles, water or dessert wine glasses, dessert fork, spoon, and place cards. This includes salt and pepper shakers, bread and butter plates, side dishes, and dinner plates. Two plates at a time are carried to the sink, and nothing is stacked or scraped in view of the guests. On informal occasions, discourage guests from leaving the table to help in a volunteer, massive, free-for-all clean-up. One family member or close friend may be the exception to this rule. Better that guests remain seated and enjoy each other's company, because lively conversation often is at its best over dessert and coffee.

Occasionally, you will see well-trained staff crumb the table before dessert is served. This means they deftly sweep off any crumbs from the tablecloth using a napkin and a plate, or a little brush with a small tray.

When serving dessert, be sure that the correct size plate is selected. I have seen a slice of pie served on a 6-inch butter plate instead of an 8-1/2-inch dessert plate. The wrong-sized plate makes it cumbersome to eat pie without having the crust slide off the plate and onto the tablecloth.

There are five accepted ways to serve a meal:

1) English- or Family-Style service, which we have already described in detail in Chapter Six;

2) American Banquet or Plate service;

3) French service, using a cart from which to serve—this is where the phrase "a la carte" originated;

4) Russian service, which was introduced by Prince Alexander Kurakin (1777–1825) while he was Russian Ambassador in Paris, and before he became the Czar in 1810. Prior to that, it was the custom for guests to eat at a U-shaped table "above or below the salt." If you sat "below the salt," which was a precious commodity, then you didn't get any and consequently "you were not worth your salt." Kurakin instructed his servants to pass platters of food around the table to each guest. Parisians loved the new dining custom, where everyone now was on equal footing. It was also during this period that floral centerpieces and place cards were first introduced.

5) Buffet service, or the offshoot of this, which is called "Stations."

American Banquet or Plate Service

Many hotels, clubs, and restaurants favor using plate service, where food is artistically arranged on the dinner plate in the kitchen and then brought into the dining room and served to each guest by the waitstaff. Plates are cleared two at a time without stacking. They are put on a tray and taken back to the kitchen. Individual desserts are then served to each guest, along with coffee.

French Service, a la carte

This a la carte service is usually done in fine restaurants where the waiters are trained to toss a Caesar salad, flambé a Steak Diane, Crêpe Suzettes or Cherries Jubilée from a side cart. The waiter prepares the dish in front of the diners and then serves it to them on their individual plates.

Russian Service

This needs to be done by a well-trained staff. Each silver or china platter is garnished in the kitchen, one with meat or fish, another platter is prepared with potatoes and/or vegetables. Two serving utensils accompany each platter. A gravy bowl and ladle may also be passed separately. Each platter and gravy bowl is brought into the dining room by a waiter and offered to the guest from the left. Using the serving utensils, the guest helps himself to a portion of food and puts it on his plate. The platters may be refilled in the kitchen and passed around in the dining room more than once.

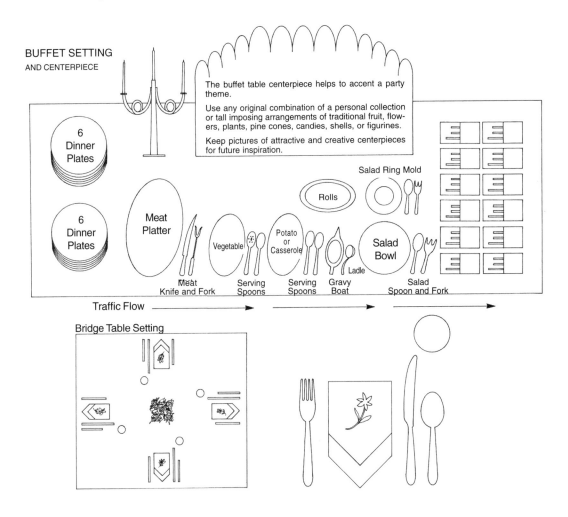

BUFFET SETTING
AND CENTERPIECE

The buffet table centerpiece helps to accent a party theme.

Use any original combination of a personal collection or tall imposing arrangements of traditional fruit, flowers, plants, pine cones, candies, shells, or figurines.

Keep pictures of attractive and creative centerpieces for future inspiration.

6 Dinner Plates

6 Dinner Plates

Meat Platter

Vegetable

Potato or Casserole

Rolls

Salad Ring Mold

Salad Bowl

Meat Knife and Fork

Serving Spoons

Serving Spoons

Gravy Boat

Ladle

Salad Spoon and Fork

Traffic Flow

Bridge Table Setting

Buffet Service or Stations

We've already discussed Buffet service somewhat, but we go into more detail here.

When you decide on serving buffet for a large crowd, to speed up service, plan to have more than one line for your guests. You can either set up a buffet starting from both ends, or have two L-shaped tables with four lines.

A well-organized buffet table ought to be arranged in logical sequence. For a buffet supper, a stack of dinner plates come first, then hot food such as meat, vegetables and casseroles, followed by cold salads and buttered rolls (unless these are served on a pre-set table). For the convenience of the guests, the flatware, often in a rolled-up napkin, is picked up last.

There are two ways to serve Buffet or Stations:

1. Guests pick up their plates from a stack of plates placed at the end of the buffet table or dinner table, and help themselves to a selection of food. When this is done, they then pick up their own silverware, which is usually rolled up in a napkin, and go sit wherever they feel like it, indoors or out.

2. Or people may serve themselves and then find a seat at a pre-set table, with a tablecloth, silverware, napkins and glasses filled with water. Salad, rolls, and butter may also be on the table.

3. When finished, the hosts or their staff clear the dinner plates and either serve dessert and coffee or the guests help themselves.

The difference between Buffet service and Stations is that with Stations, a choice of food is offered from more than one table. These are smaller than the traditional long buffet table. For instance, appetizers are served in one corner of the room and perhaps soup in another corner. Or one station offers meat and another offers fish. There could also be a pasta station and a vegetable/casserole station and a dessert/fruit station. For some occasions such as large parties, conferences or meetings, it's preferable and pleasant to have people walk about, mingling to stop and chat, and then move on.

Check the Menu

Finally, when it comes to actually setting the table, check your menu first, before deciding what china and utensils are needed. Are you planning to have a vegetable dish, salad plate, and butter plate all on the table at the same time? Do you have enough room? You need to allow 20 to 30 inches between the center of one plate to the center of the next plate. If there isn't enough room, you may need to revise the menu, or plan serving the salad as a separate course.

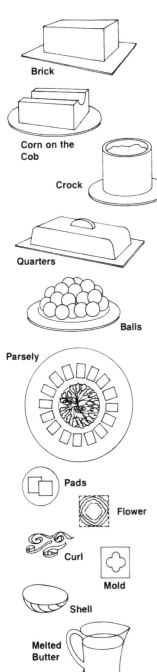

Brick

Corn on the Cob

Crock

Quarters

Balls

Parsely

Pads

Flower

Curl

Mold

Shell

Melted Butter

Ten Ways to Serve Butter!

A sprig of fresh green parsley, tiny herb leaves, or flowers always add to the butter presentation.

For formal dinners, butter plates used to be excluded, but today practicality overrules convention. When using an individual butter plate at the table, you have the following choices:

Butter Pads: Square butter pads are served on butter plates, which are placed to the left of the diner. My handy aluminum tool cuts out 16 butter pads at a time.

Butter Flowers: For this, butter pads must not be soft but firm, not chilled. Press the corner of the individual butter pad toward the center with the tip of a fork.

Butter Balls: To make butter balls: 1) scoop out butter ball with a melon ball scoop; or 2) using two special wooden serrated paddles, which have been chilled, carefully roll out butter balls. (This is a trick similar to pulling a rabbit out of a hat! It takes practice.) Keep butter balls in ice water until ready to serve.

Butter Curls: For this you need a tool called a butter curler. Dip curler in hot water before pulling it lightly across firm but not chilled butter. Store in ice water until ready to serve.

Butter Molds: Decorative butter molds with plungers are the easiest to use. Condition first by holding mold under boiling water—then plunging at once into ice water. Cut butter into 1/3-inch thick slices. The mold determines the size of the squares.

Butter in Shells: Fill small individual shells with butter. Chill.

Butter by the Brick: Remove wax paper and put on serving plate. During the fresh corn-on-the-cob season, indent brick 3/4-inch by melting the top down to a slight concave form. To butter corn, guests place their corn-on-the cob on the butter brick, then give it a quick turn to butter evenly.

Butter in the Crock: For informal occasions.

Butter in Quarters: A stick of butter may be served in a covered butter dish at the table.

Melted Butter: Melted, drawn or clarified butter may be served either in a small pitcher or for dipping in a glass container, or over a small burner.

Royal Kitchen Tours—A Rare Treat

If anyone is really interested in the history of cooking and dining, I strongly urge gourmets to visit two historic kitchens in England and one in France. The restoration of the *grande cuisine* in Paris was only begun in 1997 and recently completed. All three kitchens are open to the public.

1) Located in southwest Greater London, Hampton Court Palace, built for Cardinal Wolsey in 1515–1530, so impressed King Henry VIII that he urged Wolsey to give it to him! The 16th-century royal kitchens are the finest of their date anywhere in the world. They are laid out for visitors as if a feast was under preparation. When I visited the historic Tudor kitchen, I noticed that there were a number of separate food preparation facilities, including large rooms for receiving produce, others for cutting meat, poultry, fish and additional separate kitchens for baking, roasting, etc. The giant kitchen complex reveals that Hampton Court Palace undoubtedly was the political and social center of its day. Hampton Court Palace is also renowned for its royal gardens, orangery, and pools, originally stocked with freshwater fish for the kitchens.

2) In the exquisite Royal Pavilion of the seaside port of Brighton, there is another must-see kitchen. Here the great chef, Carême, prevailed in the 50-foot high kitchen, which is enhanced by four iron and copper palm tree columns. Chef Carême, the inventor of caramel, was brought to England from France in 1817. A dozen cooks worked under him at a time using gleaming copper saucepans, boilers, fish kettles and herb trays. It was considered to be the most up-to-date kitchen of its day. J. W. Croker noted that, "The kitchens and larders are admirable—such contrivances for roasting, boiling, baking, stewing, frying, steaming and heating: hot plates, hot closets, hot air and hot hearths, with all manner of crocks for hot water and cold water, and warm water and steam, and twenty saucepans all ticketed and labeled, placed up on their necks in a vapour bath." The steam tables are gone now, but the room is substantially the same as it was when it was built. The Prince Regent once dined here with his servants, but only after a red cloth was spread under his feet on the floor.

3) The next time I go to Paris I will head for the newly renovated kitchen of the Musée Nissim de Camondo, which gives visitors a behind-the-scenes glimpse of how an aristo-

cratic household functioned during the early 1900s. Endowed by Moise Camondo, his entire home and its contents were given to the Museum of Decorative Arts in 1936. The kitchen walls are covered with gleaming white tiles and a hotel-sized oven stands in the center of the room. There is a separate room for ripening fruit, and a cold room for meats and vegetables. There are additional rooms to wash china, glass, silver, pots, and pans as well as an office for the chef. Adjacent to the kitchen is the servants' dining room, reserved for the *maitre d'hotel*, valets, laundresses, maids and cooks, who ate as formally downstairs as their employers upstairs—much like the popular TV series "Upstairs, Downstairs." The museum is closed Mondays and Tuesdays.

Chapter Nine

The Party Calendar

"Time has no divisions to mark its passage, there is never a thunderstorm or blare of trumpets to announce the beginning of a new month or year. Even when a new century begins it is only we mortals who ring bells...."

—Thomas Mann, author

Fashions zip in and out so quickly nowadays that by the time this book is off the press the current craze may be totally passé; therefore, the calendar which follows is designed around more or less permanent themes. But freshness and originality are always welcome, so by all means capitalize on up-to-the-minute trends in creating individual themes for your party. This may include designing a party that is synchronized with a Master's Golf Tournament, the Oscar Awards ceremony, Wimbledon tennis matches, or a family reunion.

January—New Year's Day

Not one, but three choices!

1. TV Brunch
Flower lovers invite friends and neighbors to view the Pasadena Parade of Roses. Invitations give time, date, place, etc. Sketch three roses in parade formation.

Menus: See Chapter Two, include chilled rosé wine.

Decorations: A driftwood "tree" centerpiece to which rose corsages or boutonnieres are attached for each guest.

2. Afternoon

Have an Open House with Holland-Dutch overtones. (The Dutch custom of calling on New Year's Day was introduced to the U.S. in what was then Nieuw Amsterdam, now New York.)

Invitations: In the form of a windmill. "Open House: It's a Dutch custom to celebrate New Year's Day with a Rijsttafel—Please join us," etc.

Menu: Do include Lucky Herring salad. It's an Old World superstition that those who eat herring on New Year's Day will always have money in the year ahead. Include dried fruits, Edam or Gouda cheese, crackers. Or offer a sweets table: rich hot chocolate or cocoa; eggnog; marzipan cakes; windmill cookies, of course.

Decorations: An arrangement using Dutch wooden shoes as a centerpiece, or blue Delft chinaware with tulips on the table.

3. Evening

Give a small dinner (see Chapter Six) for your closest friends. Have a Rijsttafel Buffet featuring shrimp or veal curry and rice.

Activity: Have each husband write down "the happiest event of the year for us as a couple"—or the most embarrassing, the most comic, etc. Have each wife do the same. Score ten for every matched event (where husband and wife both agree). The highest scoring couple wins an appointment book each.

Other suggestions: Have each person share this year's New Year's resolution. Or read tea leaves, or hire a fortune teller.

January 19—Birthday of Paul Cézanne

(1839–1906) French painter and father of modern art

1. Afternoon

Invitations: Use postcards (available at most art museums) depicting the work of Cézanne.

Decorations: Use red apples for a centerpiece, of course! Pale green cloths. For Moulin Rouge posters, etc., see Sources of Supply.

2. Evening: Beaux-Arts Ball or formal Bal Moderne (see Chapter Seven).

Dress: Black tie or costumes.

Activity: Have artists make sketches of guests. Dance the Apple Dance: Each couple dances with one apple held between their foreheads. The couple who keeps the apple there longest wins—a good Cézanne print or book to each winner.

Chinese New Year

This holiday begins on the first full moon after January 21 and lasts for 15 days.

Invitations: Mail bright red invitations with gold lettering.

Greet guests with *Gung Hay Fat Choy*!, which means "Wishing you more money." Wear a red Chinese dress with mandarin collar, quilted jacket, or straw hat.

Decorations: Hang a Chinese travel poster, map, newspaper, fan, or a pair of chopsticks on the front door.

On a red tablecloth, borrow if necessary, a Chinese statue or vase and decorate with yellow/gold mums. Or use Chinese newspapers as placemats. I once obtained Chinese paper placemats with the Chinese signs of the zodiac from a Chinese restaurant.

Menu: Serve sweet 'n sour pork chops (Chapter Five) with rice. Or order Chinese take-out. Offer chopsticks.

Serve Chinese mandarin oranges, tea, and fortune cookies. (Just for fun you can insert your own made-up fortunes!)

Entertainment: I once hired someone to shoot off firecrackers outside our window after dessert was served.

January 24, 1848—Gold Discovered in California

Evening: Wild, Wild West Party

Invitations: Glue a playing card and poker chip on each invitation, with the date January 24, 1848. "Here is a *golden* opportunity to celebrate any occasion—a birthday, reunion or anniversary. Please join us! [Give date, time and place, etc.]"

Decorations: Checked tablecloths, sawdust on the entrance floor. Spray rocks gold to simulate nuggets and use these for centerpieces. Serve cold cuts at a "Free Lunch" counter; include hard-cooked egg, pretzels, and popcorn.

Music: Player piano, singing waiters, or barbershop quartet.

Dress: Pass out false handlebar mustaches to men, fancy garters and hair ornaments to women.

Activities: Roulette table, dice games, poker, black jack. (Give guests phony paper money to gamble with, and prizes to those who have the most money at the end of evening.) Stage a phony hold-up. (See Sources of Supply.)

February—Resort Weepers Party for Stay-At-Homes

Evening

Invitations: Mail invitations on Palm Beach, Acapulco, or Sun Valley postcards, saying, "Wish you will be here on . . . ," etc. Give date, place, time, etc. of party.

Dress: Summer sportswear, or ask everyone to dress in the native costume of the place they would most like to be. This will bring out a variety of bullfighters, Hawaiian dancers, ski outfits, and bikinis. Over "public address system" announce arrival and departure of airliners and ships from exotic foreign ports.

Decorations: Bright paper flowers (see Crêpe Paper Rosettes), travel posters. Move garden furniture, umbrellas, folding chairs, and swings indoors. Fill sand pails with potato chips, pretzels, etc. Serve frosted rum drinks.

Activities: Dance to "summertime" music. Play ping pong, indoor golf and putting games. Use live fish in a fish bowl as a centerpiece.

Crêpe Paper Rosettes

Crêpe paper rosettes are inexpensive floral centerpieces that can be made in quantity, weeks in advance and they won't wilt! Each rosette equals an entire bouquet; they are attractive in any and all colors—orange for Mardi Gras, red for St. Valentine's, or black and yellow for Hallowe'en. Edges may be sprayed with glitter, hearts, confetti, silver or gold paint. I have even used them outdoors to brighten up a green hedge in the garden for theme parties!

Directions to Make Crêpe Paper Rosettes:

1. Take one roll of crêpe paper, unroll it, and lay it flat on the floor, then fold in half lengthwise. Starting at one end, tightly gather the folded side with both hands, forming the stem. As you gather, make a quarter-turn until you reach the end of the roll.
2. Wrap stem tightly with light fishing wire or heavy string about 1-1/2 inches from the bottom.
3. Gently separate the edges and fluff paper rosette vigorously.
4. With both hands, using heel of your palm and not fingertips, gently stretch crêpe paper edges on the outside edges going around and around toward the center. This teasing of the crêpe paper gives it the desired ruffle effect similar to a carnation or peony. Shake the rosette again vigorously and you will have a lovely bouquet.

February 12—Lincoln's Birthday
Or the third Monday in February, Presidents' Day

Evening
Invitations: Make your own invitations by pasting Lincoln-head pennies on a card. "Please help us celebrate Lincoln's Birthday on February 12th." [Give time, place, etc.]

Centerpiece: Use black stovepipe hat as centerpiece (see Sources of Supply). Invert hat, add container, fill with flowers. Run a ribbon from under hat to each dinner plate.

During dinner, have guests pull their ribbon one at a time. Attached to the end will be a question, such as:

Q. With whom did Lincoln hold his great debate?
A. Douglas.
Q. On what denomination currency is Lincoln's portrait?
A. $5 bill.
Q. Is it full face or profile?
A. Full face.

After-dinner debate: Divide the group into three teams. Present one team with the pro and the other team with the con of any age-old argument, such as, "Should a woman be president of the U.S., yes or no?" But avoid too controversial topics! Limit time for presentation. (The third team acts as jury and rotates so that each group is jury at least once.)

Stunt: Supply men with false whiskers when they arrive.

Addenda: Lincoln loved a good joke. When a fat lady accidentally sat on his stovepipe hat he said, "I would have told you that the hat wouldn't fit before you tried it on!" Another time he commented, "My father taught me to work—but not to love it!"

February 14—St. Valentine's Day

1. **Afternoon:** Champagne Tea (Chapter Three).
Invitations: Traditional hearts and flowers, or cupids.
Decorations: Red velvet and satin accented with white lace.
Activity: A good opportunity for an organization to sponsor a spring fashion show with a lively commentator. Confer with your local dress shops.

2. **Evening:** Famous Lovers party, dinner dance.
Dress: Suggest couples dress as famous lovers. Full costume or headdress only.
Activity: Color one half of a heart pink, the other blue. Tear each heart roughly in half. Give pink to woman, blue to man. Matching halves are dinner partners.
Valentine Dance: One couple starts dancing for a few minutes. The music stops and each person chooses a new partner; repeat until everyone is dancing.

Decorations: Lots of red and white balloons and rosettes, candles, paper lace doilies. Or use swaths of billowing net around the room.

Menu suggestions: Heart-shaped molds, candies.

Alternate evening party: Duplicate Bridge session. Contact American Contract Bridge League, 2990 Airways Blvd., Memphis, TN 388116-3847; 1-800-264-2743 or ACBL@acbl.org.

February 22—George Washington's Birthday
Or the third Monday in February, Presidents' Day

1. Tea or House Tour for benefit of Historical Society. Time: 2:30–4:30.

Invitations: Glue 13 gold stars in a circle to represent original 13 states.

Decorations: Early American theme—red, white, and blue. Use White House address on front door: 1600 Pennsylvania Ave.

Menu suggestion: See Chapter Two for tea ideas. Serve strawberry or cherry sauce over pudding or Martha Washington's Trifle. (See Chapter Two.)

2. Dinner Dance and Hunt Ball

Decorations: Fox and hounds with *fleur-de-lis* and eagles from Washington's coat of arms. (George Washington was truly the Country Gentleman who loved to hunt and ride with the hounds. He also loved dancing, hence the Hunt Ball in his honor.)

Dress: Black tie or pink coats. Three-cornered hats or wigs for men, fans for the ladies. (See Sources of Supply.)

Alternate suggestion: In temperate climates, a river boat party simulating "down the Potomac to Mt. Vernon."

March 11—Commemorates Johnny Appleseed (1774–1847)
Patron Saint of the American Orchard, and an early conservationist

Any time of day! Plan a morning coffee or afternoon tea. Theme for annual meetings of associations of block clubs, conservationists, or beautification programs.

Invitations: Staple a small packet of seeds to a card giving time, place, etc.

Centerpiece: Use a basket of shiny red apples and/or artificial sprigs of apple blossoms on a dark green tablecloth.

Door prize: Jars of apple blossom honey.
Music: Have pianist play "In Apple Blossom Time."
Menu suggestions: Serve chilled apple cider and doughnuts.

Mardi Gras

Celebrated 40 days before Easter and the day before Ash Wednesday, the beginning of Lent

Invitation: Written on a sketch of an elegantly decorated mask.
Dress: Elaborate costumes with masks.
Decor: Costume jewelry, beads, crowns, jesters, and royal trappings Musical instruments and dance theme.
Music: New Orleans jazz band. Grand March.
Menu: Café Royale, shrimp creole and rice, or turkey gumbo (Chapter Five), French bread, pecan pie.

March 17—St. Patrick's Day

Evening: Disc-Delight for young people.
Invitations: Write invitations on green shamrock.
Decor: Irish travel posters, maps, leprechauns.
Centerpiece: Potted shamrock plant. Use dark green or lace tablecloths.
Menu suggestions: See corned beef (Chapter Five) or set up a "do-it-yourself" ice cream bar with assorted flavors and sauces, fruits, toppings, green pistachio nuts, green mints, or pistachio ice cream.
Activity: Sing Irish songs. Invite everyone to bring his favorite disc. Ask a local disc jockey or appoint someone with the gift of gab to program the recordings.
Play Categories: Give each guest paper and pencil and have them write a five-letter word like "saint" vertically. Across the top, name four categories such as songs, artists, cars, sports, states. Guest fill each space with a word whose first letter corresponds with the letter in the vertical column. Give time limit. Score 5 points for each box.
Prizes: Bar of Irish Spring soap.

March 21—First Day of Spring & Johann Sebastian Bach's Birthday

German composer, born 1685

Morning: Musicale, Luncheon or Tea by Music Group.
Invitations: Write on a copy of Bach's sheet music the time, date, and place.
Decorations: See Symphony Luncheon sketch (Chapter Two).
Place cards: White card with musical clef.
Menu: Symphony Luncheon (see Chapter Two).
Memo: Programs will include the price of the luncheon in the double-fold invitation.
Inside:

Spring Musicale *Mon., March 21* *at 10:30 o'clock* *The Little Club* *Reservations*	
	Reservations *Luncheon* *LI 7-6543* *12 o'clock* *Kim Smith* *(price)*

April 1—April Fool's Day

Evening: Mystery Party!
Invitations: Staple time, place, etc., to a mask or cut colored paper in shape of mask. (If the party is to be held at a club or hotel and the identity of the host is to remain secret, request return address be sent c/o a post office box number.)
Decorations: Cut giant black question marks from poster board and sprinkle with glitter.

Activities: Charter a bus and take the whole gang on a surprise trip to a road-house, bowling alley, swimming pool or what you will. Or, engage magicians and comedy waiters, cartoonists for the evening.

Memo: Get trick silverware, etc. from trick store.

Dress: Men could wear women's hats and women could wear men's hats. Guests may remove masks before dinner is served.

Music: Play the song "Who?" by Irving Berlin before announcing the name of the host.

Addenda: Giving a Mystery Party on someone's birthday or anniversary is sometimes kinder than giving a Surprise Party. Being surprised robs one of the pleasure of anticipation.

Easter Tea

See Chapter Three.

April 21—Rome Founded in 753 B. C.

This day is celebrated in Italy as "Natale Di Roma."

Evening: Roman Orgy for a club-sponsored annual ball, or several couples may combine in giving this lavish party.

Invitations: Roman letters on parchment scroll tied with purple ribbon.

Decorations: Use purple satin tablecloths. For centerpiece use small, gilded harps entwined with ivy. Scatter reclining garden furniture indoors and drape with brightly colored fabric or sheets. Simulate Roman columns and statues. Use torches and braziers outdoors.

Menu suggestions: Large punch bowls. Oyster bar. Long buffet table loaded with whole roasted fowl, roasts, platters of whole fish (bass, salmon, trout). Olives. Serve Caesar salad, artichokes. Red and white wines. For dessert pass large platters of grapes, figs, dates, pomegranates, and assorted fresh fruit, nuts, and cheeses.

Entertainment: Professional juggler or magician.

Dress: Togas, sandals. Provide men with laurel wreaths. Ladies with flowers.

Music: One or more harps and violins.

Memo: Ancient Romans made parsley garlands to hang around their necks, thus preventing intoxication!

April 23—William Shakespeare's Birthday
English poet and dramatist, born 1564

1. **Matinee:** Theater Party.
Invitations: Facsimile of theater ticket.
Activity: Charter bus to drive young people to theater. Serve refreshments, box lunch (see Chapter Two).

2. **Evening**
Invitations: Let's "ham" it up together for Willie Shakespeare!
Decorations: Theatrical masks.
Menu suggestions: Baked ham with lima beans and pear casserole (see Chapter Five).
Activity: Let guests give short excerpts of readings from Shakespeare's plays with modern, ad-libbed translations. Have several copies of his works available for reference. For props, provide wigs, scarves, swords, etc.

May 1—Kentucky Derby, Churchill Downs
Louisville, Kentucky

Noon: Usually given by a group or club for fun or fundraising.
Invitations: Red and white checkered card.
Decorations: Red tablecloths with horseshoe flower centerpieces and silk banner saying, "Good Luck."
Menu suggestions: See Chapter Five for barbecue recipes. Menu suggestions described below.

Digestive Track Run Down:

1. Mint Julep — cool at the start!
2. Merry-Go-Round Pie — no long shot!
3. Cole Slaw — may be a toss!

4. Tomato Pudding — sure to come out of the red!
5. Chicken Bar-B-Que — usually well done!
6. Dilli Bread — good track record!
7. Cheese Pie — carries added weight!

Activity: Form a betting pool. Each guest picks a horse in the Kentucky Derby race to win, place, or show. Give prizes.

Music: Play "In My Old Kentucky Home" and other Stephen Foster melodies.

May 5—Arbor Day

Morning Coffee or Lunch: For garden club members. Spring clean-up.
Invitations: See sketch.
Activity: Rake, dig, plant, prune, spray.
Music: Country. Attach extension cord to hi-fi speaker and place outdoors.
Menu suggestions: Planter's Punch (Chapter Four)
                           Sandwiches (Chapter Three)
                           Dessert: Serve fruit-flavored ice cream in paper cups set
                           in small clay flower pots. Place a real flower in the center.

Now Dig This!
Dress Sloppy
Come Early
Bring Tools
Work Fast
Stay Late
Drink Planter's Punch, etc.
Eat Garden Variety
     Sandwiches
and be Merry!

May—Mother's Day
Second Sunday in May

Noon: Could be co-hosted by all grown or married daughters and daughters-in-law. (A grand opportunity to celebrate for mothers, who avoid celebrating birthdays.)

Invitations: Send snapshot of Mother occupied in her favorite activity and follow through on that party theme: bridge or bingo, painting or ping-pong, tennis, golf or boating. Give date, time, and place (give party either at mother's, son's, or daughter's home; or a public or private picnic ground where small children can run and play), etc.

Decorations: Mother's favorite flowers.

Menu suggestions: Have each person prepare one course.

Activity: Prepare poems, songs, skits. Have grandchildren sing "I'm a Little Teapot."

Memo: Invite Mother's closest friends too!

May 30—Memorial Day
Western Country Theme

1. Flapjack Breakfast
Invitations: Staple a card giving time, place, etc., on a swatch of a bandana or a whole bandana.

Decorations: Gingham tablecloths, kerosene lamps, flags. Instead of numbers for tables, use cards with brands such as Diamond T, Circle C, Double U, etc. Paint a farm wagon orange and use it as the buffet table. Twine yellow artificial roses around wagon wheels. At night use spotlights.

Menu suggestions: Flapjacks, maple syrup, butter, bacon, sausage, fresh fruit and berries.

2. Evening: Barn Dance Outdoors.
Menu suggestions: Bob's barbecued beefsteak on buns, corn relish, cole slaw, potato salad, pecan rolls or donuts.

Dress: Blue jeans and gingham.

Music: Old-time fiddler.

Activity: Pitch horseshoes, volleyball, etc. Plan children's games, sack race, relay race, tug of war. Give medals or ribbons to winners.

Entertainment: Lasso demonstration.

June 11—Kamehameha Day

Birthday of the first king of Hawaii. Celebrated with parades, floats, and pageants

How to make a Hawaiian flower lei

Most children who live in Hawaii are quite expert at making flower leis at a moment's notice. It's that simple!

Take a darning needle and some heavy thread and any mainland flowers such as asters, carnations, dahlias, daisies, chrysanthemums, gladioli and draw a needle through the center of the flower, adding flowers until the lei is about a yard long. Tie ends together and you are done.

Keep leis fresh by sprinkling with water and keeping them in a plastic bag in a cool place until ready to use.

Invitations: Staple the date, time, place, etc., to a paper lei and mail in a box wrapped in batik print paper (see Sources of Supply).

Decorations: At the entrance, welcome guests with Hawaiian torches. Make an island scene using miniature palm trees, grass shacks, outrigger canoes, dolls, ukeleles, etc. Use Hawaiian print cloths or placemats of attractive brown and black batik paper goods (see Sources of Supply).

Menu suggestions: Beachboy screwdriver cocktail, sweet 'n sour pork chops (Chapter Five), kona coffee. Include pineapple, papayas, coconut, macadamia nuts with choice of dessert.

Music: Play Hawaiian records. Invite hula dancers and ukelele players.

Seat guests on straw mats spread on the ground. Place folding card tables or aluminum tables 8 inches off the ground.

Memo: One can be terribly extravagant and order fresh flower leis, anthurium, ti leaves, birds of paradise flown in direct from Hawaii. I gave them the date of the party and they shipped flowers to insure delivery the day before (see Sources of Supply).

June 23—Midsummer's Eve

Occurs near the time of the summer solstice, the great turning point in the sun's career

Shakespeare's *Midsummer Night's Dream* is based on this ancient festival celebrated with bonfires throughout Europe.

Evening: After dusk in the garden.

Invitations: Handwritten on torn parchment in Old English script.

Decorations: String Christmas tree lights in trees and shrubbery. Hang Christmas tree icicles from branches to give dreamy effect (see Sources of Supply). Use eerie green and blue spotlights or insert candles in paper bags filled partially with sand.

Use fairy dolls (King Oberon and Queen Titania) as centerpieces surrounded by candle-light and flowers.

Music: Engage strolling minstrels or madrigal singers dressed in 16th-century costumes.

Entertainment: Contact local little theater group or university drama department to stage a one-act play.

Menu suggestions: Wine punch bowl, raw vegetable bouquet, onion trees, marinated mushrooms, hot prunes wrapped in bacon, smoked ham, lima bean and pear casserole, Dobos torte (Chapter Five).

June—Father's Day

Third Sunday in June

1. Breakfast: Crown Dad King for the Day!

Menu suggestions: Caviar Omelet (see Chapter Two).

Symbol of the Day: The rose and a gold crown.

Activity: Plan a family cookout (Mother does the barbecuing?), a picnic, fishing trip, boating excursion, or order tickets for the ball game, help Dad with a pet project. Present him with a scrapbook of his achievements.

2. Evening:

If you take him out to dinner—don't let him pick up the check!

If you stay home, prepare his favorite food, and if he smokes, pass him a fine cigar after dinner.

Family Activity: Show him home movies or color slides. Play Monopoly, Scrabble, or other favorite game.

July 4—Independence Day

1. **Noon:** Pool party or picnic for young and old!

2. **Evening:** Get-together before or after firework display.

Invitations: Glue miniature American flags on folded invitations. Surround with gold stars in shape of number "4."

Decorations: Use red and white striped tablecloths, blue cornflowers. At night use red, white, and blue candles, sparklers and/or torches.

Order a patriotic kit (see Sources of Supply) and/or make your own firecracker centerpieces. (To make simulated firecrackers of assorted sizes, use red, white and blue construction paper. Staple paper into the shape of a cylinder or use rolls which held paper towel etc. In matching-sized plastic lids, make a dollar-sized hole, pull a coil of heavy red, white and blue wool yarn partially through hole, cut yarn, place lid on cylinder and *presto!* you have an attractive firecracker.)

Menu suggestions: Iced orange tea (Chapter Three), turkey salad, garnished fudge cake (Chapter Three). Add miniature flags on cake.

Music: Sousa's marching band music

Activities: Invite guests to give a two-minute humorous campaign speech either for the office of President of the U.S. or local dog-catcher! Have a soapbox handy. Gift wrap bars of soap for souvenir prizes. Or play comedy records. Or organize a baseball game, or sing songs around a campfire.

July 14—Bastille Day
National French holiday

Evening: "Saucisson-Vin-Rouge" Party

Invitations: "Viva la France!," "Bon Jour!," "Bon Appetit!" A French poodle holding the French flag. Colors: Red, white and blue.

Decorations: Put a few chairs and small tables, garden umbrella in front of the house on the sidewalk or make a sign over the front door: "Cafe de la Paix." Decorate the tables with red and white checked tablecloths, candles in wine bottles, miniature Eiffel Towers,

Arc de Triomphe, decorate walls with French posters and pennants (available from travel agency or French consulate). Use paper table accessories with French motif. For towers, arc, posters, pennants, and paper goods, see Sources of Supply. Irises for flower arrangements.

Menu suggestions: Serve a great variety of saucisson (sausages). A string of linked together sausages may be hung as decorations or arranged as artistically as a still-life. Serve *vin rouge* (red wine), preferably Beaujolais, in earthenware pitchers and coarse country bread with slabs of butter. A variety of cheeses is optional, along with a luscious green salad such as Camembert Salad a la Rothschild (see Chapter Five). A big basket of fruit, sliced melons and strawberries are the right finishing touches.

Music: Play popular French records by Maurice Chevalier, etc., or dance to a combo.

Activity: Have a cartoonist draw pictures of the guests. Show travel pictures or art films. Or plan a make-believe cruise down the Seine on a boat. Provide sketch pads for each person to do a self-portrait.

August or Any Time—Secret Desire Party!

Evening

Invitations: Mail flat key with tag attached giving time, date, place, etc. On reverse write, "The key to open the door to your personality! Come as the person you'd most like to be!"

Decorations: Sketch keys of all kinds on poster board: old keys, padlocks, etc., to unlock "My secret desire is to be. . . ." For centerpiece on table make a mobile of assorted keys and locks. These could be sprayed any color. Create dreamlike effects by draping large pieces of gauze around room and spotlight these with blue and green lights. Hang reproductions of Dali paintings on wall.

Dress: Wear the outfit of the person you'd most like to be! Have guests write, "My secret desire is . . ." and why.

Menu: Barbecue, corn on the cob, tomato pudding, salad, Rum Savarin Ring with fresh fruit.

August—African-American Blues or Jazz Festival

Evening

Invitations: Fold blue construction paper double and cut out a musical note. Use inside fold for invitation. "Dig this crazy sound, man!" Give time, date, place, etc.

Dress: Sharp.

Decorations: Combine all shades of blue from the palest blue to the deepest purple for tablecloths and background. Use blue spotlights. Use corrugated paper rolls 48" x 25" blue lines against white with black musical notes "Melody." For centerpieces, spray toy instruments various shades of blue and decorate with honeysuckle vines (Sources of Supply).

Music: Contemporary jazz for dancing or listening. "Birth of the Blues," "Basin Street Blues," "Born to Be Blue," "Blue Monday," "When Sunny Gets Blue," "Blues in the Night," "Blues."

Menu suggestions: Barbecued chicken, rice with peanuts, cole slaw, peach cobbler.

Activity: Invite guests to bring their instruments for informal jam session.

September—Labor Day or Harvest Festival

First Monday of the month

Why not plan a German Harvest Festival celebration for a change?

German Bierstübe! Start any time of day and just keep it rolling!

Invitations: Write on a white card in green ink, "Ein Prosit! Elbow-bending with German Gemutlichkeit" and give date, time, etc., or check Sources of Supply for "Bierstübe" informals.

Decorations: God's great outdoors is more than enough! Use green and white checked tablecloths trimmed with ivy, cedar, or pine. For centerpieces use leafy green and red cabbages. Gently roll leaves down and insert roses in cabbage with stems placed in individual plastic tubes available from your florist. For indoors, use Bierstübe wall panels 5' x 25', posters and coat of arms. (See Sources of Supply.)

Costumes: Tyrolean hats, vests, suspenders, aprons.

Music: An Oom-pah-pah German brass band playing lots of polkas for dancing.

Activity: The schnitzelbank song is a must! For sheet music, chart, instructions, pointers, see Sources of Supply.

Menu suggestions: Serve chilled beer on draught or in a pitcher with pretzels and sauerkraut, of course! (An annual event may be inaugurated by organizing an assembly line to slice cabbage and put it in crocks to ferment, then invite the same group back next year to sample the results.) Serve bratwurst, knockwurst, potato salad, coleslaw, apple strudel.

Memo: Order booklet with recipes, "How to have a Bierstübe" (see Sources of Supply).

September—Bonfire Lobster Cookout or Shipwreck Party

Invitations: Write time, place, etc., on paper lobster bibs.

Decorations: Fishnet tablecloths over coral, shiny vinyl petticoats. Sea shells and starfish surrounding bowl of live tropical fish. Supply guests with sand pails for lobster shells. (See Sources of Supply.)

Activity: Boating, fishing, ping-pong, tennis, sunbathing, swimming, nature walk. Treasure hunt on the beach.

Activity: Give guests false mustaches; bandanas, eye patches, earrings, pirate hats to wear; supply a map with X marking the spot where the refreshments are to be found!

Music: Harmonica players would be popular now, especially around a bonfire!

September 16—Independence Day in Mexico

Cocktail-Supper Fiesta

Invitations: Sprinkle a spoonful of confetti in an envelope and write invitations on yellow paper with green ink.

Decorations: Welcome your guests with a sign: "Bien venido amigas, amigos!" Decorate the front door with a Mexican tin mask against a turquoise background. Cover the tables with a black cloth trimmed with a red, white, and green border or use striped beach towels trimmed with fringe. Use Mexican pottery or pre-Columbian figures with chunky candles accented with gardenias, camellias or roses. Or float poinsettia blossoms (known in Mexico as the flame leaf) in a shallow dish.

Dress: Informal. Supply men with sombreros and ladies with mantillas or flowers and fans.

Music: Hire a marimba band or a flamenco guitarist or play mariachi recordings.

Toast: "Salud amor y pesetas pare gastarlos!" (Good health, love, and money, forever!)

Menu suggestions: Margaritas, Mexican broad beans and pepitas for nibblers. Tamale pie (Chapter Five), coffee Kahlua.

Activity: Hang a piñata (hollow paper fish bird, pig, etc.) from ceiling. Be sure to fill piñata with trinkets. Blindfold several guests and give them sticks. When they break the piñata, souvenir gifts fall to the ground for everyone to scramble to retrieve them. (See Sources of Supply for Mexican party accessories.)

October—Any Day, Including October 12, Columbus Day

Evening: Wine Festival.

Invitations: Choose invitations with wine or grape drawings.

Decorations: Let your guests pass through a grape arbor at the entrance. For indoors, use grape garlands in baskets, posters, candles in wine bottles, etc. On the tables use shiny cloths heaped with mountains of grapes.

Music: Hire an Italian organ grinder (with or without monkey!) or play Neapolitan songs, "O Solo Mio."

Menu suggestions: Hard-cooked eggs. Remember Columbus' famous egg debate? When Columbus was told by a cynic that anyone could have discovered the New World, he placed a hard-cooked egg on the table and asked the room full of noblemen if any could make the egg stand on end. When all failed, he cut off the egg's tip and easily stood the egg on the flat surface. With typical showmanship he said, "Once accomplished, it seems so easy!"

Raw vegetable bouquet, spaghetti, spinach salad, Italian hard rolls, spumoni ice cream, Bel Paese cheese and crackers. (For free wine-tasting booklet, see Sources of Supply.)

October 31—Charles Addams Party—Hallowe'en

Time: After dark!

Invitations: Sketch spiderweb on invitations. Give time, date, place, etc.

Decorations: Orange, yellow, and black colors. Scoop out pumpkin and fill with a container of flowers for centerpiece. Hang vampire bats, spiders from ceiling. Use chunky black candles and white tapering candles around the room. Make charcoal sketches of bats, octopus, skeletons or skulls and place in frames over existing pictures on walls

Make giant spiderwebs and attach to four corners of room. (How to make spiderwebs: Nail 6 nails or tacks in the shape of a hexagon to a board, any dimension you choose.

Wrap twine criss-cross from nail to nail, then tie twine in circular fashion knotting as you go along, forming a spiderweb. Spray with liquid starch. Let dry and repeat several times. Remove nails and spiderweb will stand alone.)

For table covers, use shiny black vinyl accented with tall gleaming silver 5-branch candelabras with orange candles. On buffet tables use raw onion trees (see Chapter Four).

Music: The choice is broad—organ music, electronic tapes, classical or pop. Include "That Old Black Magic" for dancing.

Activity: A game of billiards, if a billiard table is available, is ideal or it might be fun to scatter small tables around the room set up with chess boards, Chinese checkers, back-gammon, etc.

Menu suggestions: A buffet with lots of seafood including an oyster bar, herring, shrimp, salmon, clams or snails, caviar (budget permitting). Cheese and sausages, crackers, party rye, celery and carrot sticks, and black olives. Dessert Finale: Café Royal (Chapter Five).

November 3—Bunka No Hi
Culture Day in Japan

All those who have contributed to the world of literature, science, art, sports, and government are honored with cultural awards on this day.

1. Afternoon: Japanese Tea, 2:00 to 4:00 P.M., might be sponsored by a service group, to recognize volunteers of the year with an award, pin, or certificate at a special recognition ceremony.

Invitations: Choose Oriental informals with apple blossom design.

Decorations: Corrugated paper rolls 48" x 25' are available in dogwood, blossom pattern or bamboo (see Sources of Supply). Use posters, Japanese lanterns, parasols, pagodas.

Music: Play recordings of *Madame Butterfly,* the *Mikado,* "Japanese Sandman." (For Japanese records, see Sources of Supply.)

Menu suggestions: Sushi, rice, and fish. Almond or fortune cookies, honey cakes, ginger candy, lychee nuts, tangerine slices. Serve tea in Japanese bowls, or Sake.

Memo: Give Japanese fans for souvenirs. Burn incense.

2. Evening: Geisha Party.

For a small group, surprise guests by renting kimonos, happicoats, straw slippers, fancy headdresses for everyone. Provide a dressing room for both men and women, along with plenty of makeup. (A friend of mine converted a heated garage into a Japanese teahouse.) Use straw mats on the floor and cushions. A door placed across a pair of low coffee tables or bricks makes a perfect dining table. Invite your guests to sit on the floor and provide them with chopsticks. Order a meal from a Japanese restaurant or serve Japanese crabmeat, butterfly shrimp, marinated mushrooms, or cubed beef over hibachi, rice and spinach salad. Serve warm Sake in tiny bowls.

November—National (and Children's) Book Week
Dates vary annually

Luncheon: Usually sponsored by the Friends of the Library, Community Centers, etc.

Invitation: Mail in form of a bookmark with John Masefield's quote, "The days that make us happy make us wise."

Decorations: Place a centerpiece on each table which depicts the title of a current bestseller. Example: For the Bible, reconstruct Noah's Ark with all the animals. Before guests are seated, give each person a slip of paper and pencil with which to jot down their guesses. Give prizes to those who guess most book titles correctly.

Menu suggestions: Match menu to the book currently at the top of the bestseller list, if possible.

Activities: Have a Children's Book Fair where people may order or purchase books for young people for holiday giving.

Alternate date: National Library Week (April, date varies).

November—Thanksgiving Football Party
Fourth Thursday of the month

Afternoon

Invitation: "Please join us on Thanksgiving Day to watch the game." Give time, date, and address.

Decorations: Football balloons, pompons, pennants. Colors: earthly tones, rust, brown, green and gold.

Menu suggestions: Set up an hors d'oeuvres table in the form of a football field (this can be started way ahead), using green felt cloth marked off with 5-inch white yard-lines. Make a miniature pair of goalposts at each end from breadsticks and surround field with cheese crackers, sausage, etc. Use toothpicks with miniature pennants. I have seen individual football players made out of black and green olives, cocktail onions, grapes, bits of cheese, pickles. Place tiny numerals on each player.

Menu: Sliced turkey buffet dinner (Chapter Five). Let everyone help themselves during "time out"!

Activity: Set up more than one TV so everyone can watch both games. Make up a pool and bet which team makes the most touchdowns in each quarter, and/or which team will win and give the correct score. Award silly prizes to the winners. In warm climates, organize a game of touch football.

Alternate date: Any football weekend.

December

The entire sentimental month of December usually climaxes the year's festivities with a medley of family gatherings, engagements, weddings, homecomings, dances, club parties, church parties, and nationality parties. In bikini climes the December holidays may be celebrated poolside or dockside, while in parka climes activities are frequently centered inside or hearthside.

North or south, wherever one lives or whatever one's age or status, people become caught up during this month with the "let's entertain" spirit. Here are a few popular ideas for holiday entertaining during the jolly season!

December 6—St. Nicholas Day

Christmas Tree Decorating Party

Invitations:
Come help us trim our tree
Outside for all to see
When we're done
We'll have fun
With a "nip" and song—R.S.V.P.!

Menu suggestions: Eggnog, Wassail Bowl, or Broken Leg.

Activity: A group may help decorate the office, club, or grounds of a hospital or church. Choose a theme from a variety of motifs—old-fashioned, modern, hobbies, toys. Group may sponsor a Christmas Walk or fundraiser for UNICEF, etc.

Options:

1) Newlyweds could invite family and friends to help trim the tree and ask each person to contribute one Christmas ornament.

2) Homecoming party for young people. (See Devonshire Tea, Chapter Three, or Platter Party described on St. Patrick's Day in this chapter.)

December 24 or 25

Gather family for Christmas dinner (Chapter Six). Open presents! Snack on Christmas cookies—or just relax and enjoy!

December 26–December 31

Kwanzaa, a spiritual and festive celebration by African-Americans on black culture and family, culminating in a feast "Karamu," featuring sweet potato pie, peanut soup, corn bread, southern fried okra, vegetarian stew, and yams. (African-American Holiday Association, www.aaha@aaha-info.org)

December 31

New Year's Eve (see Chapter Five). Several couples plan to divide the menu, share the work, and double the fun.

Movable Feasts and Holidays

Dates vary.

January–February

Chinese New Year date depends on the constellation of the moon.

The Party Calendar

February–March
Mardi Gras falls on the day before Ash Wednesday, marking the end of the carnival season.

March–April
Purim; Jewish Passover.

April
Palm Sunday, Easter Sunday.

May
Mother's Day: Second Sunday in May.

June
Father's Day: Third Sunday in June.

September
Labor Day: First Monday in September.

September–October
Rosh Hashana, Yom Kippur.

October
Aloha week: Dates vary on each island in Hawaii.

November
Election Day: Second Tuesday in November.
National Book Week: Dates vary.
Thanksgiving: Fourth Thursday in November.

December
Hanukkah, Jewish Festival of Lights: Date depends on the constellation of the moon.

Sources of Supply

Sources of Supply

African-American Holiday Associaton. Kwanzaa & wedding information. <www.aaha@aaha-info.org>

Airlines and Travel Agents. Foreign country posters.

American Society of Travel Agents. 1-703-739-2782. <www.astanet.com>

Aloha Lei Greetors. Ships flower leis worldwide. Toll-free 1-800-367-5255. Or 1-808-951-9990. <www.superpages.gte.net>

American Rental Association. 1-800-334-2177. <www.ararental.org>

American Spoon Foods, Inc. Dried cherries, brandied cherries, ginger plum grilling sauce, fruit salsa, plum jam, dried Michigan morel mushrooms, corporate gift baskets. Toll-free 1-888-735-7600. Fax 1-800-647-2512. <www.spoon.com>

Bronner's Christmas Wonderland. Catalog available for party theme accessories list. Corrugated paper rolls, hand-painted murals, colored lights, pagodas, musical notes, smorgasbord accessories, Japanese records, and much more. Christmas supplies available all year. Frankenmuth, MI 48734. Toll-free 1-800-255-9327. <www.Bronners.com>

Chef's. All gourmet cookware for kitchen preparation. Toll-free 1-800-338-3232. <www.chefscatalog.com>

Crate & Barrel. Bundt forms; other gourmet cooking utensils, including omelet-making equipment. Toll-free 1-800-323-5461.

Epicurious. Recipes from *Bon Appetit* and *Gourmet* magazines, wine recommendations. <www.epicurious.com>

Florists. Large standards for flowers, arches, decorative fences and screens, etc.

Foreign Consulate. May sometimes recommend or supply material for local color. (I once borrowed an authentic French peasant costume for an April in Paris Party through the Alliance Française.)

Greetings from the President. Special official presidential greeting for a birth, wedding, 50th (and plus) anniversary. Allow 4 weeks for each request. The White House, Greetings Office, Room 39, 1600 Pennsylvania Avenue NW, Washington, DC 20500-1600.

Hammacher Schlemmer. Imprinted plastic containers, omelet pans, etc. 147 East 57th Street, New York, NY 10022. Toll-free 1-800-543-3366. <www.hammacher.com>

Hawaii Lei Company. Customized chill boxes for leis (mainland shipping). Toll-free 1-888-393-5347 or 1-808-595-6499. <www.hawaiileicompany.com>

International Special Events Society. Toll-free 1-800-688-ISES. <www.ises.com>

Jordan's Old Virginia Smokehouse. Smoked Virginia ham. PO Box 324, Richmond, VA 23202.

Leading Caterers of America. Toll-free 1-800-743-6660. <www.leadingcaterers.com>

National Association of Catering Executives. <www.nace.net>

Martha By Mail. Smoked trout, salmon, party decorations, etc. PO Box 60060 Tampa, FL 33660-0060. Toll-free 1-800-950-7130. <www.marthabymail.com>

Maytag Dairy Farms. Blue Cheese Wheel, etc. (catalog available). Box 506, Newton, IA 50208. Toll-free 1-800-247-2458.

Paradise Products, Inc. Full-color catalog describes supplies for varied party themes: smorgasbord, Moulin Rouge, George Washington's birthday, French, Mexican, Japanese, Pagoda, Hawaiian. Party accessories: roulette table, stovepipe hat, paper, etc., Japanese records. PO Box 568, El Cerrito, CA 94530. 1-510-524-8300. Fax 1-510-524-8165.

Panache. Party equipment, chair, tables, china, luminaries, accessories. 19458 S. LaGrange Ave., Mokena, IL 60448. Toll-free 1-800-454-6587. <www.Panache.com>

Places, a book by Hannelore Hahn, A Tenth House Enterprises, Inc., publication, Box 610, Gracie Station, New York, NY 10028. 212-737-7536.

Plath's Meat, Inc. Smoked whitefish, ham, bacon, pork, chicken, turkey, sausage. Box 7, Rogers City, MI 49779. 517-734-2232. Fax 517-734-2500.

Recipes. The Internet features over 8,000 recipes, including some from *Gourmet* magazine and *Bon Apetit*. <food.epicurious.com>

Replacements, Ltd. China, crystal silver, old and new. Toll-free 1-800-737-5223. Fax 1-336-697-3100 <www.replacements.com>

Stumps One Party Place. Complete decorating and party catalogs available. PO Box 305, South Whitley, IN 46787-0305. Toll-free 1-800-227-2789. Fax 1-219-723-6976. <www.stumpsparty.com>

Williams and Sonoma. Scottish salmon, smoked ham, cheeses, pastries, gourmet kitchen cookware, dishes, glassware, flatware, dining accessories. Toll-free 1-800-541-2233. <williams.sonoma.com>

Wine Answers. <www.wineanswers.com>

Yellow Pages telephone directory. Check local listings for Wedding Supplies and Services, Party Supplies, Costumes–Masquerade and Theatrical.

Index

Index

Index

Check out these exciting titles in our Know-It-All™ series, available at your favorite bookstore: